PICK® BASIC
A PROGRAMMER'S GUIDE

JONATHAN E. SISK

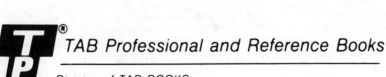

W0006558

TPR®

TAB Professional and Reference Books

Division of TAB BOOKS
Blue Ridge Summit, PA

Pick and PICK/BASIC are trademarks of Pick Systems.
Utlimate is a trademark of Ultimate Corporation.
Microdata and REALITY are trademarks of McDonnell Douglas
Computer Systems Company.

FIRST EDITION
FOURTH PRINTING

© 1987 by **TAB Professional and Reference Books**, an imprint of TAB BOOKS.
TAB BOOKS is a division of McGraw-Hill, Inc.
The TAB Professional and Reference Books logo, consisting of the letters "TPR"
within a large "T," is a registered trademark of TAB BOOKS.

Library of Congress Cataloging-in-Publication Data

Sisk, Jonathan E.
      PICK BASIC : a programmer's guide / by Jonathan E. Sisk.
          p.   cm.
      Includes index.
      ISBN 0-8306-2845-2
      1. PICK/BASIC (Computer program language)   I. Title.
      QA76.73.P225S57   1987
      005.13'3—dc19   87-18357
                                                                CIP

TAB BOOKS offers software for sale. For information and a catalog, please contact
TAB Software Department, Blue Ridge Summit, PA 17294-0850.

Questions regarding the content of this book should be addressed to:

Reader Inquiry Branch
TAB BOOKS
Blue Ridge Summit, PA 17294-0850

Contents

Foreword

THE RUMOR THAT I WROTE PICK/BASIC IN ORDER TO BE ABLE TO PLAY "STAR TREK" IS not true. However, I did play a lot of "Star Trek" while developing the language. I needed to test the product. Didn't I?

Since that time, I have seen a lot of PICK/BASIC programs. Nearly all of the programs did what they were supposed to do nearly all of the time. But some programs were not very easy to understand. Some were so hard to understand that it was cheaper to throw them away and start over than to change them.

But in all this time (about 12 years) there have been no books about PICK/BASIC other than the system manuals. Jon Sisk's new book not only shows how to write PICK/BASIC programs, but it also shows how to write PICK/BASIC programs that are easy to understand. Jon's years of teaching PICK/BASIC help to make this book an excellent learning tool. I recommend it to anyone who would like to learn PICK/BASIC. I also recommend it to anyone who already knows PICK/BASIC and would like to see how good programming standards can be applied to the language.

KEN SIMMS

Preface

THE POPULARITY OF THE PICK OPERATING SYSTEM HAS CONTINUED TO GROW OVER THE years. Recent estimates put the installed Pick base at roughly 70,000 systems, ranging in size from desktop systems, like the IBM XT and AT, all the way up to mainframe-class systems such as the IBM 4300 and 9370, with dozens of micro and super-micro systems in between.

For many years, most people who had machines that ran Pick didn't know that it was Pick they were using. Pick went under "brand" names, like Ultimate and REALITY. Today the system is no longer being sold in plain brown wrappers.

My experience has been that most of the Pick-based systems in use today are managed by people who do not have a lot of experience with other operating systems. In many ways this is an advantage—the single largest one of which is that they do not have to be "retrained" into the Pick way of doing things.

Most companies do not have a "professional" in-house staff to do programming and analysis work, and thus have to do it themselves—unless, of course, they rely on outside consultants or software vendors to perform technosurgery on their software. This book is for those of you who want to learn how to do it yourselves. It's also aimed at those who don't want to do it themselves, but want to be able to talk intelligently to those who do.

This book was developed from the course materials for my programming sessions in "The Pick System Educational Series." Naturally, every little nuance about PICK/BASIC can't be covered in one book, but this book is intended to provide a broad introductory overview about the powerful PICK/BASIC language.

The method by which this book attempts to explain PICK/BASIC is through step-by-step tutorials. In the first chapter, the basics of logging onto the system and creating your account are provided, along with a very cursory overview of the Pick Editor. From there, basic programming principles and terminology are discussed in Chapter 2. Chapter 3 takes the reader into the exciting world of programming in PICK/BASIC by providing a ready-made program which will be entered into the system, compiled, then run. A detailed explanation of each instruction and principle follows immediately after the source listing.

The objective is to cover the instructions used most often in the language, in a practical, objective, and logical order. The rest of the book follows this tutorial format, with each program building upon principles introduced in preceding examples while introducing new topics along the way.

As the first tutorial on the PICK/BASIC language, this book may serve as the pioneer by which future similar attempts are measured. Pioneers, especially in the data processing community, are easily identified: they are the ones with the arrows sticking out of their backs. I hope this book will provide the reader with a broad enough introduction to be able to understand the principles and mechanics of the PICK/BASIC language. Maybe it will even provide the courage necessary to start writing code from scratch. But more important, it is intended to encourage its readers to get out there and discover, ponder, and even maintain the existing code on their machines.

I welcome all comments and suggestions. Please direct them to me in care of the publisher.

Acknowledgments

I WOULD ESPECIALLY LIKE TO THANK KEN SIMMS, TRISH BAEZ, BILL MEYER, HENRY EGGERS, Harvey Rodstein, Karen Schaltenbrand, Holley Humphrey, Mark Lewis, Ron Powers, and Doug Rose for their valuable contributions to this book.

Introduction:
The Ground Rules

IN WRITING *PICK/BASIC: A PROGRAMMER'S GUIDE,* CERTAIN "GROUND RULES" HAD TO BE established. Without setting boundaries, the job would never have been completed and no one could have benefitted from the information. The ground rules are listed here so you might understand the working concepts used to create this textbook.

1. This is not an encyclopedia or dictionary; it is intended to be a textbook. It will provide a general understanding of nearly every instruction in the language, and the principles behind putting them to use.

2. It is not as important to identify which version of PICK/BASIC does what. The intention is to thoroughly explain the standard instructions and features. Tying specific capabilities to specific manufacturers is therefore given low priority.

3. This textbook does not replace your existing system documentation. There is still a need for standard system reference manuals.

4. Manufacturers change their versions of PICK/BASIC, eliminating bugs and adding features, frequently without acknowledging the existence of any problems. For this reason, every known bug, change, improvement or modification is not documented.

5. To further expand on point 1, there are actually several very good reasons that not every instruction is covered. Some instructions, like "INPUT @" and "INPUTTRAP," don't work consistently. Other instructions,

like "RETURN TO *statement.label*" make programs too hard to debug. Still others, like "SADD," are specific to one manufacturer, but are listed here for reference purposes.

About PICK/BASIC

The Pick System comes equipped with a very powerful programming language: PICK/BASIC. It has some remote similarities to standard Dartmouth BASIC (Beginners All-purpose Symbolic Instruction Code), but far exceeds it in features and benefits.

The comparison of PICK/BASIC to the "standard" BASIC ends its similarities at the READ, WRITE, and PRINT statements. Outside of a few intrinsic functions, PICK/BASIC is significantly enhanced and different in syntax. For example, statement labels in PICK/BASIC are optional. When they are used, most versions of Pick still require numeric statement labels, while some now allow alphanumeric statement labels.

The language is very well suited to dealing with strings of characters. This is particularly convenient in a system where *everything* is stored as a string. A special set of intrinsic functions, like INSERT, REPLACE, and DELETE, are provided to deal with the Pick "three-dimensional" data (item) structure. This means that items (records) are composed of attributes (fields), which in turn are optionally composed of "multivalues" (sub-fields), and finally, "subvalues" (sub-sub-fields?). Through PICK/BASIC, you tell the computer what you want to do to an item, not how to do it. This is why it is beneficial to have a general understanding about the Pick file and item structure before jumping into updating files.

PICK/BASIC programs are primarily used to capture and validate data before storing it on disk. They also can be used to format reports and menus, but generally these functions are done in ACCESS and PROC, respectively.

The many other features of this unique language are covered throughout this text. The bottom line is, if you have used "standard" BASIC, you will find PICK/BASIC to be a much more elegant alternative. If you have not used standard BASIC, congratulations; here's your chance to be exposed to a sophisticated, flexible, and easy-to-learn programming language.

This book deals with "generic" PICK/BASIC code; that is, the programs in the tutorials are designed to be used on any implementation of the Pick System, unless otherwise mentioned in the text.

About the Intended Reader

This book assumes that you already are familiar with the Pick Editor (EDIT) and the Pick file structure. Some of the Editor commands are provided in the tutorials, but there are many features of the Editor which are not discussed.

A background in programming in any language would be helpful, but it's not absolutely vital in order to comprehend and make use of this book. For newcomers to programming, it is important to read the section called "If You Are New To Programming." Even if you have programmed before, this section is suggested reading.

There are also several other books that can be used as companion references for this one. *Exploring the Pick Operating System* (Sisk and Van Arsdale) covers the fundamental principles of Pick: the Editor, ACCESS, PROC, TCL, file-handling, and the spooler.

The *Pick Pocket Guide* (Sisk) provides the syntax and a brief explanation of every command in the operating system; there are separate versions of the *Pocket Guide* for Ultimate and McDonnell Douglas systems. Finally, William Meyer's forthcoming *Advanced PICK Programming* is the logical next step up from this book, covering list maintenance and processing, on-line processing and reporting, integrated systems, recursion, and other topics.

What to Expect

Using a "cookbook" approach, this book takes you through practical working examples of nearly every command in the PICK/BASIC language. Some instructions, like the trigonometric functions, are not called upon very frequently where the majority of Pick systems are actually used, such as in accounting departments. Thus, these and other esoteric instructions are omitted.

After going through all of the program examples and quizzes, you will have the tools necessary to write straightforward, maintainable programs. More importantly, you will be able to read the programs that you already have. By *read*, I mean that you will be able to figure out the syntax of nearly every instruction in any PICK/BASIC program. Figuring out the *logic* is another matter altogether. Every programmer has their own style of writing code. Coupling this with the fact that the Pick System is technically very forgiving to even the sloppiest "spaghetti code," produces lots of different approaches to problem solving.

As you explore existing application programs, you will probably find many cases where improvements may be made from techniques obtained in this book. Don't hesitate—put them in! Often a single change won't provide an obvious increase in the performance of your computer; cumulatively, however, each little piece adds up to a big improvement, like the old adage that "the whole is greater than the sum of its parts." For this reason, attention is paid to programming standards and conventions, in addition to technical aspects. Current hardware is so fast that even inefficient programs run at blazing speed. This compensates for bad code, but nothing compensates for code that can't be supported.

Representation Conventions

Certain typographic conventions are used throughout this book and have the same meaning each time they are encountered.

Any text in all uppercase characters indicates the text is shown exactly as it is displayed by the computer or exactly as you must enter it. Most implementations of the Pick System are generally sensitive to the case of commands, instructions, statements, etc. If they are not entered in the right case, they won't work.

The <cr> symbol is used to represent a carriage return. This is sometimes referred to as the "Enter," "Newline," or "Line Feed" key. They all mean the same thing: press the Return key.

If You Are New to Programming

If you have never touched a computer before and expect to learn how to program from scratch using this book, your task may be more than a little difficult. This book is an introductory approach to the PICK/BASIC language. Many principles of programming are covered in the course of the text, but to keep this book from running about 1500 pages, some topics had to be skipped. For this reason, you may want to explore your local library or bookstore for books that explain the general concepts of programming. Another excellent source for this information is your local community college or university. Don't expect to find university courses on Pick just yet, but we're working on getting it in there.

If you have a reasonable "digital aptitude," however, this book may provide everything you need to understand programming in PICK/BASIC.

Chapter 1 explains some terms that you will need to understand throughout this book. Study them carefully. The glossary contains a much more complete list of Pick terminology.

Pick Terminology and Concepts

THE PICK SYSTEM USES TERMS TO DEFINE ITSELF THAT ARE UNIQUE IN THE DATA PROCESsing world. Most of these terms are defined the first time they are mentioned, and a glossary of these and other Pick terms is found among the appendices.

ACCOUNTS AND FILES

Accounts are collections of logically related files, much like departments within a company. Each department has its own set of file cabinets. The name of the account is entered at the "LOGON PLEASE:" message to gain access to the system.

Files are collections of logically related items, much as a file cabinet contains file folders made up of similar types of information. For example, one file cabinet may hold file folders which contain information about your customers, while another cabinet may hold the folders for your suppliers. In the Pick System, the number of items that may be put into a file is only limited by the capacity of the disk.

PICK/BASIC programs, each of which is considered an *item,* are stored in a file commonly called BP. Note that BP (short for "Basic Programs") is used as a convention only; as with all files, the filename is free-form.

The Pick System gains much of its elegance from the fact that it has only one file structure available. It is known as a *random access* file structure because records physically reside in the file in random order. The Pick System is excellent for developing on-line, interactive application systems, since accessing data from files is very fast and independent of the size of the file.

An *item* is a collection of logically related attributes or fields. (Other computer systems typically call this a "record.") For example, an item in the CUSTOMER-FILE might contain the name and address for a customer. All the items in the same file are typically formatted in a similar manner. For example, the first attribute in each item might be the customer's name, the second attribute might be the address, and so on.

The method by which Pick manages items is unique. Quite simply, any item in the Pick System is a collection, or *string,* of characters. Pick uses the ASCII[1] coding scheme for representing characters. This character set represents 256 unique characters. Since the upper- and lowercase alphabet, numbers, punctuation, and control characters barely use up the first 128 characters, there are plenty of unused characters available for other purposes. Recognizing this fact, the Pick System uses the last four positions in the ASCII coding scheme, numbered 252 through 255, as special characters to be used by the file system. (Computers generally begin counting at zero, which explains why the last four characters are 252 through 255, rather than 253 through 256.)

Since the Pick System treats each item as a string of characters, there is no concept of "type" of fields. Other systems store data differently depending on the type of the data. The primary "types" of data on other systems are numeric (binary, floating-point decimal, Comp-1, Comp-3, packed decimal, etc.) and character fields, used for storing names and other string-type data.

Item-IDs

Each item must have its own unique identifier. This is called its *id,* (pronounced "eye-dee" in most of the world, and "ahh-deee" in Texas) or *item-id.* This is often referred to by some as the "key," and by others as the "primary key." The item-id may be virtually any combination of alphabetic, numeric and (most) punctuation characters. Those characters that may not be used are: space ( ) ^ ' " \ and any control character. Choosing the item-id for items is not a trivial process. How the item-id is structured has a significant effect on how the item-id "hashes" to a file. A discussion of this selection process is presented in Chapter 13.

The Relationship of Files and Items

It might be helpful to consider the method by which Pick has implemented its file structures, and to see how items fit into this scheme. Each item ("record") that is placed into a file *must* also have a unique item-id, or key. This item-id is then *hashed,* or internally massaged to calculate the storage location where the item is to be placed. To retrieve an item, the unique item-id must be provided to the process, which then hashes it once again to the same location. This requires that the item-id be logical or easily known, because if you don't know the item-id, you can't get to an individual item. There are facilities provided to access the entire file, or even a "selected" subset, if the item-id is not known.

---

1. Acronym for American Standard Code for Information Interchange, a standard 8-bit information code used with many computers and terminals.

It is important to emphasize that since there is only one file structure in the Pick System, it is used not only by programmers, developers, and users, but by the operating system itself. This is both very powerful and vastly different from other operating system environments that provide their users/programmers with multiple file structures for the use of data and a different set of hidden file structures for use by the operating system or its various utilities.

In the Pick System, all files and items are accessible. From the data files up to the system files, everything is available to the user/programmer, who can greatly enhance the functionality of the system.

ATTRIBUTES, VALUES, AND SUBVALUES

An *attribute* (which some people call a ''field'') is an object or a collection of logically related objects, like an address or list of addresses, within an item. In the Pick System, these objects are typically referred to as *values*.

For example, if there were an item called ''100'' in a file called CUSTOMER-FILE, and you were to display it by copying it to the terminal, it would appear as shown in Fig. 1-1. From visual inspection, it is apparent that the item has five attributes. All of the attributes have only one value, with the exception of second, which has two values, both of which are separated by a special ''reserved'' character called a *value mark*. It is displayed as a right-hand square bracket. Note that each value is similar in nature. That is, they are both addresses, but there must be a way to separate them. That's where *multivalues* come into use. There may be as many separate values as needed in an attribute, provided that each is separated by a value mark. This allows treatment of each value as one entity.

Values may, in turn, be broken up into multiple *subvalues*. The special reserved character to separate subvalues is called, creatively enough, a *subvalue mark*. It is displayed as a backslash (\ ). There'll be more about values and subvalues in Chapter 13, which discusses array management.

Each line number (along the left side of the screen) corresponds to an attribute. When writing programs in PICK/BASIC, each attribute *must* contain a legal statement or expression (i.e., no blank lines).

```
>COPY CUSTOMER-FILE 100   (T)  <cr>
```

100	Item-id
001 HAPPY CAMPERS MOTOR LODGE	Attribute 1
002 2600 MOOSE STREET]P.O. BOX 1777	Attribute 2
003 EAST OVERSHOE	Attribute 3
004 MN	Attribute 4
005 80808	Attribute 5

Fig. 1-1. Sample display of an item.

3

WHY A VARIABLE-LENGTH ITEM STRUCTURE?

An attribute, or field, in a Pick item is merely a string of characters within an item that also is a string of characters. Pick distinguishes one attribute from another by attaching one of the special reserved characters previously mentioned to the end of the attribute. This is the character numbered 254 from the ASCII coding scheme. Not surprisingly, this is called an *attribute mark*.

This means that when the Pick System accesses an attribute, it merely "scans" the item one character at a time until it reaches an attribute mark. It doesn't matter how many characters occur between attribute marks, other than the fact that most Pick systems impose a maximum size limitation of 32K (about 32,267) characters on any single item. Consequently, items, attributes, values, and subvalues may be of *variable length,* which allows items to expand and contract as changes are made.

Most other computer operating systems utilize a fixed-length field concept which requires that each field within a record have indicated a specific length, along with a beginning and ending character position, to specify where the field is found or stored in the record. The total of all of these fixed-length fields indicates the record size.

The classic problem with this scheme is the five-digit ZIP code. When the record was originally laid out, five positions were provided to allow for the storage of a ZIP code. When the ZIP code expanded to nine characters, all the fixed-length-field victims had a real problem. They had to resize their record structures, rewrite their programs, and tell their bosses to wait.

This problem doesn't occur in the Pick System. With Pick, you simply change the programs to accept and display nine positions, change the dictionary items used by ACCESS for reporting, and life goes on.

The concept of using *delimiters* to separate attributes (fields), values, and subvalues significantly simplifies the problem of data management. All you tell the Pick System is what you want, not how to do it. It then scans through the item, counting the delimiters along the way, until the requested location is found. Simple.

This scheme leads to a phenomenon commonly referred to as the *three-dimensional item structure.* Attributes may contain *multiple values,* each of which is separated by a *value mark.* Values, in turn, may contain multiple *subvalues,* each of which is separated by a *subvalue mark.* Figure 1-2 illustrates the logical structure of the Pick System.

Systems are made up of **accounts.**
Accounts are made up of **files.**
Files are made up of **items.**
Items are made up of **attributes.**
Attributes are made up of **values.**
Values are made up of **subvalues.**

Fig. 1-2. Summary of the Pick data structure.

IF YOU HAVE WORKED ON OTHER SYSTEMS

Most systems which impose the fixed-length field and record structure require individual programs to be stored in separate source code files, with each 80-character record representing a single line or statement of source code.

Since Pick does not impose this fixed-length mentality, source programs in the Pick System are stored differently. Typically, a single file is created to contain multiple programs of a certain application such as "AR.BP," to contain "Accounts Receivable" programs. Each item in the file is a program. Each attribute (or field) in the (program) item is a single PICK/BASIC line of source code. Remember that Pick has only one file structure, which accommodates variable-length items, attributes, values, and subvalues. The only constraint is that the total length of the program cannot exceed 32,257 characters, which is too much to place in one program, anyway.

Since each attribute (field) is of variable length, there is no concept of a continuation character used by other systems when a given line of source code exceeds the space allocated within the 80-character constraint. Also, there is no concept in the writing of PICK/BASIC source programs (unlike Fortran, for example) that the statements must start in the 7th or 8th column position of the line and end in the 72nd or 73rd column. PICK/BASIC source statements may begin in any column position.

The concept that multiple source programs (items) are stored in the same source code file affects how you indicate to the various utilities the program that you want to edit, compile, and run. This is covered in Chapter 2, but basically you have to tell the various utilities that the program is in a certain file and has a certain name (item-id). This is no different than the way Pick manipulates items in other files: there is only one file structure.

Experienced programmers, just beginning to understand and appreciate the Pick file and item structure, soon realize that this environment easily provides the ability to write PICK/BASIC programs which can write other PICK/BASIC programs. There are several excellent "code generators" commercially available to the Pick System.

By now you are realizing that the Pick operating system provides many powerful features that address many problems plaguing other computer environments with the fixed-length record structures. The Pick System provides a very powerful language called PICK/BASIC. It is almost unfortunate that it is called "BASIC," because of the association with earlier and simpler BASIC languages. Pick has more high-level loop control constructs available than the ever-present COBOL language, plus an exceptional environment for tracing and analyzing program "bugs."

Since Pick provides this unique file structure with variable-length items, many additional functions also are provided to manipulate these structures of character strings. The concept that Pick retrieves a field without knowing what the data represents (no data typing) means that the Pick system provides an ideal environment for creating *parameter-driven* application systems. This provides the ability to write programs that read data files which contain the parameters and instructions which instruct the programs how to function. Parameter-driven systems avoid the necessity to "hard code" the functions of a program into its source code, which then requires recompilation if changes are needed. Such systems are typically more flexible and generic in application. This is a great aid for software developers.

Another distinction of the Pick System is the way it stores time and date values. In the instances where a date needs to be stored, it may be stored as a string, such as

07/04/1997, or you may utilize a function which converts the date to an integer representing the number of days that have elapsed since the reference date of 12/31/1967. This process is known as *internal conversion*. Dates before 12/31/1967 have a minus sign preceding the integer number of days. For example, if you were to take the date, 12/31/1967, and convert it with the date conversion function, the function yields the result 0 (zero). The string 1/3/1968, converted with the same function, yields the result 3, and 12/29/1967 yields −2.

The advantages of this internal conversion process are many. First, it makes it extremely easy to perform calculations on dates, since they are stored internally as integer numbers. Second, it optimizes disk storage, given that dates in ''internal format'' require less room than their ''external-format'' equivalents. Third and finally, it assists in ''sorting'' dates, since it is easy to compare two integer numbers to determine which is greater. Extensive functionality exists in Pick to utilize this format and to present dates in many different external formats. These are discussed at length in Chapter 7.

The storage of time has a similar internal conversion scheme. Hours and minutes are internally converted to an integer number that represents the number of seconds that have elapsed since midnight.

This unusual world of Pick, where items (records) automatically expand and contract and no attempt is made to ''type'' the data stored in fields means that an attribute in an item, which previously had been used to contain customer address information, may be changed quite easily—and without breaking any rules—to accommodate a numeric value, such as the person's age.

TERMINOLOGY OF THE PICK/BASIC LANGUAGE

Now let's examine some standard programming concepts as they are implemented in Pick.

Statements

A *statement* is a list of words which comprise the detailed instructions from which the computer makes its decisions and performs its duties. It normally consists of constants, variables, expressions, and/or the special commands of the PICK/BASIC language. The PICK/BASIC language allows multiple statements to be put on one physical line (attribute) provided that each statement is separated by a semicolon (;). The first line of code in Fig. 1-3 illustrates what happens when this feature is abused.

```
PRINT "ENTER NAME " ; INPUT NAME ; IF NAME = "" THEN STOP
(first statement)        (second)         (third)

COUNTER = 0          ; * SET NUMBER OF ITEMS COUNTER TO ZERO
(first statement)      (second statement)
```

Fig. 1-3. Poor and acceptable uses of multiple statements on one source line.

As a rule of thumb, however, it is recommended to put only one statement per line. This makes programs more visually appealing and, consequently, easier to maintain. The one exception to this rule is when a comment, or remark, is included on a source line, as illustrated by the second line.

Constants and Literals

A *constant* is a value which remains unchanged. Numeric constants do not have to be enclosed in quotes. For example:

```
SECONDS.PER.HOUR = 3600
```

This replaces the current value of the variable SECONDS.PER.HOUR with the value 3600. "3600" is the constant.

Literal constants are any strings enclosed in single or double quotes, or between backslashes (\ ). Any number of characters, up to the maximum item size of 32K, may occur between the quotes or backslashes. For example:

```
REPORT.TITLE = "PHYSICAL INVENTORY REPORT"
```

where "PHYSICAL INVENTORY REPORT" is the literal constant.

```
PRINT.LINE = 'NAME' : '    ' : 'PAY RATE'
```

where 'NAME', '   ', and 'PAY RATE' are the literal constants.

Other acceptable literal constants include:

```
PROMPT ""
```

where the two double quotes represent the "null" string, meaning no value.

```
AGE = "0"
```

where "0" is the literal constant. Purely numeric values do not have to be enclosed in quotes. The equivalent statement is:

```
AGE = 0
```

Since no data typing occurs in Pick, these two statements produce the same effect.

Variables

A *variable* is a symbol that represents and contains a data value. As its name implies, the value, or contents, of a variable may change during program execution. Some other systems call these "data names."

In many versions of BASIC, as well as in languages such as Pascal, Ada, and PL/I, the "type" of a variable must be declared prior to storing data in it. This means that the

7

Self-explanatory form:	The "Guess What" form:
AGING.TOTAL = 0	**AT** = 0
IF **EXIT.FLAG** THEN STOP	IF **X** THEN STOP
MATREAD **CUSTOMER.ARRAY...**	MATREAD **CA...**

Fig. 1-4. Sample variable names.

computer is told what type of data to expect in a particular variable—whether it will be a number or a combination of both letters and numbers. In other versions of BASIC, variable names are typically single alphabetic characters for numeric variables, which are used in arithmetic operations. "String" variable names are usually single alphabetic characters followed by a "$" character. "String" variables contain alphabetic and/or punctuation characters and, on occasion, numbers.

In PICK/BASIC, no concept of data type exists. Variable names may be any length and therefore may be descriptively named. Variable names may include alphabetic characters, periods and dollar signs, but must begin with an alphabetic character. Figure 1-4 illustrates samples of variable names that are all valid in PICK/BASIC.

Assignment

Variables may be *assigned* an initial value in a program. For example:

ITEM.COUNTER = 0

This assigns the value of 0 (zero) to the variable named ITEM.COUNTER. This is also known as the process of *replacement*. When a variable name appears on the left side of an equals sign, then the result of whatever appears on the right side of the equals sign will be placed there. Typically, what appears on the right side is a function which produces some result, or a literal string enclosed in quotes, or even a number, as in the example.

This phenomenon is extremely important. There are many instances of using assignment throughout a program. These are examined throughout the tutorials.

When the program assigns the value of 0 (zero) to the variable ITEM.COUNTER, the variable is *initialized*. Initializing means that the program is making the first reference to a variable. The result of not initializing a variable before it is referenced results in an error message:

[B10] VARIABLE HAS NOT BEEN ASSIGNED A VALUE; ZERO USED!

It's a good idea to systematically assign initial values to variables.

The most important aspect of variables with regard to initializing is that they must be declared on the left side of an equals sign *before* referring to them on the right side of an equals sign. Part A of Fig. 1-5 illustrates the correct approach to initializing variables,

```
 A    003      TOTAL.AMOUNT = 0
      .
      .
      .
      007      PRINT "ENTER DOLLAR AMOUNT OF CHECK " :
      008      INPUT CHECK.AMOUNT
      .
      .
      014      TOTAL.AMOUNT = TOTAL.AMOUNT + CHECK.AMOUNT
 B    .
      .
      .
      014      TOTAL.AMOUNT = TOTAL.AMOUNT + CHECK.AMOUNT
```

Fig. 1-5. Example of A) properly initializing a variable, and B) failing to initialize.

while part B illustrates what happens when a variable is not initialized. TOTAL.AMOUNT appears at line 14 for the *first* time in this program, and will generate the runtime error message cited above.

Functions

Functions are operations on one or more variables, constants, or expressions (see *nuclear tokens*), which generate a single value. They are one of the kinds of elements that may be used in a PICK/BASIC expression. (The other two are variables and constants). Functions perform relatively complicated operations, like removing all extraneous blanks from a string or converting dates to alternate formats. Functions ordinarily do not stand alone in a statement. They are typically assigned to a variable or output with a PRINT statement. Here are a few of the various functions available in PICK/BASIC:

```
PRINT STR("!",25)
CUSTOMER.ITEM(1) = TRIM(RESPONSE)
CURRENT.TIME = TIME()
```

There are some rare occasions, however, where functions may effectively "stand alone." One such case is when a function is passed to an external subroutine. Essentially, the rule is that functions may be used anywhere an expression may be used.

Functions which are native to a language are called *intrinsic functions*. The intrinsic functions within PICK/BASIC have one syntactical common denominator. They are always immediately followed by a set of parentheses. Sometimes, depending on the type of function, there are one or more *arguments* or *expressions* within these parentheses. In a few exceptional cases, there are no expressions within the parentheses. Table 1-1 is a partial listing of PICK/BASIC intrinsic functions, showing required number of expressions within the parentheses.

Table 1-1. Partial Listing of Functions Showing Arguments Required.

Functions which require no expressions:*

    COL1( )

    COL2( )

    TIME( )

    DATE( )

    TIMEDATE( )

Functions which require one expression:

    RND(*numeric.expression*)

    INT(*numeric.expression*)

    NUM(*numeric.expression*)

    ASCII(*string.expression*)

Functions which require two expressions:

    COUNT(*string.expression,string.expression*)

    STR(*string.expression,numeric.expression*)

    ICONV(*string.expression,conversion.expression*)

    OCONV(*string.expression,conversion.expression*)

Functions which require three expressions:

    FIELD(*string.expression,string.expression,numeric.expression*)

    INDEX(*string.expression,string.expression,numeric.expression*)

Functions which require four expressions:

    EXTRACT(*array.variable, numeric.expression, . . .*
    . . . numeric.expression, numeric.expression)

    DELETE(*array.variable, numeric.expression, . . .*
    . . . numeric.expression, numeric.expression)

Functions which require five expressions:

    INSERT(*array.variable, numeric.expression, . . .*
    . . . numeric.expression, numeric.expression, . . .
    . . . string.expression)

    REPLACE(*array.variable, numeric.expression, . . .*
    . . . numeric.expression, numeric.expression, . . .
    . . . string.expression)

*According to one leading Pick expert, the TIME( ), DATE( ), and TIMEDATE( ) functions would be more accurately called "global system variables." They just happen to have a syntax that makes them appear confusingly similar to functions.

Operators

Operators are characters, and sometimes words, which perform logical, arithmetic, relational, or string-modifying operations. Operators include: $+ - / * <> <= >=$ # : and a few others. A detailed explanation of the operators is found in Appendix A. Figure 1-6 illustrates some of the operators available in PICK/BASIC.

The operators can be classified into three distinct categories. *Arithmetic operators* include $+$ (addition), $-$ (subtraction), $/$ (division), $*$ (multiplication), and $^$ (exponentiation). *Logical operators* are used in comparison operations, and include $>$ (greater than), $<$ (less than), $>=$ (greater than or equal to), $<=$ (less than or equal to), and # (not equal to, which may also be represented by $<>$ or $><$). *String operators* include : (concatenation, or "linking" strings together) and the MATCHES relational operator, which detects "patterns" of characters.

In the first line of Fig. 1-6, "$>$" is a logical operator which means "greater than," and "$+$" is an arithmetic operator for addition. In the second line, "MATCHES" is a relational operator which checks patterns of characters, and "$:$" is a string-modifying operator which means concatenate. *Concatenate* is another way of saying "link together."

Expressions and Arguments

An *expression* is a valid series of constants, variables, and functions, connected by operators. These are also frequently referred to as *arguments*. The simplest expression is a single constant, variable or intrinsic function. For example:

```
TOTAL = TOTAL + NEXT.AMOUNT
```

This is an arithmetic expression, one which adds the two (presumably assigned) variables together and stores the result in a variable called TOTAL.

Expressions produce a result, like a string of characters or a number. The result they produce determines the type of expression. It is important to distinguish types of expressions in attempting to explain the capabilities of PICK/BASIC.

Some functions, for example, test for a "true" or "false" condition, which could be classified in this case as a *conditional expression*. As you proceed through the tutorials, you will see a variety of expressions, such as "string" expressions and "numeric" expressions. Each new type of expression is explained as it is encountered. For example:

```
ELIGIBLE.FOR.RETIREMENT = (AGE >= 65)
```

This is a known as a *relational, logical* or *boolean expression*. Boolean expressions use

---

```
IF CHECK.AMOUNT > 0 THEN CHECK.TOTAL = CHECK.TOTAL + CHECK.AMOUNT

IF PART.NUMBER MATCHES "1A4N" THEN TITLE = TITLE : " " : RESPONSE
```

Fig. 1-6. Examples of using operators.

11

the operators $>$ $<$ $>=$ $<=$ $<>$ $><$ #. Any such expression evaluates to a numeric nonzero value (normally 1) if true, and a 0 (zero or null) if false. This statement assigns the value 1 (one) to the variable ELIGIBLE.FOR.RETIREMENT if the variable AGE is greater than or equal to 65; otherwise, it is assigned a 0 (zero) if not true.

The parentheses not only clarify, but also determine the meaning of the statement. By the way, if you don't put the parentheses around the expression, then it will not work on some versions of Pick.

Logical or boolean expressions are used within conditional expressions like the IF-THEN and LOOP-UNTIL constructs. They also have the property of being able to stand alone in an assignment statement.

This process of combining expressions continues in an ever-expanding combination of syntactical permutations when parentheses and the logical operators OR and AND are included. Figure 1-7 illustrates the use of parentheses and logical operators.

Functions and Nuclear Tokens

In the initial definition of functions it was mentioned that functions always are followed immediately by a set of parentheses, often containing one or more expressions. This is where the concept of "nuclear" or "atomic" tokens needs to be discussed. Effectively, a *nuclear token* is the smallest part of an expression. Functions may also contain other expressions, which in turn may contain other functions. This is known as an *infix* notational language. An example of this is the statement:

```
PRINT ABS(INT(X * Y))
```

In evaluating expressions, the computer starts from the innermost set of parentheses and works outward. This example has "X * Y" at its core. "X" and "Y" themselves are nuclear tokens, because they are variables which already contain a result by an assignment or a calculation. When X is multiplied by Y, the result itself becomes the nuclear token for the INT function. The INT function retrieves the integer portion (the numbers to the left of the decimal point) of the number, which becomes the nuclear token for the ABS function, which retrieves the absolute value of a numeric expression. The absolute value is always the positive value of a numeric variable; hence, the ABS function strips off the leading minus sign if the result is a negative number.

```
ELIGIBLE.FOR.RETIREMENT = (AGE >= 65)
IF ELIGIBLE.FOR.RETIREMENT AND (YEARS.WORKED > 1 AND YEARS.WORKED < 10) THEN
    RETIREMENT.GIFT = "TIMEX WATCH"
END
IF ELIGIBLE.FOR.RETIREMENT AND (YEARS.WORKED > 10) THEN
    RETIREMENT.GIFT = "ROLEX WATCH"
END
```

Fig. 1-7. Using parentheses and logical operators.

12

MAINTAINING STANDARDS AND CONVENTIONS

Once you know how to program in one language, you discover that most of the same principles apply in almost all languages: programs are used to capture, manipulate, store and retrieve data on the computer. In current technology, data is stored on "hard" or "fixed" disks. In a few years, hard disks may be obsolete, but the principles of dealing with new media will remain the same. There will still be a need to have programs to organize and administer data management.

In any programming language as flexible as PICK/BASIC, it is important to consider adopting "standards." These are "standard" methods of doing things. In programming textbooks and training classes, discussion of "standards" often is left until the end, after habits are already started. Introducing some of the concepts early on allows you to take advantage of them from the start.

Many programming shops have lists of "programming standards." These are the guidelines which programmers follow in order to produce programs that everyone can understand and maintain. This text suggests many standards, such as the variable naming conventions about to be discussed. You may choose to implement some and/or use some of your own.

Most versions of Pick are implemented using the ASCII coding scheme.[2] Any variable may contain a number or a character string. Since there are no "typed" variables in the Pick System, it is suggested that you use some variable naming conventions. For example, all variables that act as accumulators could have. TOTAL for the suffix. The next few sections illustrate some of the conventions that are used throughout this text.

File Variables. A *file variable* is used to refer to a DATA or DICT file and is always declared in an OPEN statement. The suggested convention is that the variable name of the file is always followed by the suffix ".FILE":

filename .FILE

For example:

```
OPEN "CUSTOMER-FILE" TO CUSTOMER.FILE...
```

Item-ID Variables. An *item-id variable* is a variable used to contain an item-id (what many people call a "key"). It's a good idea to always follow the name of the variable with the literal, ".ID":

variable.ID

For example:

```
INPUT CUSTOMER.ID
```

---

2. Some newer versions of Pick, notably the IBM 4300 and 9370 implementations, use the EBCDIC coding scheme. EBCDIC is an acronym for Expanded Binary Coded Decimal Interchange Code. This is an 8-bit coding scheme, similar to ASCII but using the eighth bit, which extends the range of characters to 256.

Array Variables. An *array variable* is the resting place for an item read in through a READ or MATREAD statement. The suggested convention is that the name of the array is always followed by the suffix, ".ITEM":

arrayname.ITEM or *arrayname*.ARRAY

For example:

MATREAD CUSTOMER.**ITEM** FROM CUSTOMER.FILE,CUSTOMER.ID...

Flag Variables. A *flag variable* typically contains one of two possible conditions: 0 (zero) or (numeric) non-zero (normally 1). These end with the suffix, ".FLG":

variable.FLG

Note that you may use any conventions that you like to name your variables. It is recommended that you do use some naming conventions, however, because many programmers have found that naming conventions make programs less difficult to create and/or modify.

SUMMARY

You have just completed the "crash course" on programming concepts. In it, you learned important principles and terms like *variables*, *expressions*, and *operators*. These principles, with few exceptions, are generalized and apply to virtually every programming language. From now on, the topics become much more specialized.

The Related
TCL Processes

2

THIS CHAPTER WILL EXPLAIN THE MOST IMPORTANT TCL (TERMINAL CONTROL LAN-
guage), system-level procedures you will have to deal with in order to begin programming in PICK/BASIC. These include using the Editor, creating and maintaining files, and
compiling and running your programs.

The PICK Editor

The Editor is the process through which programs are entered into the computer. It
allows the creation, update, and deletion of items in a file. A brief tutorial on the most
essential Editor commands is provided in this chapter.

In general, editors fall into two categories. There are *line editors*, like the one about
to be discussed, and there are *full-screen editors*. A line editor is much more primitive
in design. In line editors, you must position the ''line pointer'' to the line (attribute) that
you want to affect using a positioning command such as ''G'' (goto line), ''U'' (move
up), and ''N'' (move down). With a full-screen editor, you use the numeric keypad or
the arrow keys to position to the line that you want to alter.

If your system has JET, or one of its derivatives such as ULTIWORD or
WORDMATE, then you actually have a full-screen editor available. Invoking the JET
editor is accomplished by using the command ''JET-EDIT'' in place of the ''ED''
command. JET has its own set of commands, many of which are similar to the commands
in the Pick line editor. If you decide to try the JET editor, press the ''?'' key once it is
activated to obtain a list of all of the available JET commands.

Activating The Editor

The following commands are essential for the use of the Editor throughout the course of this book:

ED or EDIT

Either of these verbs may be used at the TCL prompt character (>) to activate the Editor. It always has the general form:

>**ED** *filename item-id* <cr>

to edit an individual item in a file, or

>**ED** *filename item-id item-id item-id...* <cr>

to edit multiple items in a file, or

>**ED** *filename* * <cr>

to edit all the items in a file, or

>**SELECT** *filename* {with selection criteria...} <cr>
n ITEMS SELECTED.
>**ED** *filename* <cr>

The ED command does not require the *itemlist* specification when following a SELECT or SSELECT command.

Before entering the Editor, the requested filename is searched for the specified item-id. If the item-id is found, the line pointer is left at the "top" of the item. If it is not found, then a "NEW ITEM" message appears and the line pointer is positioned to the top of an otherwise empty item. Once the Editor has been invoked, there are a number of commands available; the next several sections describe those that are used the most often.

Inserting New Lines

The Insert Editor command inserts one or more lines:

I

For an example, examine the terminal dialogue in Fig. 2-1. Note that while you are in "insert mode," each new line (attribute) is given a line number. To get out of insert mode, press the carriage return key while the cursor is positioned immediately to the right of a "plus" (+) sign. This returns control to the Editor command mode.

```
>ED filename item-id        activates Editor
NEW ITEM                    indicates new item
TOP                         indicates "top" of item
.I<cr>                      starts inserting lines
001+* this is line 1 <cr>
002+* this is line 2 <cr>
003+<cr>                    gets out of insert
```

Fig. 2-1. Using the Insert command.

Replacing Existing Lines

To replace a portion or all of an attribute, or a range of attributes, use the Replace command:

R

For example:

`.R/PRINT/CRT`

replaces, on the current line, the first occurrence of the word "PRINT" with "CRT." The command

`.RU999/PRINT/CRT`

replaces, in the next 999 lines, all occurrences of "PRINT" with "CRT."

Listing Items to the Screen

To list a specified number of lines on the screen, use the List command:

L

See Fig. 2-2 for an example of using the List command. The "EOI 011" message means that the "End Of Item" has occurred at line 11. There are no more attributes or lines after this message.

The Shortcut Way to List Items. Most versions of Pick allow "prestored" commands in the Editor:

P

Normally, the only one that is defined automatically is P0 (zero), and it issues an "L22" command. To test this, enter the **P** command at the Editor command prompt (Fig. 2-3).

17

```
>ED filename item-id <cr>          activates Editor
TOP                                indicates top of item
.L22<cr>                           lists 22 lines
001 * this is line 1
002 * this is line 2
003 * and so on...
    .
    .
011 * this is the last line...
EOI 011
```

Fig. 2-2. Using the List command.

```
>ED filename item-id <cr>
TOP
.P<cr>                                      lists 22 lines
001 * this is line 1
002 * this is line 2
003 * and so on...
    .
    .
011 * this is the last line...
EOI 011
```

Fig. 2-3. Using the Editor's prestored commands.

Deleting Lines

To delete one or more lines, use the Delete command:

DE

or

DE_n_

For example:

```
014 * this line needs to go away...
.DE<cr>
```

This does away with the current line, which in this case is line 14. Or, you can use the DE command on multiple lines:

```
014 * this line is going away...
.DE3
```

18

This deletes line 14 and the next two lines, for a total of three lines.

Moving the Line Pointer

To move the pointer to a particular line *n*, use the Goto command:

    G*n*

or

    n

For example:

```
014 * this is line 14
.G7<cr>
007 * this is line 7
```

The "G" is optional. You may also simply enter the line number:

```
014 * this is line 14
.7<cr>
007 * this is line 7
```

Reviewing Changes: The F Command

To review changes in an item, use the Flip command:

    F

This command "flips" Editor buffers. Get used to this. You must use this command before you may review any changes that have been made to an item:

```
014 * this is line 14
.F<cr>
TOP
.
```

Saving and Exiting

The File command is used to save (or resave) the item being entered or modified. Entering

    FI

files the item, saving all changes made. For example:

```
014 * this is line 14
```

```
.FI<cr>
'item-id' filed.
```

Exiting without Saving Changes. To abort the edit of an item, use the Exit command. Entering

```
EX
```

exits the item without saving any changes. For example:

```
014 * this is line 14
.EX<cr>
'item-id' exited.
```

Note: Unlike other systems, the Editor doesn't have the logic (in most versions of Pick) to warn you to save the item before exiting, if any changes have been made. *Be careful!* Some implementations now ask "ARE YOU SURE? (Y/N)" when using the EX (and FD) commands.

Deleting an Item

This command deletes the current item from the file:

```
FD
```

Some versions of the Editor ask if you are "sure" you want to do this; most other versions don't. *Caveat emptor*. A TCL command called "RECOVER-FD" typically is available to recover a deleted item, but there's a catch. The only time it works is if you use it to try to recover the last item that was edited and deleted.

GETTING INTO THE SYSTEM

Now we will walk through the process of getting into the system, creating your account and files, and entering your programs.

Logging On

To begin a session, the first thing to do is "log on" to the system. Every Pick system has an account called "SYSPROG." This very powerful account contains the commands used to do most of the system administration functions, such as backups, restores, and maintenance.

Find a terminal, turn it on, and enter "SYSPROG" at the "Logon Please" message.

```
LOGON PLEASE:SYSPROG<cr>
```

If the next prompt is "PASSWORD?", then you must find out what the password is and enter it before you may continue.

20

After a brief introductory message, which typically welcomes you to the system and tells you the current system time and date, the computer displays the TCL (Terminal Control Language) prompt. On all systems other than the Microdata (McDonnell Douglas) version of Pick, TCL is indicated by the ">" prompt character. Microdata uses the ":" symbol as its prompt character.

The activity generated by entering a command at the TCL prompt is referred to as a *process*. While the Pick system is capable of handling multiple processes within an account, for safety's sake you are encouraged to create your own account. This will protect you from the other users of your system, and vice versa.

Creating Your Own Account

Enter the following command at the TCL prompt character:

>**CREATE-ACCOUNT**<cr>

Before we continue, an explanatory disclaimer is required. The "CREATE-ACCOUNT" procedure varies operationally among different implementations of Pick. This means that the questions asked of you by the CREATE-ACCOUNT process may be in a different order or format, but essentially the same information is needed by all the different versions.

ACCOUNT NAME?**your.account.name**<cr>

The name of your account is up to you. There are certain characters to avoid in your account name (or any item-id, for that matter). These characters include: spaces, arrow keys, single or double quotes, slashes or backslashes, and never any control characters. Enter your account name and press Return. If you can't think of one, use "CLASS" as your account name.

L/RET CODES?<cr>

This cryptic prompt is for the security (retrieval) codes for this account. Retrieval codes are better left alone. Press Return.

L/UPD CODES?<cr>

This is for the entry of the update codes. Ignore this for now. Maybe forever. Press Return.

MOD, SEP?**29,1**<cr>

This prompt allows you to specify the size (modulo) of the MD (Master Dictionary) file in the account you are about to create. Normally, there is a default value here of "29,1." If not, enter 29,1 and press Return. This means that 29 contiguous frames will be set aside for the new MD. This will most likely be adequate for the next decade or two, or until you add lots of items to the MD, in which case you might consider increasing the modulo. Choosing modulo is not trivial. Fortunately, that's why there is normally a default provided here.

PASSWORD?<cr>

An account password is up to you. If you use it, you will be asked for it each time you log on to your account.

PRIVILEGES?**SYS2**<cr>

The privilege level is important. Privilege level two (SYS2) allows access to anything that is in or available to the account. That's what you want. A detailed explanation of privilege levels is found in *Exploring the Pick Operating System* or the standard Pick System reference manuals.

This is normally all the information that you need to enter. One or two more questions may be asked of you. Do the best you can. It's not likely that you'll hurt anything. If the process completes normally, control returns to TCL. If not, consult your system manuals for troubleshooting.

Now it's time to try your new account. Enter this:

>**LOGTO your.account.name**<cr>

The LOGTO command allows you to leave the current account to access another. Control normally returns to TCL on the new account.

Creating Your Work Files

Before getting into the PICK/BASIC tutorial, some work files must be created. These will hold the data, programs, and PROCs created during the tutorials. These files are established with the CREATE-FILE command (see Fig. 2-4).

The CREATE-FILE command places a new file in the current account. The numbers following the filename indicate the starting disk address, modulo, and separation for the dictionary and DATA levels of the file, respectively. For the sake of brevity, the messages

---

```
>CREATE-FILE BP 11,1 29,1 <cr>

[417] FILE 'BP' CREATED. BASE = fid. MOD = 11. SEPAR = 1
[417] FILE 'BP' CREATED. BASE = fid. MOD = 29. SEPAR = 1
```

Fig. 2-4. An example of the CREATE-FILE command.

output from the following CREATE-FILE commands have been left out.

```
>CREATE-FILE STAFF 7,1 11,1 <cr>
>CREATE-FILE PROCS 1,1 11,1 <cr>
>CREATE-FILE STATES 1,1 11,1 <cr>
```

The numbers following the filename specify the size of the file. These are called the *modulo* and *separation*, and a detailed explanation of these is found in *Exploring the Pick Operating System*.

Preparing the Source File

The file in which PICK/BASIC programs reside needs to have a minor operation performed prior to being able to compile programs. This is accomplished by using the Editor to change the "D-pointer" (the file definition item) in the MD. Note: readers with Ultimate or McDonnell Douglas computer systems do not need to do this!

Here are the steps involved in preparing the BP file pointer:

```
>ED MD BP<cr>
TOP
.1<cr>
001 D
.R/D/DC<cr>
001 DC
.FI
'BP' FILED.
```

The reason that this has to be done is that PICK/BASIC object code has to be handled differently than "normal" data items. *Source code* refers to the human-readable list of instructions to perform as a program. In the Pick System, source code resides in the DATA section of files. *Object code* is produced by compiling source code into executable, machine-readable code. When a program is compiled, a "pointer" item is placed in the dictionary of the source file[1]. This pointer item tells the system where the object code will be found for execution. The name of the pointer item is the same as the source program item. Incidentally, this is exactly the same way that "lists" are handled with the SAVE-LIST command.

Note for Ultimate Users: Ultimate Corporation added a verb called UPDATE-FILE in release 122, when "security" was implemented. This was ostensibly to prevent users from damaging file definition items (D-pointers). This change does not have to be done to source files on Ultimate systems, because any file may contain source and/or object code. However, if you do feel like doing this to a file, you must use the UPDATE-FILE verb; otherwise, you may damage or even destroy the file!

---

1. This scheme does not currently apply to computers from McDonnell Dougls (Microdata). Rather, the executable object code is created as an item in the same file as the source code. The object code item-id is the program name preceded by a $.

```
>ED BP HELLO<cr>
NEW ITEM
TOP
.I<cr>
001+IF TIME() < 43200 THEN PRINT "GOOD MORNING"<cr>
002+IF TIME() > 43200 THEN PRINT "GOOD AFTERNOON"<cr>
003+END<cr>
004+<cr>
TOP
.FI<cr>
'HELLO' FILED.
```

Fig. 2-5. Entering the HELLO program example.

The ED Command and HELLO Program

PICK/BASIC programs are typically entered through the standard Pick Editor, although any editor will do. The Pick Editor is activated with the ED or EDIT command. Follow the instructions in Fig. 2-5, and enter the program shown. This program is now ready to be compiled, which must be done before it may be run.

Note: The instructions in this program test the current system "time." In Chapter 1, the internal representation of time was discussed. The important point to remember is that time is stored internally as the integer number of seconds past midnight: "43200" is 12:00 (noon), which is 12 (hours) multiplied by 3600 (seconds per hour).

The command line "ED BP HELLO" entered at the TCL command prompt (>) instructs the Pick System to activate the Editor. The program goes into the file called "BP," and its item-id is (or will be) "HELLO."

PICK/BASIC Program Names (Item-IDs)

Since Pick stores individual programs as items (records) in a single program file and Pick does not limit the length of the item-id[2] (program name), you may use descriptive item-ids. One warning, however: *Never use a program name that has the same name as the source file in which it will reside!* These are some invalid program names:

>ED BP BP

or

>ED AR.BP AR.BP

Actually, the Pick system will let you get away with this—for the moment. It catches up with you later when it destroys your file. The next section discusses the BASIC command, which is used to compile source code into (executable) object code. Normally,

---

2. Older versions of the Pick System limited the length of the item-id to 50 bytes.

when a compile takes place, a pointer to the object code of the program is placed in the dictionary level of the source file, using the same item-id as the source item. If there is a program with the same name as the file, there is a potential danger of the object pointer writing over the *file pointer* (the pointer to the DATA section of the file). If this happens, all your program source items will be lost! Some versions of Pick have built-in protective mechanisms to prevent this problem.

COMPILING PROGRAMS: THE BASIC COMMAND

The BASIC command activates the PICK/BASIC compiler to translate the source code into object code. The following examples illustrate the BASIC command and some of its available options.

```
>BASIC BP HELLO<cr>
***
'HELLO' COMPILED.  1 FRAMES USED.
```

Each * represents one source line successfully compiled into executable object code. A listing of the program may be produced with the L option:

```
>BASIC BP HELLO (L)<cr>

001 IF TIME() < 43200 THEN PRINT "GOOD MORNING"
002 IF TIME() > 43200 THEN PRINT "GOOD AFTERNOON"
003 END
'HELLO' COMPILED.  1 FRAMES USED.
```

The listing may be routed to a printer by including the P option:

```
>BASIC BP HELLO (LP)<cr>
```

Other options are available. These options are discussed in Appendix B.

ACTIVATING PROGRAMS: THE RUN AND CATALOG COMMANDS

There are two ways to load and execute a compiled program. The first is the use of the RUN verb:

```
>RUN BP HELLO<cr>
GOOD MORNING
```

(Unless it's after 12:00 P.M., of course, in which case the program displays ''GOOD AFTERNOON'').

25

The second way is to CATALOG the program. This effectively makes a verb out of the program:

```
>CATALOG BP HELLO<cr>
'HELLO' CATALOGED.

>HELLO<cr>
GOOD MORNING
```

The rule with regard to cataloging programs is that the only programs which *must* be cataloged are those which are considered "external" subroutines. While all of your programs do not have to be cataloged, it's still a good idea. Note that external subroutines do not have to be cataloged on Ultimate systems, unless the subroutine resides in a different file from the program that calls it.

From now on in the tutorials, compile all of your programs with the BASIC command, and then CATALOG each program.

IF IT DIDN'T WORK

If you had any problem with the example called "HELLO," check the code using the Editor. It must be entered exactly as it appears in the text.

There are many possible reasons why programs don't compile. Here is a partial list of the most common compile failures:

1) Functions or instructions are misspelled. For example:

```
PRINT "HELLO THERE"
```

2) Quotation marks, used in printing or assigning "literals" are "unbalanced," meaning, an odd number exists. For example:

```
PRINT "HELLO THERE
```

3) A GOTO or GOSUB statement which instructs the program to transfer control to a nonexistent statement label. For example:

```
001    10    PRINT "HELLO"
002          GOTO 99
003          END
```

4) An IF-THEN or IF-THEN-ELSE statement isn't properly terminated with an END directive. Or, worse, is terminated with too many END directives. For example:

```
IF QTY.ON.HAND < REORDER.POINT THEN
    PRINT "PRODUCT NEEDS TO BE REORDERED!"
(HERE IS WHERE THE "END" STATEMENT SHOULD HAVE BEEN)
    .
and the code goes on...
```

This has the unpleasant side effect of using the *next* END directive that the compiler encounters as the terminator for the THEN initiator. Don't worry about this for now. The proper way to prevent this problem is explained in Chapter 4, at the end of the narrative on Example 2.

5) Having a blank or "null" line in the source program. Currently only Ultimate and a few other licensees allow null source lines. For example:

```
001
002 * This program is used to enter General Ledger accounts
```

Again, the programs in this book were tested and they worked on our test machines. The most important thing to do is to compare your program listing line-by-line with the program listings from the book. You may find that you left out a character or two here and there. Don't feel bad if your programs don't always compile the first time; it happens to everybody.

3

Fundamental
PICK/BASIC
Statements
and
Instructions

IN THE FIRST PROGRAM, MANY OF THE MOST FUNDAMENTAL PRINCIPLES OF PROGRAMMING in PICK/BASIC are discussed. Topics, statements, and functions covered include: comments (remarks), PROMPT, PRINT, INPUT, ABS, SQRT, ALPHA, NUM, END, IF-THEN, STOP, the null string, and LEN.

Enter the program in Fig. 3-1. An explanation of each instruction and technique follows. Note that most of the spaces in the tutorial programs are put there for visual esthetics. The easier a program is to read, the easier it is to maintain. Generally, spaces are optional, but there are some cases where they are not. To be safe, enter the programs exactly as shown in the examples.

Having entered the program, you are now ready to compile and run it. From now on, after entering each program example, compile it with the BASIC verb, catalog it with the CATALOG verb, then type the program name at the TCL prompt. Once again, here's an example:

```
>BASIC BP EX.001<cr>
**********************************************
SUCCESSFUL COMPILE!  1 FRAMES USED.

>CATALOG BP EX.001<cr>
'EX.001' CATALOGED.

>EX.001<cr>
```

Fig. 3-1. Program Example 1.

```
>ED BP EX.001
TOP
.I<cr>
001+* EX.001
002+* BASIC TERMINAL I/O AND CONDITIONAL EXPRESSIONS
003+* mm/dd/yy : date last modified
004+* JES : author's initials
005+*
006+    PROMPT ":"
007+    PRINT
008+*
009+* GET NAME
010+*
011+    PRINT "PLEASE ENTER YOUR NAME " :
012+    INPUT NAME
013+    PRINT
014+*
015+* CHECK TO SEE IF THEY WANT TO STOP
016+*
017+    IF NAME = "" OR NAME = "QUIT" THEN STOP
018+    PRINT "HELLO THERE " : NAME
019+    PRINT
020+*
021+* NOW GET STRING OR NUMBER
022+*
023+    PRINT "PLEASE ENTER A NUMBER OR A STRING OF LETTERS " :
024+    INPUT RESPONSE
025+    IF RESPONSE = "" OR RESPONSE = "QUIT" THEN STOP
026+    PRINT
027+*
028+* CHECK TO SEE IF STRING IS NUMERIC
029+*
030+    IF NUM(RESPONSE) THEN
031+        PRINT "ABS VALUE OF " : RESPONSE : " IS " :   ABS(RESPONSE)
032+        PRINT "THE SQUARE IS " : RESPONSE * RESPONSE
033+        PRINT "THE SQUARE ROOT IS " : SQRT(RESPONSE)
034+        STOP
035+    END
036+*
037+* CHECK TO SEE IF STRING IS LETTERS ONLY
038+*
039+    IF ALPHA(RESPONSE) THEN
040+        PRINT "THE LENGTH OF " : RESPONSE : " IS " : LEN(RESPONSE)
041+        STOP
042+    END
043+*
044+* STRING MUST CONTAIN NON-ALPHA AND NON-NUMERIC   CHARACTERS
045+*
046+    PRINT "YOUR RESPONSE WAS NOT CONSIDERED NUMERIC OR ALPHABETIC"
047+    END
048+<cr>
.FI
```

Once the program loads and begins execution the following prompt appears on the screen:

PLEASE ENTER YOUR NAME:

A feature of this book is the detailed explanation of each new topic, or derivatives of earlier topics, following the tutorial programs. The instruction, or group of statements and instructions, are repeated where the narrative explains them. This technique minimizes the amount of backtracking that you will have to do in order to examine the actual source instructions.

A note for Fortran and COBOL programmers learning Pick. After a quick visual scan of the program EX.001, or any other PICK/BASIC program, you will notice the total absence of data typing via implicit assumptions by virtue of the first character in the data/field names (i.e., variables beginning with I through N do not imply integer data). Nor do you find the ever-present "DATA DIVISION" that all COBOL programs must contain. Remember that no data typing exists in the Pick System. A field is a field is a field.

PROGRAM NAMES AND COMMENT SECTIONS

The first five lines of Programming Example 1 consist of comments:

```
001 * EX.001
002 * BASIC TERMINAL I/O AND CONDITIONAL EXPRESSIONS
003 * mm/dd/yy : date last modified
004 * JES : author's initials
005 *
```

The Pick System is very flexible regarding the manner in which files and items are named. This usually results in some rather diverse item-ids, particularly when naming programs. (A program is stored as an item in the Pick System, so a program name is an item-id). For instance, a programmer may decide to call a program "AP101," which may mean to him that this is the program to enter and update the accounts payable vendor file. Others go to the extreme of identifying the nature of the program in its item-id. For instance, another programmer may call this same program "ENTER.ACCOUNTS.PAYABLE. VENDOR."

Rather than trying to explain the entire program in the program name, it may be more useful to decide on a simple item-id and explain the purpose of the program through remarks in the program. A *comment section* is simply a standard set of remark statements that appears at the beginning of each program. Remark statements have little effect on the execution of the program. This technique makes it easier to work with program files.

The Program Name

It's a good idea to use line 1 of each program to repeat the program name:

```
001 * EX.001
```

The reason for this is that programs which are considered external subroutines require a SUBROUTINE statement on this line, so you can't always count on this line being available. Note: Instead of placing a remark on line one, it is permissible to put the word "PROGRAM," followed by the program name. This little-known feature has been present for years in the Pick System.

The Program Description

Line two contains a single-line description of the program:

```
002 * BASIC TERMINAL I/O AND CONDITIONAL EXPRESSIONS
```

Other examples could be "UPDATE THE ACCOUNTS PAYABLE VENDOR MASTER FILE," or "EXTRACT CUSTOMER LISTS FROM DATABASE."

Date Last Modified and Author's Initials

The "date last modified" is the last date the program was changed:

```
003 * mm/dd/yy: date last modified
```

Follow a consistent date format, like *mm-dd-yy*, for example:

```
003 * 12/15/97 : date last modified
```

The comment on line 4 gives the initials of the last person who changed the program, which is useful for finding and persecuting the guilty party.

```
004 * JES : author's initials
```

"Spacer" Remark Lines

Line 5 is a "spacer remark line," which provides a visual separation of the comment section from the actual executable code of the program:

```
005 *
```

This treatment is for visual esthetics only and has no impact on the actual execution of the program; it just makes the program look more organized for the benefit of the programmer. Once again, the easier code is to read, the easier it is to maintain.

THE PROMPT STATEMENT

The PROMPT statement defines the character to display on the screen when an INPUT statement is executed:

```
006 PROMPT ":"
```

Any expression which produces a single character may be used as the argument. When this statement is left out of the program, the default prompt character is a question mark.

THE PRINT STATEMENT AND BLANK LINES

The PRINT statement is used to print data on the screen or printer. All by itself on a line, it simply skips a line on the output device:

```
007 PRINT
```

When followed by an expression, the current value of the expression is displayed or printed. Chapter 15, Example 13, discusses routing output to the system printer with the PRINT-ER ON statement.

ANNOTATING THE PROGRAM

Comments, also called *remarks*, have been discussed at several points already throughout this book. The block of comments in lines 8-10 serves two purposes:

```
008 *
009 * GET NAME
010 *
```

First, it provides the visual spacing to make the source code more readable to those who must maintain it and, second, the comment on line 9 reminds the programmer about the task at hand.

THE PRINCIPLE OF PSEUDOCODE

One important principle of program design is "pseudocode." "Pseudocode" is the process of describing program logic in plain English. Since a program is simply a set of instructions to perform a task, it is often necessary to plan out the logic of the problem before starting to write the code that will accomplish it. This may be done by organizing the logic in plain English statements, in the form of remarks. This way, the logic may be debugged before even one line of executable source code is ever written.

For example, if you wanted to teach a robot how to "make toast," you have to tell it the steps to perform. For instance, the robot would have to go to the kitchen, find the bread, remove a slice, find the toaster, put the bread in the toaster, push the button, wait for it to cook, remove the bread, and then find a plate to place it on. Once this sequence of events has been "programmed," all you need to tell the robot the next time you want toast is simply "make toast." The same principle applies to telling the robot how to make coffee, eggs, juice, etc. After the robot has been taught all of the individual routines, you may then put them all together by telling the robot to "make breakfast." To the robot, this means make toast, make coffee, make eggs, etc. Although this may seem like an elementary example, it introduces the principle of *modularity*. Programs typically are comprised of a series of individual, self-standing modules, each of which performs a specific task.

As this relates to the subject at hand, the entire logic of any program problem may be written first in comments, as in this example. Once the logic is in place, the source instructions of the appropriate language may be inserted after the comments, hence the principle of pseudocode.

MORE ON THE PRINT STATEMENT

The PRINT statement in line 11 displays "PLEASE ENTER YOUR NAME" on the screen and positions the cursor two spaces to the right of the word NAME. Note that the space between the word NAME and the " character is to force the space between the literal and the cursor.

```
011 PRINT "PLEASE ENTER YOUR NAME " :
```

Throughout this book, many other forms of the PRINT statement are explained, including its ability to print at specific coordinates on the screen or to do special functions like erase the screen. The PRINTER ON and PRINTER OFF statements also affect the output of PRINT statements.

THE INPUT STATEMENT

The INPUT statement causes the program to wait for the user to enter something on the keyboard:

```
012 INPUT NAME
```

When input is received, it is placed into the variable following the INPUT statement, which in this case is the variable NAME. Generally, what the user enters on the keyboard must be followed by a press of the Return key, although Pick provides the ability to automatically issue the Return when a certain number of characters have been received.

THE IF STATEMENT AND NULL STRINGS

The IF statement is used to determine whether or not a certain condition applies before continuing execution. IF statements are always followed by *conditional expressions,* which are expressions which derive either a "true" or "false" value. In the Pick System, "true" is represented by a numeric nonzero (normally 1), and "false" is represented by 0 (zero) or null.

```
017 IF NAME = "" OR NAME = "QUIT" THEN STOP
```

This IF statement checks to see if the variable NAME contains any data. The portion of the statement NAME = "" reads like this: If the NAME is null, which means that you simply pressed the Return key, then the conditional expression is true; if you entered a $<cr\alpha>$, then the variable NAME will be cleared (set to null). In PICK/BASIC, the *null string* is represented as *""* or *''*. The ":" prompt character previously defined in the PROMPT statement appears to the immediate left of the cursor.

```
IF ANSWER = "Y" THEN ...
IF AMOUNT > 0 THEN ...
IF OLD.AMOUNT # NEW.AMOUNT THEN ...
```

Note: The situations where the equivalence to 0 (zero) of a null value, which is typically represented by two quotation marks with nothing between them, occurs in other places in the Pick System. For example, if you attempt to add up fields which normally contain numeric data, such as money amounts, and one or more fields contain null (or any other nonnumeric data), then these fields are treated as though they contained the value 0 (zero).

A good way to check how your system handles nulls is to try the following statements in a test program:

```
001   A = ""
002   B = 0
003   IF A = B THEN PRINT "YES" ELSE PRINT "NO"
```

On most versions of Pick, this will print "NO."

BOOLEAN OPERATORS

Two or more conditional expressions may be connected by a *boolean operator*, which is one of the words AND or OR. Normally, when only one conditional expression follows an IF instruction, then the statement (or statements) following the THEN is (are) executed if the expression evaluates true. Otherwise, unless an ELSE is present, control "falls through" to the next physical line of the program. The ELSE initiator is optional in the IF construct, and is explained at the end of Example 2 in Chapter 4.

When two conditional expressions are connected with an OR, then either of them evaluating true causes the statement(s) following the THEN initiator to be executed. Having an AND connect the conditional expressions means that both expressions must evaluate true in order for the statement(s) following the THEN initiator to be executed.

This line has two possible choices for executing the STOP statement which follows the THEN initiator. Either a null (carriage return or line feed) or the word QUIT would have caused the STOP statement to be executed.

Here are sample conditional expressions using boolean operators:

```
IF ANSWER = "Y" OR ANSWER = "" THEN ...
```

This statement indicates that if *either* of the conditional expressions evaluate to true, then the statement (or statements) after the THEN initiator will be executed.

```
IF BALANCE.DUE > 0 AND INTEREST.FLAG = "Y" THEN ...
```

This second statement indicates that *both* of the conditional expressions must evaluate true in order to execute the statement (or statements) following the THEN initiator.

BAIL-OUT MECHANISMS: THE CONCEPT OF "ESCAPE PODS"

Eventually (if it hasn't happened to you already) you will run a program that prompts you to enter something and you will not know exactly what it wants. Maybe it needs something in a particular format, like a date or money amount, but you have no way of knowing. So you try pressing Return and it displays something like "INPUT REQUIRED!" and prompts you again. You try "END" or "QUIT" or "?" or "HELP." Then you try your favorite obscenity, again to no avail. In frustration, you try the data entry operator's last resort—the BREAK key—and find that it has been disabled. At times like this you reconsider your future in data processing and consider a less frustrating career, like religious cult management or being an air traffic controller.

To make a long story short, it is a very thoughtful touch to allow operators an escape or "bail-out" mechanism. This means that any time in your programs that an operator is prompted to input data, one consistent response is always available. This word (or character) is their panic button. In all of the tutorial examples, QUIT is used as the magic word. You may choose anything you want, but whatever you choose should be the first thing you teach your data entry operators. Tell them that when they enter this word, it means "*Get me out of here!*"

Implementing the escape pod principle has some remarkable side effects. First, it greatly reduces the fears of your users, assuring them that they may always escape in an orderly fashion from any program without hurting anything. Second, it allows you, the programmer, the benefit of cleaning up any unfinished program business before returning the user to the process or menu that sent them there.

The most important aspect of implementing your escape pod scheme is that you remain consistent in what you check or test for to allow them to bail out. Don't make it "X" in one place, "QUIT" in another, and "END" in yet another.

Line 17 is waiting for either a null or "QUIT" to allow the operator to get out. If that's what the operator inputs, then the program stops.

THE STOP STATEMENT

The STOP statement immediately terminates the execution of a program:

```
017 IF NAME = "" OR NAME = "QUIT" THEN STOP
```

If the program was activated from TCL, by entering >RUN BP EX.001, or >EX.001, then control returns to the TCL prompt character. If, however, the program had been executed from a menu, perhaps written in the PROC (procedure) language, then control automatically returns to the menu. The ABORT statement is the first cousin to the STOP statement. The difference is that when the ABORT is executed, control returns unconditionally to TCL, regardless of how the program was activated.

PRINTING EXPRESSIONS WITH PRINT

This statement prints the literal "HELLO THERE " on the screen and prints the current value of NAME, meaning, whatever you entered previously at the prompt to enter your name. Note that there is a space after the word "THERE" to force a space between the word "THERE" and your name.

```
018 PRINT "HELLO THERE " : NAME
```

This print expression was composed by a concatenation operation. First the literal "HELLO THERE " was concatenated (or linked) to the current value of the NAME variable. Once the concatenation was complete, the entire expression was printed.

Avoiding Redundancy and Repetition. Many of the instructions that have been covered up until now, such as PRINT, INPUT, IF-THEN, PROMPT, and comments, are used extensively throughout the rest of the tutorials. Rather than explaining the same things over and over, they will not be documented hereafter unless some new twist or nuance is being introduced.

THE NUM FUNCTION

The NUM function is one of several Pick intrinsic functions considered to be a "self-standing" conditional expression, i.e., one which evaluates to either a zero or null for "false," or a numeric nonzero value (normally 1) for "true."

```
030 IF NUM(RESPONSE) THEN
031    PRINT "ABS VALUE OF " : RESPONSE : " IS " : ABS(RESPONSE)
032    PRINT "THE SQUARE IS " : RESPONSE * RESPONSE
033    PRINT "THE SQUARE ROOT IS " : SQRT(RESPONSE)
034    STOP
035 END
```

This statement tests the string received in RESPONSE to determine whether or not it is a number. In the Pick System, a number is a string of digits with an optional period or decimal point. If it is determined to be a number, then all of the statements, up to and including line 34, are executed. If the response is not a number, then execution continues after the next END statement (which occurs on line 35).

An important note: Some, but not all, versions of the Pick System consider "null" to be numeric. This adds a level of complexity to your IF statements when they determine whether something is numeric; it must additionally be checked to see if it is null or not null, as the case may be.

If you did enter a number, then the statements on lines 31-35 are executed.

THE ABS FUNCTION

The ABS function produces the absolute (positive) value of a numeric string:

```
031 PRINT "ABS VALUE OF " : RESPONSE : " IS " : ABS(RESPONSE)
```

Suppose that you had entered −123.45 as your response; Line 31 would display:

```
ABS VALUE OF -123.45 IS 123
```

The ABS function comes in handy when printing the bottom-line totals of profit and loss reports for unstable companies.

Note that no range checking took place on the numbers you entered. This program may produce unusual results if the number is too large.

FINDING SQUARES AND SQUARE ROOTS

The next two lines utilize the PRINT statement and the SQRT function to determine squares and square roots.

```
032 PRINT "THE SQUARE IS " : RESPONSE * RESPONSE
033 PRINT "THE SQUARE ROOT IS " : SQRT(RESPONSE)
```

The statement in line 32 prints the message ''THE SQUARE IS '', followed by an expression which takes the value of RESPONSE and multiplies it by itself. This is here simply to demonstrate the fact that formulas may be 1) performed in the same line as a PRINT statement, or 2) may be ''assigned'' to a variable on a separate source line and have the value displayed here. Both ways are discussed throughout this book.

There is also the intrinsic function EXP, which may be used to raise a number to other exponential values, as well as the ^ operator that also indicates exponentiation. See Appendix B for the syntax.

The SQRT function produces the square root of a numeric expression. This displays the message shown, followed by the square root of RESPONSE.

THE END STATEMENT

When an IF-THEN statement or IF-THEN-ELSE statement spans more than one physical line of a program, it must be terminated with an END statement:

```
035 END
```

This principle is referred to as the *initiator/terminator relationship*, and is discussed immediately following this example. This particular END statement terminated the THEN initiator which started at line 30.

THE ALPHA FUNCTION

The ALPHA function, like the NUM function discussed earlier, is also considered a conditional expression, one which evaluates to a true (numeric nonzero) or false (zero or null) condition. They are most often used in IF-THEN, IF-THEN-ELSE, and in CASE constructs:

```
039 IF ALPHA(RESPONSE) THEN
040    PRINT "THE LENGTH OF " : RESPONSE : " IS " : LEN(RESPONSE)
041    STOP
042 END
```

This statement tests the variable RESPONSE to determine if it contains only alphabetic characters. This means no characters other than the letters A through Z (upper- or lowercase). If this evaluates true, then the statements up to the next END statement are executed. Otherwise, execution of the program continues after the next END statement, which happens to occur on line 42.

If this message appears, then it means that the response that you provided to the variable RESPONSE was not considered either entirely numeric or alphabetic:

```
046 PRINT "YOUR RESPONSE WAS NOT CONSIDERED NUMERIC OR
    ALPHABETIC"
```

Consequently, this line displays the message shown and program execution stops at the next line.

THE LEN FUNCTION

If you enter a string of characters that is considered to be composed entirely of alphabetic characters at the INPUT statement on line 24, then the LEN statement on line 40 will be executed:

```
040 PRINT "THE LENGTH OF " : RESPONSE : " IS " : LEN(RESPONSE)
```

The LEN function determines and reports the number of characters in a string or string expression. Suppose you enter ''ARISTOTLE'' into the variable RESPONSE. Line 40 then displays

```
THE LENGTH OF ARISTOTLE IS 9
```

THE FINAL END STATEMENT

The END statement (more accurately called a *compiler directive*) occurs in two places in PICK/BASIC. The first occurrence is when it is used as a terminator for a multiline IF-THEN or IF-THEN-ELSE statement. The second and final form is as a *program terminator*, meaning that this is the logical end of the program. On most Pick systems, if the final END statement is left out, one is automatically assumed at the end of an item (remember, even programs are considered "items"). You should include the final END statement just for consistency. This END statement on line 47 terminates the program.

This finishes the first example. Before moving on to Example 2, take a closer look at the IF statement.

THE IF-THEN STATEMENT

The IF statement has perhaps the greatest variety of possible syntactical forms of any instruction in the language. Since it is one of the most frequently used statements, it is important to understand the mechanics of how and when they are used. The examples and discussions will first focus on the "simplest" forms. As you progress through the examples, more sophisticated cases and uses are uncovered. Example 1 illustrates the forms.

The Single-Line Form

The "single-line" form means that the entire logic test, and the instructions which are to be executed when it evaluates true, are contained in one physical source line. The first general form has a syntactical form which appears as:

IF *conditional.expression* **THEN** *statement*

If the conditional expression evaluates true (numeric nonzero), then the single statement after the THEN initiator is executed and program execution continues on the next line of the program. If it evaluates false (zero or null), program execution continues from the next line.

Since statements may be delimited by a semicolon, the next form of this occurs as:

IF *conditional.expression* **THEN** *statement* ; *statement* ; *statement* . . .

When this conditional expression evaluates true, all of the statements following the THEN initiator are executed. There is no logical limit to the number of statements that may be put here but, as a rule of thumb, use the multiline form of the IF statement when more than a few statements are to be executed.

The single-line form is useful when there is only one statement to execute upon evaluation. There are, however, many cases in programs where many statements need to be performed on a true condition. Rather than trying to place these all on one physical line with semicolons between the statements, there is the next logical extension to the IF-THEN construct.

The Multiline IF-THEN Construct

The multiline IF-THEN construct has the general form:

IF *conditional.expression* **THEN**
   statement
   statement

```
IF conditional.expression THEN<cr>                    (starts "level 1")
    statement(s) . . .
    IF conditional.expression THEN<cr>                (starts "level 2")
        statement(s) . . .
        IF conditional.expression THEN<cr>            (starts "level 3")
            statement(s) . . .
        END                                           (ends "level 3")
    statement(s) . . .
    END                                               (ends "level 2")
statement(s) . . .
END                                                   (ends "level 1")
```

Fig. 3-2. Nesting conditional statements.

statement . . .

END

The multiline form introduces the concept of the initiator/terminator relationship. When the THEN instruction appears as the last word in an IF-THEN statement, it is considered an *initiator*, meaning that it must be terminated later with an END statement. When the conditional expression evaluates false, program execution continues with the first executable statement after the END statement.

There are cases where "nested" IF statements are needed (Fig. 3-2). When they are the last word on a source line, remember to terminate every THEN or ELSE with an END.

Avoid having too many levels of nested IF statements. It makes programs more difficult to figure out and increases the probability of logic and syntax errors (see the use of the CASE construct in Chapter 9). Also, to assist in making the program more readable, try to align the END statement underneath the IF statement that initiated it.

Note that many instructions in the PICK/BASIC language allow (or require) the THEN and/or ELSE construct. Anywhere they are allowed/required, the single- or multiple-line forms may be used.

Note also the fact that on all versions of Pick the first END compiler directive encountered which is not part of a THEN/ELSE construct above, causes the program to stop compiling.

This concludes Example 1. Now it's time to take a review quiz on the principles discussed. (The answers are found in the appendix.)

REVIEW QUIZ 1

1) What is a variable?

2) How are PICK/BASIC programs entered into the computer?

3) After a program is entered, what two things must be done to activate it?

4) What are remark statements, and why are they used?

5) What characters may safely be used to separate multicharacter variable names?

6) What statement terminates the execution of a program?

7) What is a conditional expression?

8) How many programmers does it take to change a light bulb?

4

The Concept of Loops

IN THE FIRST PROGRAMMING EXAMPLE, AN IMPORTANT ASPECT OF PICK/BASIC WAS COVered: data has to be checked to be sure that it adheres to some sort of format or condition. This is called *data validation*. Even though the Pick System has no concept of data types, as programmers and users we must ensure that data entered via the terminal is checked. We cannot effectively use a system if the contents of its items are not reliable.

Program Example 2 continues in this exploration of editing techniques and introduces the principles of reiteration ("looping"), string manipulation, and some expansions on the IF-THEN construct. Statements and functions covered include: MATCHES, GOTO, COUNT, TRIM, IF-THEN-ELSE, LOOP-UNTIL-REPEAT.

The first seven lines of the example reiterate principles, concepts, and instructions covered in Example 1. From this point on in the book, only new topics and new ideas on previous topics are examined.

Call up the Editor and enter Example 2, shown in Fig. 4-1.

A Note about Program Execution. A PICK/BASIC program begins executing at the first executable (non-remark) statement in the program and then "walks down" through the program, one statement at a time, until it runs out of statements and the program stops. Various statements are used to overcome this default sequence of events. The IF statements are used to control which statements are executed, depending on the outcome of tests conducted in their conditional logic. The GOTO statement makes the program resume execution at a location other than the next physical source line, by transferring program execution to a *statement label*. Various other statements provided in PICK/BASIC allow the program to overcome the default sequential execution of a program.

Fig. 4-1. Program Example 2.

```
>ED BP EX.002
TOP
.I
001 * EX.002
002 * DATA VALIDATION, BRANCHING AND LOOP STRUCTURES
003 * mm/dd/yy : date last modified
004 * JES : author's initials
005 *
006    PROMPT ":"
007 *
008 10 * GET VALID SOCIAL SECURITY NUMBER
009 *
010    PRINT
011    PRINT "ENTER SOCIAL SECURITY NUMBER (nnn-nn-nnnn) " :
012    INPUT SOCIAL.SECURITY.NUMBER
013    IF SOCIAL.SECURITY.NUMBER = "QUIT" THEN STOP
014 *
015 * CHECK RESPONSE TO SEE IF IT MATCHES THE ACCEPTABLE PATTERN
016 *
017    IF SOCIAL.SECURITY.NUMBER MATCHES "3N'-'2N'-'4N" THEN
018       PRINT "THAT'S A GOOD NUMBER" ; * MUST BE GOOD. LET'S CONTINUE
019    END ELSE
020       PRINT "SORRY, NOT A GOOD NUMBER.  TRY AGAIN "
021       GOTO 10   ; * MUST NOT BE GOOD.  MAKE THEM TRY AGAIN.
022    END
023 *
024 20 * GET VALID DATE
025 *
026    PRINT
027    PRINT "ENTER A DATE (mm-dd-yy) " :
028    INPUT TEST.DATE
029    IF TEST.DATE = "QUIT" THEN STOP
030 *
031 * CHECK "FIXED" PATTERN MATCH FIRST
032 *
033    IF TEST.DATE MATCHES "2N'-'2N'-'2N" THEN
034       PRINT
035       PRINT "DATE PASSED FIXED PATTERN MATCH" ; * YUP. IT PASSED.
036    END ELSE
037       PRINT
038       PRINT "DATE FAILED FIXED PATTERN MATCH" ; * NOPE.  NO GOOD.
039    END
040 *
041 * NOW, CHECK VARIABLE PATTERN MATCH
042 *
043    IF TEST.DATE MATCHES "1N0N1X1N0N1X2N0N" THEN
044       PRINT
045       PRINT "DATE PASSED VARIABLE PATTERN MATCH"
046    END ELSE
047       PRINT
```

```
048           PRINT "DATE FAILED VARIABLE PATTERN MATCH"
049       END
050 *
051 * GET STRING FOR ALPHA AND MATCHES TEST
052 *
053       LOOP
054          PRINT
055          PRINT "ENTER A WORD FOR THE ALPHABETIC TEST " :
056          INPUT ALPHA.STRING
057       UNTIL ALPHA(ALPHA.STRING) DO
058          PRINT
059          PRINT "SORRY, THAT FAILED THE ALPHA TEST. TRY AGAIN"
060       REPEAT
061       IF ALPHA.STRING = "QUIT" THEN STOP
062 *
063 * PASSED ALPHA, NOW TRY IT WITH "MATCHES"
064 *
065       IF ALPHA.STRING MATCHES "0A" THEN     ;* THAT'S A ZERO!
066          PRINT
067          PRINT "THAT ALSO PASSED THE MATCHES TEST"
068       END
069 *
070 * GET SENTENCE FOR "COUNT" TEST
071 *
072       PRINT
073       PRINT "ENTER SEVERAL WORDS EACH SEPARATED BY A BUNCH OF  SPACES "
074       INPUT WORD.STRING
075       IF WORD.STRING = "QUIT" THEN STOP
076 *
077 * DETERMINE THE NUMBER OF SPACES
078 *
079       NUMBER.OF.SPACES = COUNT(WORD.STRING," ")
080 *
081 * TELL OBSERVER HOW MANY SPACES THERE ARE
082 *
083       PRINT
084       PRINT "YOUR RESPONSE CONTAINED " : NUMBER.OF.SPACES :   " SPACES"
085 *
086 * STRIP EXTRA SPACES
087 *
088       WORD.STRING = TRIM(WORD.STRING)
089 *
090 * DETERMINE NUMBER OF SPACES AFTER STRIPPING WITH TRIM
091 *
092       NUMBER.OF.SPACES = COUNT(WORD.STRING," ")
093 *
094 * TELL OBSERVER THE NEW NUMBER
095 *
096       PRINT
097       PRINT "AFTER TRIMMING, THERE ARE " : NUMBER.OF.SPACES : " SPACES"
098 *
```

```
099 * SHOW OBSERVER THE STRING AFTER THE TRIM
100 *
101    PRINT
102    PRINT "HERE'S WHAT THE STRING LOOKS LIKE AFTER THE TRIM : "
103    PRINT
104    PRINT WORD.STRING
105    END
```

USING STATEMENT LABELS

There are occasions in a program where execution may have to transfer to a point other than the next immediate line. Most often this is because a section of code must be repeated, or to bypass certain instructions. This phenomenon is known as *looping* and involves the use of statement labels. (Note that there are other, even better methods available to perform loops.)

On most Pick systems, a statement label is a number at the beginning of a source line. In our example:

008 **10** * GET VALID SOCIAL SECURITY NUMBER

Note that the *attribute* (or line) *numbers* ("008" in this example) have nothing to do with statement labels ("10" in this example). Line numbers are placed on the left side of the screen by the Editor.

Statement labels are optional in PICK/BASIC. They are only used to indicate the destination of a GOTO or GOSUB statement elsewhere in the program. It is a good idea, however, to insert them only when they have a purpose. Unnecessary statement labels might be misleading during debugging and maintenance.

Spaces are generally not important to the syntax of a program. Some compilers are sensitive to the placement of spaces between variables and keywords (PICK/BASIC instructions), so it is advisable to put spaces between each keyword/variable in a statement. When a statement label is placed on a source line in a program, it must be the *first* non-blank character on the line and *must* be followed by a valid PICK/BASIC statement. One popular convention is to have only remark statements on source lines that contain statement labels, as in the previous example.

Some implementations of Pick allow statement labels to contain or consist of alphabetic characters. For example, on systems which support alphabetic labels, as illustrated in Fig. 4-2.

```
033   GOSUB PRINT.DETAIL.LINE
  .
  .
  .
127   PRINT.DETAIL.LINE:    ;*  ROUTINE TO PRINT DETAIL LINE ON CHECK
```

Fig. 4-2. Using alphabetic statement labels.

THE MATCHES RELATIONAL OPERATOR

On line 17, a test is made to determine whether the input matches a predetermined pattern, using the MATCHES relational operator:

```
017 IF SOCIAL.SECURITY.NUMBER MATCHES "3N'-'2N'-'4N" THEN
```

If it does match, then the message "THAT'S A GOOD NUMBER" appears on the screen, and program execution continues after the END statement on line 22. If it does not match the pattern, then the message "SORRY, NOT A GOOD NUMBER. TRY AGAIN" appears on the screen and program execution transfers, via the GOTO statement, back to line 7, where the statement label "10" appears. Using the GOTO statement in this form illustrates one means of setting up a repetitive loop function.

The MATCHES (or MATCH) relational operator checks data against a pattern. Three pattern-match operators are available: "N" for numeric, "A" for alphabetic and "X" for wildcards (any character). These pattern-match operators must be preceded by an integer number (or zero), which indicates the exact length of the number of characters that will be accepted. In addition to the three pattern-match operators, literals may be specified by enclosing literal strings in quotes. Parts A through D of Fig. 4-3 illustrate various pattern matches.

The pattern-match string in line 17 of the program indicates that the only string that will be accepted is one in which the first three characters are numbers, followed by a hyphen (-), followed by two numbers, another hyphen, and four more numbers. (When a pattern match operator is preceded by a zero, any number of the character type are accepted.)

Part A of Fig. 4-3 shows a form similar to line 17, here applied to dates. This form is technically correct but is not very flexible; it forces the operator to precede the one-character months (like May) and days of the month (like the fifth) with a 0 (zero) during entry. Further, it only allows the "-" as a delimiter.

	Match expression	Acceptable input	Unacceptable input
A	"2N' - '2N' - '2N"	12-01-97	12/01/97 12-1-97
B	"1N0N1X1N0N1X2N0N"	12-12-97 12/12/1997 2-2-97	1DEC97 12-12 1- -1
C	"1A2N1A3N"	A22T003	A2T03
D	"1A0A', '1A0A"	PALMER, ARNIE	ARNIE PALMER

Fig. 4-3. Examples of pattern matching expressions for A) date input, B) generalized date input, C) combined alphabetic and numeric entries, and D) common data entry conventions.

The Pick System does not require leading zeros or any specific delimiter between months, days, and the year. The only rule is that the delimiter must be non-numeric, and consistent. The next pattern match (Part B) accepts virtually any valid "external" date format.

This expression literally reads, "Look for one number (1N) followed by any length of numerals (0N), which also includes zero numerals, followed by any character (1X) as a delimiter, and so on." This very "generalized" date pattern match handles just about any valid date. Using this technique prevents you from having to code individually all the possible pattern matches in a complex IF-THEN statement using multiple OR clauses.

Part C of Fig. 4-3 illustrates a pattern composed of letters and numbers. It specifically requires one alphabetic character, followed by two numbers, followed by another single alphabetic character, followed by three numbers. Part D illustrates a pattern of alphabetic characters, separated by the comma. This shows how the MATCHES operator may be used to enforce data entry conventions, which assist in standardizing the methods by which data is entered.

THE IF-THEN-ELSE CONSTRUCT

At the end of Example 1 there was an explanation of the single-line IF-THEN and the multiline IF-THEN constructs. The other extension to the IF statement is the ELSE construct, which in this example appears in lines 17-22:

```
017 IF SOCIAL.SECURITY.NUMBER MATCHES "3N'-'2N'-'4N" THEN
018    PRINT "THAT'S A GOOD NUMBER" ; * MUST BE GOOD. LET'S
       CONTINUE
019 END ELSE
020    PRINT "SORRY, NOT A GOOD NUMBER.  TRY AGAIN "
021    GOTO 10 ; * MUST NOT BE GOOD. MAKE THEM TRY AGAIN.
022 END
```

The THEN initiator precedes the statement, or statements, and executes when the conditional expression evaluates true (numeric nonzero). The ELSE construct precedes the statements and executes on a false condition (i.e., zero or null).

The Single-Line Form

The first, and simplest, general form of the single-line IF-THEN-ELSE construct is:

IF *conditional.expression* THEN *statement* ELSE *statement*

This reads, "If the conditional expression evaluates true, then the single statement after the THEN initiator is executed and program execution continues on the next line of the program; if the conditional expression evaluates false, then the single statement after the ELSE initiator is executed and program execution continues on the next line of the program."

Since statements may be delimited by semicolons, the next form of this construct occurs as:

IF *conditional.expression* **THEN** *statement* ; . . .
. . . *statement* **ELSE** *statement* ; *statement* . . .

(Note that this is still the single-line form!) If the conditional expression evaluates true, then the statements after the THEN initiator are executed in turn. If it evaluates false, then all of the statements after the ELSE initiator are executed. Once again, there is no limit to the number of statements that may follow the THEN or ELSE clause, but when there's more than one, it makes the program much more maintainable to have each statement on a separate line.

The Multiline Form

As discussed earlier in the explanation of the single-line form, it is generally accepted that when there is more than one statement to perform after the THEN or ELSE initiator, then the multiline form is used. This version has the general form:

IF *conditional.expression* **THEN** < cr >
   statement
   statement
   statement . . .
END ELSE
   statement
   statement
   statement . . .
END

This form also relies upon the initiator/terminator relationship introduced earlier. When the THEN appears as the last word on a line, it is considered an *initiator*, which means that it must be *terminated* on a subsequent source line with an END statement.

The same situation holds true with the ELSE clause. When the ELSE appears as the last word on a line, it too must be terminated later with an END statement.

When the conditional expression evaluates true, all of the statements up to the next END ELSE statement are executed. Because of the ELSE clause, after these statements execute, execution transfers to the first executable statement after the next END statement. When the conditional expression evaluates false, execution transfers to the statements following the END ELSE statement, and after execution, program execution continues with the next executable statement after the END statement.

THE GOTO STATEMENT

The GOTO statement makes the program resume execution at the first statement following the label number that follows the GOTO statement. (Remember that the source line numbers along the left side of the screen are placed there by the Editor, and have nothing to do with statement labels.) If this line is executed, program execution transfers to statement label "10," which happens to occur on source line 8.

```
021 GOTO 10 ; * MUST NOT BE GOOD. MAKE THEM TRY AGAIN.
```

Here is another example of the GOTO statement:

```
001     COUNTER = 0
002  10 COUNTER = COUNTER + 1
003     PRINT COUNTER
004     IF COUNTER = 5 THEN STOP
005     GOTO 10
```

This illustrates the logic behind using the GOTO statement to perform loops. In this case, the variable COUNTER is assigned an initial value of zero on line 1. On line 2, COUNTER is incremented by taking its current value and adding 1 to it. The result of the calculation is assigned to the variable COUNTER so that its value is now 1 (one). Line 3 prints the current value of COUNTER, which outputs a 1 (one) on the next line on the screen. Line 4 is where the test takes place. The logic of line 4 indicates that if the current value of COUNTER is 5, then the program stops. Since there is no ELSE clause in the IF-THEN statement, the logic "falls through" to the next line (5) each time through the loop until the value in COUNTER reaches 5. The GOTO statement on line 5 unconditionally transfers program execution to line 2, where it finds the statement label "10."

While some programmers use GOTO statements as a standard practice, many programmers never use them. The reason that GOTOs are forbidden in some programming shops is that when they are overused and/or used incorrectly, they make program logic much harder to analyze—leading to what is often called "spaghetti code."

Forbidding GOTO statements is a technique that is frequently associated with the concept of *structured programming*, which is discussed in Chapter 13, following the discussion of subroutines and loops.

FIXED AND VARIABLE PATTERN MATCHES

This block of code illustrates the principles mentioned earlier in the explanation of pattern matches:

```
033 IF TEST.DATE MATCHES "2N'-'2N'-'2N" THEN
034   PRINT
035   PRINT "DATE PASSED FIXED PATTERN MATCH" ; * YUP, IT PASSED.
036 END ELSE
037   PRINT
038   PRINT "DATE FAILED FIXED PATTERN MATCH" ; * NOPE, NO GOOD.
039 END
```

Specifically, the program is waiting for the input of a date. After receiving the input, on line 33 it is tested for a "fixed" pattern of 2 numbers followed by a "-" delimiter, two more numbers, another dash, and two more numbers. If the input adheres to this format, the message from line 35 displays; otherwise the message from line 38 displays.

The pattern match on line 43 is much more flexible about accepting input. Although it looks much more complicated, the benefit achieved in using it outweighs the complexity of coding it.

```
043 IF TEST.DATE MATCHES "1N0N1X1N0N1X2N0N" THEN
044    PRINT
045    PRINT "DATE PASSED VARIABLE PATTERN MATCH"
046 END ELSE
047    PRINT
048    PRINT "DATE FAILED VARIABLE PATTERN MATCH"
049 END
```

Specifically, this pattern match looks for at least one number, followed by any character, at least one number, another character, and then at least two numbers.

THE LOOP CONSTRUCT

The concept of loops was introduced earlier in this example. There are actually several methods available to perform loops. Coincidentally, this one is called ''LOOP'':

```
053 LOOP
054    PRINT
055    PRINT "ENTER A WORD FOR THE ALPHABETIC TEST " :
056    INPUT ALPHA.STRING
057 UNTIL ALPHA(ALPHA.STRING) DO
058    PRINT
059    PRINT "SORRY, THAT FAILED THE ALPHA TEST. TRY AGAIN"
060 REPEAT
```

The LOOP construct has nearly as many possible forms as the IF-THEN statement; for the most part, however, there are several relatively ''standard'' methods of use. One such form is illustrated in Fig. 4-4.

```
001    COUNTER = 0                ;* Assign initial value
002    LOOP                       ;* Start/Return Point
003        COUNTER = COUNTER + 1   ;* Increment Counter
004        PRINT COUNTER           ;* Display Counter
005    UNTIL COUNTER = 5 DO       ;* Check to see if done
006    REPEAT                     ;* Not done, return to LOOP
007    STOP                       ;* We're outta here...
```

Fig. 4-4. Standard form of the LOOP construct.

This standard form effectively does the same thing as the loop described earlier, which used the GOTO statement. Note that the LOOP form does not require statement labels or GOTO statements.

On line 1 of Fig. 4-3, the variable COUNTER is initialized to zero. On line 2 the LOOP statement appears, which indicates the beginning of a LOOP process. This is the point at which program execution returns when the next REPEAT statement is executed. The statements on lines 2 and 3 execute unconditionally, incrementing the value of COUNTER by 1 (one) and printing its value.

At line 5, the conditional expression test takes place to determine when to exit the loop. Line 5 reads, "If the current value of COUNTER is NOT 5, then REPEAT the process." Otherwise, when COUNTER does reach 5, execution transfers to the next statement after the REPEAT statement. In this case, that's line 7.

THE UNTIL CLAUSE AND DO INITIATOR

Each time the LOOP statement is initiated, there *must* be an UNTIL (or WHILE) clause:

```
057 UNTIL ALPHA(ALPHA.STRING) DO
```

The UNTIL/WHILE is always followed by a conditional expression and the initiator, DO, in the form:

UNTIL *conditional.expression* DO

or

WHILE *conditional.expression* DO

On line 57, the conditional expression tests the contents of the variable ALPHA.STRING to determine if it is entirely composed of alphabetic characters. The logic of this line reads, "If ALPHA.STRING contains only alphabetic characters, meaning that the ALPHA function evaluates true, then exit the loop." This means that program execution continues at line 61. Otherwise, the message "SORRY, THAT FAILED THE ALPHA TEST. TRY AGAIN" prints, and the REPEAT statement forces the loop to start over from line 53, where the LOOP statement occurs.

The basic difference between the UNTIL and the WHILE clause is in its logic. The UNTIL form works until a true (or positive) result occurs as a result of its conditional expression. The inverse of this is the WHILE form, which works while its conditional expression evaluates as true (numeric non-zero), or until it evaluates as false (zero or null). Fortunately, since they are so close in meaning, you may use one form for nearly every loop.

Note: On Ultimate systems, the UNTIL and WHILE clauses are optional in the LOOP construct. The EXIT statement may be used to terminate the loop.

A COMPARISON OF MATCHES AND ALPHA

Line 65 of the example, using the MATCHES relational operator, checks the input to determine if it is composed entirely of alphabetic characters, just like the ALPHA function did earlier:

```
065 IF ALPHA.STRING MATCHES "0A" THEN
066    PRINT
067    PRINT "THAT ALSO PASSED THE MATCHES TEST"
068 END
```

This illustrates an important principle in the Pick System. There is virtually always more than one way to do something[1]. These two separate functions only appear to be identical. The ALPHA function is, in fact, more efficient in terms of the amount of CPU "horsepower" required to perform the function. This happens to hold true when the NUM function is compared with the MATCHES "0N" as well, but the NUM function is more efficient than its "MATCHES" counterpart. This means that:

ALPHA(*string*)   is better than **MATCHES** *"0A"*

and that

NUM(*numeric.expression*)   is better than **MATCHES** *"0N"*

The moral of this story is: Use the MATCHES statement only for "composite" or complex pattern matches, like dates or general ledger account numbers. Use the intrinsic functions, NUM and ALPHA, on purely numeric or alphabetic data, respectively.

Note that some characters, notably the hyphen and period will "pass" as acceptable numeric characters in the NUM function but are not accepted with the MATCHES "0N" statement.

THE COUNT FUNCTION

The COUNT statement is used to determine the number of occurrences of a character, or a string of characters, within another string of characters. This example simply determines the number of spaces in the string of characters that you entered, and reports it on line 84:

```
079 NUMBER.OF.SPACES = COUNT(WORD.STRING," ")
```

---

1. Mr. Pick himself calls this "rope," as in, "Give someone enough rope . . . "

For another example of the COUNT function, consider this example:

```
STRING = "ABC*DEF*GHI*JKL"
SEARCH.STRING = "*"
NUMBER.OF.STARS = COUNT(STRING,SEARCH.STRING)
```

Upon execution, the variable NUMBER.OF.STARS contains the number 3, since there are three occurrences of the ''*'' (asterisk) in the variable STRING. This statement and its counterpart, the DCOUNT statement, are particularly useful in PICK/BASIC, especially in situations when you need to determine how many values appear in an attribute. The DCOUNT function is covered in Example 4.

Note that there is a potential problem when using COUNT or DCOUNT with overlapping strings. For example:

```
COUNT("XXXXXXXXXX","XXX")
```

produces ''8'' as the result, while

```
DCOUNT("XXXXXXXXXX","XXX")
```

produces ''9'' as the result. This means that you must carefully make sure that you use DCOUNT only with a single character as the delimiter, or make sure that the delimiter is not repeated if null fields are possible within the string being counted.

THE TRIM FUNCTION

The TRIM statement is very useful for removing extraneous blanks from a string of characters. When a string is ''trimmed,'' all leading and trailing blanks are removed, and any occurrences of two or more spaces within the string are replaced by a single blank. On line 88, the string that you entered is trimmed, and the result is placed back into the same variable:

```
088 WORD.STRING = TRIM(WORD.STRING)
```

Consequently, on line 92, where the number of spaces within the string is counted, the number is dramatically reduced. Line 97 reports the number of spaces now present in the line, and line 102 displays the result of the TRIM function.

REVIEW QUIZ 2

1) The INPUT statement prints a character before waiting for input. How is this character assigned?

2) How could you make the ''>'' (right angle bracket) the prompt character?

3) What is a statement label?

4) What are two of the six methods to transfer program execution to another location in a program? (Use the techniques discussed in this chapter)

5) What relational operator checks input to make sure that it adheres to a particular format?

6) What pattern matches are required to validate the following formats?

   A) 02-4000-01
   B) A1000/101
   C) CLAUS,SANTA
   D) 12/1/89
   E) 1000.15

7) What two purposes does the END statement serve?

8) Where are spaces significant in a source program?

9) Where else are spaces used, and when?

10) What statement is required to print the number of occurrences of the letter ''i'' in ''Mississippi?''

Calculations and the Principle of Precedence

IN PROGRAM EXAMPLE 3, THE PRINCIPLE OF *PRECEDENCE* IS DISCUSSED, AND SEVERAL OF the intrinsic functions related to numbers are covered. This program also includes a simple guessing game, which further illustrates the principle of decision points and branching within a program. Topics, statements, and functions covered include precedence, RND, and REM.

Now enter Program Example 3 (Fig. 5-1).

ARITHMETIC OPERATIONS AND PRECEDENCE

Expressions are evaluated in a program in accordance with the rules of precedence. The highest precedence is parentheses. When parentheses are present in an expression, operations within the innermost set of parentheses have the highest precedence. The second highest priority is exponentiation. Multiplication and division both comprise the third level. When two functions of the same level of precedence occur in an expression, they are evaluated from left to right. The fourth level is addition and subtraction (with the same left-to-right evaluation scheme). Level five in the Pick System, is "print masking," followed on level six by concatenation. Level seven is for relational operators (such as ">" for "greater than"), and finally, on level eight, are the logical operators AND and OR.

Two operators may not be used in succession unless they are separated by parentheses. For example, the expression:

$$X \wedge -Y$$

Fig. 5-1. Program Example 3.

```
>ED BP EX.003
TOP
.I
001 * EX.003
002 * PRECEDENCE OF MATH OPERATIONS AND A FEW MATH FUNCTIONS
003 * mm/dd/yy : date last modified
004 * JES : author's initials
005 *
006    PROMPT ":"
007 *
008 * SHOW THE EXPRESSION WITHOUT PARENTHESES
009 *
010    PRINT
011    PRINT "HERE IS WHAT HAPPENS WHEN WE RELY ON PRECEDENCE : "
012    PRINT
013    PRINT "10 + 20 * 5 - 12 / 3 = " : 10 + 20 * 5 - 12 / 3
014 *
015 * NOW SHOW IT WITH PARENTHESES
016 *
017    PRINT
018    PRINT "HERE IS WHAT HAPPENS WHEN WE PARENTHESIZE EXPRESSIONS : "
019    PRINT
020    PRINT "((((10 + 20) * 5) - 12) / 3) = " : (((( 10+20) * 5) - 12)/3)
021 *
022 * GET NUMBERS FOR DIVISION TEST
023 *
024    PRINT
025    PRINT "ENTER A NUMBER TO DIVIDE " :
026    INPUT NUMERATOR
027    IF NUMERATOR = "QUIT" THEN STOP
028 *
029    PRINT "ENTER NUMBER TO DIVIDE BY " :
030    INPUT DENOMINATOR
031    IF DENOMINATOR = "QUIT" THEN STOP
032 *
033    PRINT
034    PRINT NUMERATOR : " DIVIDED BY " : DENOMINATOR :
035    PRINT " LEAVES A REMAINDER OF " : REM(NUMERATOR,DENOMINATOR)
036 *
037 * NOW, LET'S PLAY GUESSING GAME...
038 *
039    MY.NUMBER = RND(10) + 1     ; * GENERATE THE RANDOM NUMBER
040    PRINT
041    PRINT "I HAVE A NUMBER BETWEEN ONE AND 10 "
042    PRINT "TRY TO GUESS WHAT IT IS "
043 *
044 * MAKE USER GUESS NUMBER
045 *
046    LOOP
```

56

```
047        PRINT "ENTER YOUR GUESS " :
048        INPUT GUESS
049        IF GUESS = "QUIT" THEN STOP   ;* MUST HAVE GIVEN UP
050     UNTIL GUESS = MY.NUMBER DO
051        PRINT "SORRY.  THAT'S NOT IT.  TRY AGAIN"
052     REPEAT
053 *
054 *
055     PRINT
056     PRINT "CONGRATULATIONS.  YOU GOT IT"
057     END
```

will not even compile, much less work. It must be written as:

$$X \wedge (-Y)$$

Use the higher precedence of parentheses to overcome situations where two operations of the same level, such as multiplication and division, occur in an expression. Table 5-1 summarizes the precedence of operations in Pick.

On line 13 of the example, the result of the calculation is printed. This results in the answer "106." Line 20 provides the result "46" because precedence has been altered through the use of parentheses.

```
013 PRINT "10 + 20 * 5 - 12 / 3 = " : 10 + 20*5 - 12/3
```

As a matter of style, and to ensure accuracy in mathematical expression, use parentheses when more than one arithmetic operator appears in an expression.

Table 5-1. Precedence of Mathematical Expressions.

Operator	Operation	Example in PICK/BASIC
$\wedge$	Exponentiation	$X \wedge Y$
*	Multiplication	$X * Y$
/	Division	X / Y
+	Addition	$X + Y$
−	Subtraction	$X - Y$
	"print masking"	PRINT X "L#25"
: or CAT	Concatenation	X : Y or X CAT Y
>, <, > =, < =, #	Relational operators	X > Y
AND and OR	Logical operators.	X < Y AND X > 0

THE REM FUNCTION

The REM function returns the remainder of a numeric expression divided by a second numeric expression:

```
035 PRINT " LEAVES A REMAINDER OF " : REM(NUMERATOR,DENOMINATOR)
```

REM also happens to be one of the few functions in PICK/BASIC where there is potential ambiguity. This is due to the fact that there is also a REM *statement,* which is an alternate means of declaring a remark statement.

When the REM appears as the beginning of a statement, the compiler interprets it as a remark statement, the same as the * and ! characters. For example:

```
REM Get user response and determine if valid
```

Otherwise, it is interpreted as a remainder function. For example:

```
PRINT REM(TOTAL.AMOUNT,2)
```

or

```
ANSWER = REM(SUB.TOTAL,BALANCE)
```

THE RND FUNCTION

The RND function generates a random integer number between zero and the numeric expression in the parentheses, minus 1.

```
039 MY.NUMBER = RND(10) + 1 ; * GENERATE THE RANDOM NUMBER
```

In line 39, the RND function would first generate a random number between 0 and 9 (which is 10 minus 1); then 1 is added to the random number, and the result is then stored in the variable MY.NUMBER. This means that MY.NUMBER is now a number between 1 and 10, inclusively.

The RND function is particularly useful for determining amounts of salary increases.

Note that the guessing game program in the example is extremely forgiving. It keeps prompting until you provide either the correct answer or QUIT.

REVIEW QUIZ 3

1) Why is precedence important?

2) What is the difference between the REM statement and the REM function?

3) What does the RND function do?

4) What is wrong with the following program samples and how may they be corrected?

```
IF ANSWER = "Y" THEN PRINT "YES" END ELSE PRINT "NO"

IF ANSWER > 0 THEN
    PRINT "ANSWER IS > 0"
  ELSE
    PRINT "ANSWER IS < 0"
END

IF ANSWER = "N" THEN
    PRINT "ENTER ALTERNATE VALUE " :
    INPUT ALTERNATE.VALUE
    IF ALTERNATE.VALUE = "" OR ALTERNATE.VALUE <= 0 THEN
        PRINT "MUST BE ANSWERED OR POSITIVE !"
END
```

6

String-Handling Intrinsic Functions

IN PROGRAMMING EXAMPLE 4, MORE OF THE INTRINSIC FUNCTIONS ARE DISCUSSED, ALONG with some programming techniques for optimizing program code. Topics, statements and functions covered include EQU, EQUATE, CHAR, COUNT, DCOUNT, SLEEP, SEQ, and STR.

Enter Programming Example 4, shown in Fig. 6-1.

THE EQUATE (EQU) STATEMENT

It is normal to place assignment statements at the beginning of the program. The EQUATE statement is also used to assign constants:

```
009    EQUATE ATTRIBUTE.MARK TO CHAR(254)
010    EQUATE VALUE.MARK TO CHAR(253)
011    EQUATE SUB.VALUE.MARK TO CHAR(252)
012    EQUATE CLEAR.SCREEN TO CHAR(12)
013    EQUATE BELL TO CHAR(7)
014    EQUATE TRUE TO 1
015    EQUATE FALSE TO 0
```

Naturally, there are some technical differences between assignment and the EQUATE statement. For example, the statement

```
EQUATE BELL TO CHAR(7)
```

Fig. 6-1. Program Example 4.

```
>ED BP EX.004
TOP
.I
001 * EX.004
002 * DEALING WITH DELIMITERS AND OTHER STRING FUNCTIONS
003 * mm/dd/yy : date last modified
004 * JES : author's initials
005 *
006 * DEFINE STANDARD CONSTANTS
007 *
008     PROMPT ":"
009     EQUATE ATTRIBUTE.MARK TO CHAR(254)
010     EQUATE VALUE.MARK TO CHAR(253)
011     EQUATE SUB.VALUE.MARK TO CHAR(252)
012     EQUATE CLEAR.SCREEN TO CHAR(12)
013     EQUATE BELL TO CHAR(7)
014     EQUATE TRUE TO 1
015     EQUATE FALSE TO 0
016 *
017 * GET SENTENCE FOR COUNT AND DCOUNT TEST
018 *
019     PRINT
020     PRINT "ENTER A SENTENCE OF ABOUT 10 TO 15 WORDS " :
021     INPUT SENTENCE
022     IF SENTENCE = "QUIT" THEN STOP
023 *
024 * TRIM EXTRA SPACES FIRST
025 *
026     SENTENCE = TRIM(SENTENCE)
027 *
028 * DETERMINE THE NUMBER OF SPACES
029 *
030     PRINT
031     PRINT "IN THE SENTENCE, "
032     PRINT SENTENCE
033     PRINT
034     PRINT " THERE ARE " : COUNT(SENTENCE," ") : " SPACES"
035 *
036 * DETERMINE THE NUMBER OF WORDS
037 *
038     PRINT
039     PRINT "AND, THERE ARE " : DCOUNT(SENTENCE," ") : " WORDS"
040 *
041 * PICK A NUMBER OF SECONDS TO SLEEP FOR...
042 *
043     PRINT
044     NAPTIME = RND(10) + 3
045     PRINT "I'M NOW SLEEPING FOR " : NAPTIME : " SECONDS"
046     SLEEP NAPTIME     ; * ZZZZZZZZZZZZ
```

```
047 *
048 * GET A CHARACTER FOR SEQ TEST
049 *
050    PRINT
051    PRINT "LET'S TEST THE SEQ FUNCTION.  PRESS ANY KEY " :
052    INPUT KEY,1
053    PRINT "THE SEQ OF " : KEY : " IS " : SEQ(KEY)
054    PRINT
055 *
056 * GET A CHARACTER FOR THE STR TEST
057 *
058    PRINT
059    PRINT "ENTER CHARACTER TO PRINT IN STR FUNCTION " :
060    INPUT CHARACTER
061    IF CHARACTER = "QUIT" THEN STOP
062 *
063 * GET NUMBER OF TIMES TO PRINT
064 *
065    PRINT "ENTER NUMBER OF TIMES TO PRINT " :
066    INPUT NUMBER.OF.TIMES
067    IF NUMBER.OF.TIMES = "QUIT" THEN STOP
068 *
069 * NOW SHOW THE FUNCTION
070 *
071    PRINT "HERE GOES..."
072    PRINT STR(CHARACTER,NUMBER.OF.TIMES)
073    END
```

Does apparently the same thing as:

```
BELL = CHAR(7)
```

The net effect is the same; that is, the constant BELL is assigned the value of the decimal character 7. It may be used to generate an audible "beep" by using the statement:

```
PRINT BELL
```

The EQUATE and assignment statements are treated differently, however. The EQUATE form is more efficient than the assignment statement using the "=" (equals) sign. This is due to the fact that the EQU or EQUATE statement is interpreted during the compilation phase, where the CHAR(7) is evaluated and object (i.e., executable) code is generated for this constant. This also saves the overhead of maintaining a variable during runtime, since there is no run-time storage allocation for this constant. (This is also the way quoted constant text strings are handled.)

With the assignment form BELL=CHAR(7), evaluation occurs at runtime, and a small amount of overhead is required during the initialization phase of the program. Admittedly this overhead is hardly noticeable, but any time that there are opportunities to optimize programs, you should jump at the chance.

Using EQU or EQUATE also has what could be considered a down side. Once the constant has been assigned, it may not be changed later in the program. For example, if this instruction appeared near the top of the program:

```
EQU VALUE.MARK TO CHAR(253)
```

and later in the program, this instruction appeared:

```
VALUE.MARK = CHAR(252)
```

An error message will appear:

```
[B121] LABEL 'VALUE.MARK' IS A CONSTANT AND MAY NOT BE WRITTEN INTO
```

The program stops, leaving you in the PICK/BASIC debugger.

Realistically speaking, you would never want to change the reference to VALUE.MARK anyway. That's why it's called a constant. After all, value marks are always value marks.

THE CHAR FUNCTION

The CHAR function converts a decimal integer into its ASCII equivalent. The ASCII character set is simply a standardized means of referring to the numeric, alphabetic, punctuation, and control characters. The same set of program lines that demonstrated the EQUATE statement in the preceding section also show the use of CHAR( ):

```
009   EQUATE ATTRIBUTE.MARK TO CHAR(254)
010   EQUATE VALUE.MARK TO CHAR(253)
011   EQUATE SUB.VALUE.MARK TO CHAR(252)
012   EQUATE CLEAR.SCREEN TO CHAR(12)
013   EQUATE BELL TO CHAR(7)
```

For example, the standard character to sound the "bell" in your terminal (and some printers) is Control-G. It would require entering a Control-G into a program to use it in program. Entering control characters directly into programs should always be avoided! The CHAR function takes care of this potential problem for you.

It is normal to see a series of assignment statements at the top of a program to define regularly used variables or constants. For instance:

```
BELL = CHAR(7)
```

or

```
EQUATE BELL TO CHAR(7)
```

When this is interpreted by the compiler, it figures out what the ASCII character equivalent of a decimal 7 is, and assigns it to the variable called BELL. Throughout the rest of the program, whenever a "beep" is needed, it may be performed with the following statement:

```
PRINT BELL
```

A bell also may be generated simply by issuing this statement:

```
PRINT CHAR(7)
```

However, it is generally considered more efficient to assign the constant BELL at the beginning of the program rather than referring to CHAR(7) every time it is required. This also tends to make the program more readable.

Example 4 illustrates the most commonly used constants in PICK/BASIC, listed in Fig. 6-2.

THE COUNT AND DCOUNT FUNCTIONS

The COUNT function was discussed in Example 2. It is used to determine and report the number of occurrences of a character (or character string) within another string.

This example asks you to enter a sentence of about 10 to 15 words. The COUNT function on line 34 displays the number of spaces in the sentence.

```
034  PRINT " THERE ARE " :COUNT(SENTENCE," ") :" SPACES"
```

Consider this, however: Since the space character is being used as a delimiter to separate words, is the number of spaces displayed an accurate count of the number of words in the sentence?

Probably not. The number of spaces is one *less* than the number of words in the sentence. This is an extremely important principle. When you are trying to determine the

Constant name	Decimal equivalent	Assigned with
ATTRIBUTE.MARK	254	CHAR (254)
VALUE.MARK	253	CHAR (253)
SUB.VALUE.MARK	252	CHAR (252)
CLEAR.SCREEN	12	CHAR (12)
BELL	7	CHAR (7)
ESCAPE	27	CHAR (27)

Fig. 6-2. Commonly used constants.

number of objects by counting the delimiters that normally separate these objects, an allowance has to be made for correcting the oversight. In other words, 1 (one) must be added to the final result, but only when the string being counted is not null. That brings us to the DCOUNT function:

```
039  PRINT "AND, THERE ARE " :DCOUNT(SENTENCE," ") :" WORDS"
```

The DCOUNT function behaves exactly like the COUNT function, but with one minor difference: it corrects for the fact that the character being counted is being treated as a delimiter and adds 1 to the result. In other words, the DCOUNT function determines the number of data items delimited by the given string, where COUNT determines the number of occurrences of the given string.

This normally happens when counting the number of attributes in an item, or the number of values within an attribute, or the number of subvalues within a value. It returns a zero only when counting a null string. Figure 6-3 illustrates the various effects of the COUNT and DCOUNT functions. (Note that the ''}'' character represents a value mark.) Note also that this DCOUNT statement works correctly only because we trimmed the string (using TRIM) before performing the DCOUNT.

THE SLEEP STATEMENT

The SLEEP (or alternately RQM) statement is used to put a process ''to sleep'' for a certain period of time:

```
046  SLEEP NAPTIME    ; * ZZZZZZZZZZZZ
```

This is useful for process control, like running a FILE-SAVE at a certain time, or when

STRING	Instruction	Result
"abc]def]ghi"	COUNT(STRING,VALUE.MARK) DCOUNT(STRING,VALUE.MARK)	2 3
"abc]def"	COUNT(STRING,VALUE.MARK) DCOUNT(STRING,VALUE.MARK)	1 2
"abc"	COUNT(STRING,VALUE.MARK) DCOUNT(STRING,VALUE.MARK)	0 1
"" (null)	COUNT(STRING,VALUE.MARK) DCOUNT(STRING,VALUE.MARK)	0 0

Fig. 6-3. Effects of the COUNT and DCOUNT functions.

you feel like annoying your data entry operators. Note: Some implementations of Pick automatically disable the break key when the SLEEP statement is executed.

There are two ways to put a process to sleep. The first is when the numeric expression following the SLEEP statement contains a number. For instance:

```
SLEEP 300
```

The number defines, in seconds, the length of program inactivity. This statement tells the PICK/BASIC program to sleep for 5 minutes. The second form consists of making the expression following the SLEEP statement contain a time in "military" (24-hour) format. For example:

```
SLEEP 23:59
```

This leaves a wake-up call for 11:59 P.M.

The RND (random) function is used in this example to generate a random number between 0 and 9, and then to add 3 to the result. This will set up in a naptime of 3 to 12 seconds. Don't worry about being quiet around a sleeping terminal. (It sometimes takes a system crash to wake them up.)

RESTRICTIONS ON THE INPUT STATEMENT

Normally when an INPUT statement is executed, up to 140 characters may be entered before pressing the Return key. The reason that 140 characters are allowed is because that happens to be the length of the Primary Input Buffer on most Pick systems. The INPUT statement also allows the name of the variable that receives input to be followed by an expression which evaluates to a number:

```
052   INPUT KEY,1
```

This indicates the maximum number of characters that will be accepted by the INPUT statement. What's more, when the designated number of characters is received, the program automatically issues a carriage return, whether or not the operator is ready.

In this example, the INPUT statement waited for one character to be entered prior to continuing execution. Any key which produces output is adequate. Some keys on the keyboard, like the Shift and Control keys, don't actually generate "output," so the INPUT statement is unable to detect that input has been provided. By the way, if you're looking for the "any" key, you won't find it. Simply press the space bar.

As a suggestion, don't use the length parameter because of the inconsistencies that it imposes on the operator. (Sometimes it does carriage returns for you, and sometimes it doesn't.)

THE SEQ FUNCTION

The SEQ function is exactly the opposite of the CHAR function covered earlier in this example. It produces the decimal equivalent of any ASCII character:

```
053   PRINT "THE SEQ OF " : KEY : " IS " : SEQ(KEY)
```

For example, if you were to press the "A" key on your keyboard at the ". . . PRESS ANY KEY " prompt, it prints the message that the sequence of "A" is 65. This function is useful for situations like determining if a control character has been entered. Control characters have decimal values in the range 1 to 31, and all characters above 127 are Pick control characters.

THE STR FUNCTION

The STR function is used to generate or print a string of characters of a predetermined length. In Program Example 4, line 72, it displays such a string based on operator input:

```
072   PRINT STR(CHARACTER,NUMBER.OF.TIMES)
```

If an asterisk and the number 20 had been entered at the appropriate prompts, line 72 would be equivalent to:

```
PRINT STR("*",20)
```

and a row of 20 asterisks would be sent to the screen or printer. This technique is much more efficient than printing the row of asterisks as a literal:

```
PRINT "********************"
```

If there's no other reason, at least you won't have to find a pencil and count the characters on your screen or program listing. It also saves object code space.

Admittedly, this is more a programmer efficiency technique than a program efficiency consideration. (Sometimes the issue of program maintenance efficiency overrides the run-time efficiency considerations.)

By the way, the STR function may be used to generate a string of spaces, just like the SPACE function. For example:

```
PRINT STR(" ",25)
```

is the same as saying:

```
PRINT SPACE(25)
```

Using the STR function, however, is less efficient than the SPACE function when generating strings of spaces.

REVIEW QUIZ 4

1) What advantage does the EQUATE statement have over an assignment statement using the "=" sign?

2) Which of the following statements is more efficient?

   ```
   EQU CLEAR.SCREEN TO CHAR(12)

   CLEAR.SCREEN = CHAR(12)
   ```

3) What is the difference between the COUNT and DCOUNT statements?

4) What does the SLEEP statement do?

5) What statement puts a process to sleep for 10 minutes?

6) What statement puts a process to sleep until 5:30 P.M.?

7) What does the SEQ function do?

8) What does the STR function do?

9) What instruction prints a row of 10 "-" (hyphen) characters?

7

Data Conversion
and Print Masking

I N THIS EXAMPLE, THE PRINCIPLES OF "CONVERTING" AND FORMATTING DATA ARE COV-ered. Topics, statements, and functions covered include print (format) masking, GOTO, ICONV, OCONV(D,MT), SPACE, DATE( ), TIME( ), and TIMEDATE( ).

Now enter Program Example 5, shown in Fig. 7-1.

THE ICONV FUNCTION

The ICONV function is used to convert data from its *external format* to its *internal format*. To explain external versus internal is relatively easy; external format is the form in which a piece of data is readable to humans; internal format, as briefly introduced in Chapter 1, most often makes sense only to the computer.

Notice that the ICONV function has two arguments. The first argument is the string of numbers or characters that are to be converted. The second argument is the *conversion code*. One example of a conversion code is the date, or "D" conversion:

```
027   INTERNAL.BIRTHDAY = ICONV(BIRTHDAY,"D")
```

The Pick System stores dates in an internal format which is a number representing the number of days that have elapsed since December 31, 1967. (Day zero on the Pick Calendar). Every night at midnight, a counter is incremented by 1. Consequently, if you were to find an item in a file which had the number 7777 stored in an attribute, it could be a date in internal format, or an amount of money, or a street address. The only person who knows for sure is the programmer who put it there.

Fig. 7-1. Program Example 5.

```
>ED BP EX.005
TOP
.I
001 * EX.005
002 * PRINT MASKING, INTERNAL AND EXTERNAL CONVERSIONS
003 * mm/dd/yy : date last modified
004 * JES : author's initials
005 *
006     PROMPT ":"
007 *
008 * GET FIRST AND LAST NAME
009 *
010     PRINT
011     PRINT "ENTER YOUR FIRST NAME " :
012     INPUT FIRST.NAME
013     IF FIRST.NAME = "QUIT" THEN STOP
014 *
015     PRINT
016     PRINT "ENTER YOUR LAST NAME   " :
017     INPUT LAST.NAME
018     IF LAST.NAME = "QUIT" THEN STOP
019 *
020 * GET BIRTHDAY
021 *
022     LOOP
023        PRINT
024        PRINT "ENTER YOUR BIRTHDAY (MM-DD-YY) " :
025        INPUT BIRTHDAY
026        IF BIRTHDAY = "QUIT" THEN STOP
027        INTERNAL.BIRTHDAY = ICONV(BIRTHDAY,"D")
028     UNTIL INTERNAL.BIRTHDAY # "" DO
029        PRINT "MAKE SURE YOU SEPARATE MONTH DAY AND YEAR WITH DASHES!"
030     REPEAT
031 *
032 * NOW LET'S SHOW OFF
033 *
034     PRINT
035     PRINT "HELLO THERE " : FIRST.NAME
036     PRINT
037     PRINT "THE CURRENT DATE IS " : OCONV(DATE(),"D2/")
038     PRINT "THE CURRENT TIME IS " : OCONV(TIME(),"MTH")
039     PRINT
040     PRINT "IF YOU WERE BORN ON " : BIRTHDAY :
041     PRINT ", THEN THE DAY OF THE WEEK WAS " :
042     PRINT OCONV(INTERNAL.BIRTHDAY,"DWA")
043     PRINT "THIS WAS DAY " : OCONV(INTERNAL.BIRTHDAY,"DJ") :
044     PRINT " OF THE YEAR"
045     PRINT
046     PRINT "THAT MAKES YOU " : DATE() - INTERNAL.BIRTHDAY : " DAYS OLD"
047 *
```

```
048 * GET NUMBER FOR SPACE TEST
049 *
050     PRINT
051     PRINT "LET'S TEST THE SPACE FUNCTION."
052     LOOP
053        PRINT "ENTER A NUMBER BETWEEN 5 AND 20 " :
054        INPUT YOUR.NUMBER
055     UNTIL NUM(YOUR.NUMBER) OR YOUR.NUMBER = "QUIT" DO REPEAT
056     IF YOUR.NUMBER = "QUIT" THEN STOP
057 *
058 * SHOW FIRST AND LAST NAME WITH SPACES BETWEEN
059 *
060     PRINT
061     PRINT "HERE'S YOUR NAME WITH " : YOUR.NUMBER : " EMBEDDED SPACES"
062     PRINT FIRST.NAME : SPACE(YOUR.NUMBER) : LAST.NAME
063 *
064 * SHOW TIMEDATE() AND MASKING
065 *
066     PRINT
067     PRINT "HERE'S TIME AND DATE LEFT JUSTIFIED IN 40 SPACES"
068     PRINT "*" : TIMEDATE() "L#40" : "*"
069     PRINT
070     PRINT "HERE'S TIME AND DATE RIGHT JUSTIFIED IN 40 SPACES"
071     PRINT "*" : TIMEDATE() "R#40" : "*"
072     END
```

Users see only the output of all the work performed by the computer. Now that you are the programmer, you need to know what type of data will be received in a program, because you have to make sure that the data is converted to its proper internal format. Otherwise, many strange things may occur.

With this first example, the ICONV statement is used to take the BIRTHDAY variable and converts it with the D (for ''Date'') conversion. This takes care of the ''internal number of days'' calculation, so it produces one of two results: Either the number of days since 12/31/67 if the date is ''valid,'' or a null if it is determined to be ''invalid.'' In the Pick System, a date is considered valid if it is received with consistent delimiters between the month, day and year. A date is invalid if the conversion fails.

Here are some valid dates for the date conversion function:

    1-1-97
    1.1.97
    01/01/1997
    01 JAN 97
    1JAN1997

(Note that leading zeros are optional.) Now here are two invalid dates for the date conversion function:

    1197
    010197

The reason they are considered invalid is that they already appear to be in internal format.

The same set of conversion codes that are available ACCESS are also available to PICK/BASIC. The conversions used most often are covered in this book.

Here's what happens when a date is converted from its external format to its internal format:

External Format	Date Conversion	Result Provided
12/12/97	D	10939
12 DEC 1997	D2	10939

Figure 7-2 illustrates the various date conversions that may be applied to internal dates.

There are many benefits in storing dates this way. First, it makes sorting easier because it's easy to compare two numbers to see which is greater. Second, it makes performing calculations on dates much easier. This might not seem significant until you have to figure out your own algorithm for calculating what 90 days is from any particular date. Finally, it is more efficient, in terms of storage, than its external counterpart.

On line 28, the contents of the variable, INTERNAL.BIRTHDAY, is examined to determine if it is null, which indicates that the internal conversion process failed. A valid external format is one in which the month, day, and year are each separated by any consistent non-numeric character. If the variable is determined to be null, then the response entered is definitely not a date, so a message is displayed and the birthday is again requested.

	Internal Format	Date Conversion	Result
10939		D	12 DEC 1997
10939		D2/	12/12/97
10939		D2-	12-12-97
10939		D-	12-12-1997
10939	(julian date)	DJ	346
10939	(numeric month)	DM	12
10939	(alphabetic month)	DMA	DECEMBER
10939	(numeric day of week)	DW	5
10939	(alphabetic day of week)	DWA	FRIDAY
10939	(4-digit numeric year)	DY	1997
10939	(quarter)	DQ	4

Fig. 7-2. Sample external date conversions.

On the other hand, if there is a value in INTERNAL.BIRTHDAY, then program execution continues from line 31.

THE OCONV, DATE, AND TIME FUNCTIONS

The OCONV statement is exactly the opposite of the ICONV statement. It takes data in its internal format and converts it to external format, using the same set of conversion codes available to the ICONV function and the ACCESS retrieval language:

037   PRINT "THE CURRENT DATE IS " : OCONV(DATE(),"D2/")

A reserved system function, called DATE( ), retrieves the current system date in its internal format. On line 37, the system date is retrieved and output converted using the "D2/" conversion. This takes the date and formats it in the form *mm/dd/yy*. Note for European readers: Many versions of Pick allow the date format to be "toggled" to European format, which this conversion formats as *dd/mm/yy*.

Time, like dates, is also stored in an internal format representing the number of seconds that have elapsed since midnight. This provides many of the same benefits as the date conversion, particularly with doing calculations:

038   PRINT "THE CURRENT TIME IS " : OCONV(TIME(),"MTH")

Figure 7-3 illustrates what happens when a time is converted from its external format to its internal format, as well as the various time conversions that may be applied to internal times.

On Line 38 of the example, the message, "THE CURRENT TIME IS ", displays, followed by the current time in the format *hh:mm*AM or *hh:mm*PM, depending on whether or not you are doing this before or after lunch.

External format	Conversion	Result
12:30	MT	45000
10:00	MT	36000

Internal format	Conversion	Result
61200	MT	17:00
61200	MTS	17:00:00
61200	MTH	05:00PM
61200	MTHS	05:00:00PM

Fig. 7-3. Time conversions.

Using OCONV with Dates

Once a date is converted to its internal equivalent, it may be output formatted with any of the many types of date conversions. This statement takes the INTERNAL.BIRTHDAY variable and converts it to the external format using the DWA conversion, which spells out the day of the week:

```
042   PRINT OCONV(INTERNAL.BIRTHDAY,"DWA")
```

Line 43 does the same with the DJ conversion, which returns the date in its Julian date format. The Julian date is the sequential number of the day within the year. For example, January 15 is the 15th day of the year and February 15 is the 46th day. This is how you may calculate the number of shopping days left until Christmas. Just for fun, the program to do just that is provided in Appendix C. It's called EX.005A.

Performing Calculations with DATE

On line 46, your age in days is calculated and displayed. This is done by taking the internal system date, DATE( ), and subtracting your birthday, which is stored in INTERNAL.BIRTHDAY. Incidentally, days before December 31, 1967 (day zero on the Pick calendar) are stored internally as negative numbers.

THE SPACE FUNCTION

The SPACE function is used to produce or display a string of spaces. The number of spaces is determined by the result of the numeric expression, in this case, the number you entered into YOUR.NUMBER:

```
062   PRINT FIRST.NAME : SPACE(YOUR.NUMBER) : LAST.NAME
```

If the value of YOUR.NUMBER were 15, for example, the statement would be equivalent to:

```
PRINT SPACE(15)
```

This prints 15 spaces at the current cursor or printer position.

The SPACE function comes in handy when formatting output on reports and screens. (Another way of doing output formatting is through the use of *print masks*, to be discussed shortly.)

THE TIMEDATE FUNCTION

When the TIME( ) and DATE( ) functions were discussed earlier, it was noted that both of these functions retrieve their respective current values in internal format. The TIMEDATE( ) function retrieves the current system time and date in its external format.

For example, the instruction:

```
PRINT TIMEDATE()
```

produces output in the form:

```
10:17:36  12 DEC 1997
```

Line 68 of Program Example 5 uses it in this form:

```
068  PRINT "*" : TIMEDATE() "L#40" : "*"
```

PRINT (FORMAT) MASKING

Print masking is the process of taking an expression and presenting it in a particular output format, typically either left- or right-justified. Print masks are composed of several elements: the justification indicator, a "fill" or "pad" character, and a number to indicate the length of the output.

```
068    PRINT "*" : TIMEDATE() "L#40" : "*"
```

Together, these three elements comprise a print mask. The print mask immediately follows the output-producing expression that it is to format.

The justification is usually either an L for left-justified or R for right-justified. Some systems additionally support extra justification codes, such as D for date justification, which effectively produces the same result as an OCONV function; only the L and R are covered here.

The second of the three elements is the single character to "pad" the output. There are three "standard" characters available:

* Fills output with asterisks.
# Fills output with blanks.
% Fills output with zeros.

The third and final element of the print mask expression is an integer number which indicates the maximum length of the output.

On line 68, an asterisk (*) is displayed. This is to indicate the beginning position of the output. It is immediately followed by the current system time and date, produced with the TIMEDATE( ) function. Notice that the output is displayed left-justified in a field of 40 blanks and followed immediately by another asterisk to indicate the "end" of the output. This appears as:

```
*8:15:34  12 DEC 1997                   *
```

On line 71, an asterisk is displayed, followed by the current system time and date,

75

right-justified in a field of 40 blanks, followed by another asterisk. This appears as:

```
*                          08:15:34  12 DEC 1997*
```

Here's a *very* important note about print masking: Did you notice that there is no character, other than an optional space, between the expression being printed and the mask expression? This is extremely important, because it directs the program to treat the "first" expression as an object of the "second" expression, which is considered a "masking" expression. Shown below are correct and incorrect use of print masking:

```
PRINT "*" : "HI THERE" "L#15" : "*"
```

outputs

```
*HI THERE              *
```

whereas, the statement:

```
PRINT "*" : "HI THERE" : "L#15" : "*"
```

outputs

```
*HI THEREL#15*
```

Not exactly what you wanted . . . .

The moral of this story is that you may use print masking anytime you need it, but remember to separate the expression being printed from its mask expression with only a space, or, of course, the ever-popular null.

REVIEW QUIZ 5

1) What does internal format mean? What does external format mean?

2) What instruction and conversion code is required to convert a date from its external format to its internal format?

3) Suppose you have a variable called BILL.DATE. In this variable is the value "12-12-1399." How could you find out what day of the week it was? If this bill were due in 30 days, how could you determine when it should be paid?

4) What instruction and conversion prints the system time in its external format?

5) What does the SPACE function DO?

6) What is print masking?

7) What output do the following examples produce?

```
PRINT "NAME" "L#15" : "ADDRESS"
PRINT "123" "R#8" : "456" "R#8"
PRINT "NAME" : "L#15" : "ADDRESS"
```

8) What function retrieves the current system time and date?

9) How do you really know when you are a programmer?

8

Numeric
Data Conversion
and Output Routing

IN PROGRAM EXAMPLE 5, TWO OF THE TYPES OF INFORMATION WERE DISCUSSED THAT must be converted internally before they are stored. The third, and perhaps most common, type of data that requires internal conversion is money.

There's an important rule for you to commit to memory here:

Money is always stored internally as the number of pennies!

That's because the Pick report writer, ACCESS, needs it this way. So, in Example 6, the conversion process for handling dollar amounts is covered.

In all of the preceding examples, each PRINT statement that was used to output a literal, variable, or expression to the screen simply printed at the next available screen line. In other words, no special screen formatting took place. Example 6 illustrates formatting screens using a set of PICK/BASIC intrinsic functions. Additionally, the MC and MR conversion codes are introduced. Topics, statements, and functions covered include the ''@'' function, ICONV, and OCONV (MR/MC).

Using the lisiting in Fig. 8-1, enter Program Example 6 now.

THE @ FUNCTION

There are a number of special cursor control functions in PICK/BASIC. These include a function that positions the cursor to a specific coordinate on the screen and a function

Fig. 8-1. Program Example 6.

```
>ED BP EX.006
TOP
.I
001 * EX.006
002 * TERMINAL OUTPUT FORMATTING, MONEY CONVERSIONS
003 * mm/dd/yy : date last modified
004 * JES : author's initials
005 *
006    PROMPT ":"
007 *
008    PRINT @(-1) : @(15,0) : "EXAMPLE 6" : @(58,0) : TIMEDATE()
009 *
010 * GET FIRST NAME
011 *
012    LOOP
013       PRINT @(5,3) : "FIRST NAME" : @(35,3) : STR("_",25) : @(35,3) :
014       INPUT FIRST.NAME,25
015    UNTIL FIRST.NAME # "" DO REPEAT
016    IF FIRST.NAME = "QUIT" THEN STOP
017 *
018 * GET LAST NAME
019 *
020    LOOP
021       PRINT @(5,5) : "LAST NAME" : @(35,5) : STR("_",25) : @(35,5) :
022       INPUT LAST.NAME,25
023    UNTIL LAST.NAME # "" DO REPEAT
024    IF LAST.NAME = "QUIT" THEN STOP
025 *
026 * PUT NAMES TOGETHER AND CONVERT TO UPPER AND LOWER CASE
027 *
028    WHOLE.NAME = FIRST.NAME : " " : LAST.NAME
029    WHOLE.NAME = OCONV(WHOLE.NAME,"MCT")
030 *
031 * GET ANNUAL SALARY
032 *
033    LOOP
034       PRINT @(5,7) : "ANNUAL SALARY" : @(35,7) : STR("_",9) : @(35,7) :
035       INPUT SALARY,9
036    UNTIL SALARY = "QUIT" OR NUM(SALARY) DO REPEAT
037    IF SALARY = "QUIT" THEN STOP
038 *
039 * GET NUMBER OF PAYCHECKS
040 *
041    LOOP
042       PRINT @(5,9) : "HOW MANY PAYCHECKS DO YOU GET EACH YEAR? "
043       PRINT @(5,10) : "PLEASE ENTER A NUMBER BETWEEN 1 & 52 " : @(-4) :
044       INPUT CHECKS
045    UNTIL (CHECKS >= 1 AND CHECKS <= 52) DO REPEAT
046    IF CHECKS = "QUIT" THEN STOP
```

```
047 *
048    PRINT @(5,11) : "THANKS.   NO MORE QUESTIONS"
049 *
050 * START CALCULATIONS
051 *
052    INTERNAL.SALARY = ICONV(SALARY,"MR2")        ; * CONVERT
053    PAYCHECK.AMOUNT = INTERNAL.SALARY / CHECKS ; * CALC.   AMT
054 *
055 * PRINT PSEUDO-CHECK
056 *
057    PRINT @(5,15) : STR("*",50)                  ; * PRINT STARS
058    PRINT @(10,16) : "CHECK 123" "L#20" :        ; * PRINT CHECK #
059    PRINT "DATE " : OCONV(DATE(),"D")            ; * TODAY'S DATE
060    PRINT @(10,17) : "PAY TO THE ORDER OF " :
061    PRINT WHOLE.NAME                             ; * PRINT NAME
062    PRINT @(10,18) : "THE AMOUNT OF " :
063    PRINT OCONV(PAYCHECK.AMOUNT,"MR2,$*15")   ; * EXTERNAL AMT
064    PRINT @(5,19) : STR("*",50)
065 *
066 * DONE.
067 *
068    PRINT
069    END
```

that clears the screen. Each of these functions is enclosed in a set of parentheses and is preceded immediately by the @ (''at'') character.

```
008 PRINT @(-1) :@(15,0) :"EXAMPLE 6" :@(58,0) :TIMEDATE()
```

The @ functions produce a string of characters. This string is most often printed immediately, but it may also be stored in a variable. Multiple @ functions may be concatenated, just like any other string. Figure 8-2 lists the most common functions used in conjunction with the PRINT statement. A more complete listing appears in Appendix B.

Line 8 of the example does the following: First, it clears the screen, using @(−1). It then moves the cursor to column position 15 on screen line (row) 0, the top of the screen.

Function	Description
@(−1)	Clears the screen.
@(−3)	Clears from the current cursor position to the end of the screen.
@(−4)	Clears from the current cursor position to the end of the current line.
@(x,y)	Positions the cursor at column (vertical axis) "x" on row (horizontal axis) "y".

Fig. 8-2. Commonly used "@" functions.

Next, it outputs "EXAMPLE 6" at the current cursor position, then moves the cursor to position 58 on screen line 0, where it next outputs the current system time and date.

Line 13 moves the cursor to position 5 on screen line 3, displays the prompt "FIRST NAME," then moves the cursor to position 35 on screen line 3, where it outputs a string of 25 "__" (underscore) characters. It then moves the cursor back to position 35 on screen line 3.

CONCATENATION

On Line 28, the two variables you had entered earlier, FIRST.NAME and LAST.NAME, are joined together (concatenated), separated by a space. The joined string is then stored in the variable WHOLE.NAME:

```
028 WHOLE.NAME = FIRST.NAME : " " : LAST.NAME
```

This is done because, on the next line of code, a conversion on the entire string is performed.

Figure 8-3 shows two examples of concatenation. Effectively, these two examples produce the same output. In Case 1, the variables are output in five separate PRINT statements. In Case 2, the variables are concatenated together and then output in one PRINT statement. There are several different schools of thought as to which of these is more efficient; I suggest that you use the one with which you feel more comfortable.

CHARACTER MASKING WITH THE OCONV FUNCTION

So far, you have seen the conversions for dates and times. A unique conversion, called the "MC" (for "Mask Character"), allows various conversions on alphabetic and/or

```
Case 1:

001     PRINT NAME      "L#20" :
002     PRINT ADDRESS   "L#25" :
003     PRINT CITY      "L#20" :
004     PRINT STATE     "L#10" :
005     PRINT ZIP       "L#11"

Case 2:

001     PRINT.LINE = NAME "L#20"
002     PRINT.LINE = PRINT.LINE : ADDRESS "L#25"
003     PRINT.LINE = PRINT.LINE : CITY     "L#20"
004     PRINT.LINE = PRINT.LINE : STATE    "L#10"
005     PRINT.LINE = PRINT.LINE : ZIP      "L#11"
006     PRINT PRINT.LINE
```

Fig. 8-3. Examples of concatenation.

numeric strings. For example, the "MCT" conversion converts the first alphabetic character in each word of a string to its uppercase form:

```
029 WHOLE.NAME = OCONV(WHOLE.NAME,"MCT")
```

Figure 8-4 illustrates some of the MC conversions and their effects on data. The MCU code converts all of the alphabetic characters to uppercase. The MCL code converts all of the alphabetic characters to lowercase. The MCN code retrieves all the numeric characters from the string, while the MC/N code retrieves all the nonnumeric characters. Similarly, the MCA code retrieves all the alphabetic characters (upper- or lowercase) from the string, and the MC/A code retrieves all the non-alphabetic characters. Finally, the MCT conversion capitalizes the first character of each word. Note that this conversion works fine for O'Brien, but not for McDonald.

MORE ON THE @ FUNCTION

Another twist on the @ function is shown in line 43:

```
043 PRINT @(5,10) :"PLEASE ENTER A NUMBER BETWEEN
    1 & 52 " :@(-4) :
```

Note that the last function directed to the screen before pausing to wait for user input is the intrinsic function, "@(−4)". Its purpose is to clear from the current cursor position (in this case, from two spaces to the right of the number "52") to the end of the line. This cleans up any "leftover" input when and if it is necessary to prompt the operator for this information again.

MONEY CONVERSIONS WITH ICONV

In Example 5 you examined the effect of date and time conversions. Here, the money conversion is introduced. The MR conversion is used to convert numeric amounts to their

Internal format	Conversion	Result
123 Main Street	MCU	123 MAIN STREET
123 MAIN STREET	MCL	123 main street
123 MAIN STREET	MCN	123
123 MAIN STREET	MCA	MAINSTREET
123 MAIN STREET	MCT	123 Main Street
SEAN O'BRIEN	MCT	Sean O'Brien
MEAGAN MCDONALD	MCT	Meagan Mcdonald

Fig. 8-4. MC conversions and their effects on data.

internal equivalents (remember that on dollar amounts the internal format represents the number of pennies):

```
052 INTERNAL.SALARY = ICONV(SALARY,"MR2")   ; * CONVERT
```

Money amounts are converted to internal format for several reasons. First, and probably the most important, is the fact that storing this way can save hundreds of hours in programming time, since it allows most output reports to be produced with the ACCESS language. (ACCESS does not work well when the data is not stored in internal format). Second, many powerful output conversion codes may be used when writing PICK/BASIC and/or ACCESS reports.

The MR conversion has quite a few forms. It is almost always followed by a number, which indicates the number of decimal positions expected. This number is normally ''2'' for dollar amounts. Another way of thinking about this number is that it represents the number of positions that the decimal point has to move to the right to convert this number to its internal equivalent. Figure 8-5 illustrates what happens when numbers are converted from external to internal format.

Figure 8-6 illustrates some of the numeric conversions that may be applied to internal numbers. The MR2 conversion places the decimal point two positions from the right end of the numeric string; when ''MR2'' is followed by a comma, the conversion places the decimal point two positions from the right end of the numeric string and puts commas in every third position to the left of the decimal point. Following ''MR2,'' with a dollar sign ($) places the decimal point two positions from the right end of the numeric string and puts commas in every third position to the left of the decimal point and precedes the string with a dollar sign.

External format	Conversion	Result
100.22	MR2	10022
100.3	MR2	10030
100	MR2	10000
10	MR2	1000
0	MR2	0
−10	MR2	−1000
−100	MR2	−10000
−100.3	MR2	−10030
−100.22	MR2	−10022

Fig. 8-5. Converting money from external to internal format.

83

Internal format	OCONV conversion	Result
123456789	MR2	1234567.89
123456789	MR2,	1,234,567.89
123456789	MR2,$	$1,234,567.89

Fig. 8-6. Numeric conversions that can be applied to internal numbers.

Using Signcodes in MR Conversions

There are five special codes to activate special features on numeric amounts, four of which are for handling negative numbers. These special *signcodes* always appear in the same parametric position illustrated in Fig. 8-7.

The D signcode instructs the conversion processor to output the literal "DB," for debit, after positive numbers; the other codes modify *negative* numbers. Conversion B in Fig. 8-7 shows the effect of not using a signcode on negative numbers. The C signcode outputs the literal "CR," for credit, after negative numbers, and the E signcode "encloses" negative amounts in the "< >" angular brackets. The M signcode "moves" the negative sign, which normally precedes negative numbers, to the right end of the number. Finally, the N signcode suppresses the leading minus sign on negative numbers. Yes, this does make negative numbers look like positive numbers. (There *are* applications for this, other than printing totals on profit and loss reports for failing companies.)

Fill Characters (Format Masking) in MR Conversions

The MR conversion provides a feature which fills the print field with either blanks, zeros, or asterisks; this is essentially the same as print (format) masking. The three fill

Internal format	OCONV conversion	Result provided
123456789	MR2,D$	$1,234,567.89DB
– 123456789	MR2,$	– $1,234,567.89
– 123456789	MR2,C$	$1,234,567.89CR
– 123456789	MR2,E$	< $1,234,567.89 >
– 123456789	MR2,M$	$1,234,567.89 –
– 123456789	MR2,N$	$1,234,567.89
123456789	MR,$ * 17	* * * *$1,234,567.89
123456789	MR2,$ * 10	$34,567.89

Fig. 8-7. Effects on data of signcodes and format masks used with the MR conversion.

operators are:

%   For filling with zeros
#   For filling with blanks
*   For filling with asterisks

The mask operator must be preceded by an integer number which tells it the number of characters to pad the field with. For example, the next-to-last line of Fig. 8-7 shows the use of format masks with the money conversion. The only "new" feature added here is the format mask itself (*17), which prints the number left-padded with * characters, so that the field is exactly 17 character positions wide.

Just for fun, watch what happens when the format mask is not wide enough to handle the number being printed, as in the last line of Fig. 8-7. In this example, the first two numbers are truncated because the number being printed is much larger than the mask allows for.

On line 52 of Example 6, the amount entered into the variable SALARY is converted to its internal equivalent. Once a number is in internal format, calculations may be performed or any of the output conversions just illustrated may be applied.

Line 53 calculates the amount of each paycheck by first taking the INTERNAL.SALARY variable and dividing it by the NUMBER.OF.PAYCHECKS variable. This result is then stored, still in internal format, in the variable PAYCHECK.AMOUNT.

The code on lines 57 through 64 prints a simulated paycheck on the screen, using functions and features previously covered. One added nuance is the treatment of the output on lines 60 and 61. Line 60 outputs the literal "PAY TO THE ORDER OF " and leaves the cursor positioned at the end of this message on the screen. It is important to remember that the colon at the end of the line means to suppress the carriage return normally printed at the end of a PRINT statement.

Line 61 externally converts the variable, PAYCHECK.AMOUNT, with the "MR2, * 15" conversion. It then prints the external amount at the current cursor position. Line 36 displays a string of 50 asterisks at position 5 on line 15.

REVIEW QUIZ 6

1) What instructions are required to:

    A)   Clear the terminal screen (two ways):

    B)   Print "HELLO THERE" on the 15th line at the 3rd position:

    C)   Clear from the cursor position to the end of the line?

2) What instruction is used to input a variable, and to limit the input to six characters?

3) What instruction is used to convert "123456.78" to its internal format?

4) What statement is used to print the external form of the number "5667788" so that it displays in the format $56,677.88?

5) What is concatenation?

6) As an exercise, modify EX.001 to validate more closely the numbers entered by the operator. Note that this program allows the operator to enter negative numbers. Prevent this from happening.

The CASE Statement
and Controlling Switches

IN PROGRAM EXAMPLE 7, A VERY PRACTICAL ALTERNATIVE TO THE IF-THEN STATEMENT is introduced: the CASE statement. Additionally, you will examine the effect of some of the "switches" available. These include the BREAK key, the ECHO flag, and the PRINTER output flag.

From Fig. 9-1, enter Program Example 7 now.

THE SUBSTRING (TEXT EXTRACTION) FUNCTION

The square brackets are used to extract a fixed number of characters from a string. This fixed number of characters is typically referred to as a *substring*:

```
017 IF OPTION[1,1] = "Q" THEN STOP   ; * SHORTCUT BAILOUT
```

If the variable called NAME contained the string "WASHINGTON," for example, executing the instruction:

```
PRINT NAME[1,7]
```

would produce "WASHING". The first numeric argument within the square brackets indicates the starting position within the string and the second numeric argument refers to the number of characters to be retrieved or extracted.

Fig. 9-1. Program Example 7.

```
>ED BP EX.007
TOP
.I
001 * EX.007
002 * THE CASE STRUCTURE, BREAK KEY CONTROL, PRINTER ON/OFF, ECHO ON/OFF
003 * mm/dd/yy : date last modified
004 * JES : author's initials
005 *
006     PROMPT ":"
007 *
008 10 * MAIN STARTING POINT AND RETURN POINT
009 *
010     PRINT @(-1) : @(20,0) : "EXAMPLE 7" :    ; * CLEAR SCREEN AND FORMAT
011     PRINT @(58,0) : TIMEDATE() :             ; * PRINT TIME AND DATE
012     PRINT @(3,3) : "A.   BREAK KEY TEST" :   ; * DISPLAY MENU
013     PRINT @(3,5) : "B.   PRINTER TEST" :
014     PRINT @(3,7) : "C.   ECHO TEST" :
015     PRINT @(3,10) : "ENTER OPTION LETTER OR 'QUIT' TO STOP " :
016     INPUT OPTION                             ; * GET RESPONSE
017     IF OPTION[1,1] = "Q" THEN STOP           ; * SHORTCUT BAILOUT
018 *
019 * MAKE DECISION BASED ON WHAT WAS ENTERED
020 *
021     BEGIN CASE
022     CASE OPTION = "A"                        ; * TEST BREAK ON AND OFF
023        BREAK OFF                             ; * DISABLE BREAK KEY
024        PRINT @(-1) : @(10,10) :              ; * POSITION FOR MESSAGE
025        PRINT "YOUR BREAK KEY IS NOW DISABLED..." ; * TAUNT OPERATOR
026        PRINT @(10,12) : "GIVE IT A TRY.   PRESS <CR> WHEN READY   " :
027        INPUT ANYTHING                        ; * AWAIT RESPONSE
028        BREAK ON                              ; * ENABLE BREAK KEY
029        PRINT @(-1) : @(10,10) : "YOUR BREAK KEY IS NOW WORKING AGAIN" :
030        PRINT @(10,12) "PRESS <CR> WHEN READY " :
031        INPUT ANYTHING
032     CASE OPTION = "B"                        ; * TEST PRINTER ON, CLOSE, OFF
033        PRINTER ON                            ; * ENABLE PRINTER OUTPUT
034        CRT @(-1) : @(10,10) : "THE PRINTER FLAG IS NOW ON." :
035        PRINT CHAR(12) ; PRINT ; PRINT ; PRINT ; * SHOULD GO TO SPOOLER
036        PRINT "PRINTER TEST IN PROGRESS"       ; * DITTO
037        PRINTER CLOSE                         ; * CLOSE SPOOLER ENTRY
038        PRINTER OFF                           ; * DISABLE PRINTER OUTPUT
039        PRINT @(10,18) : "THE PRINTER FLAG IS NOW OFF " :
040        PRINT @(10,20) : "PRESS <CR> WHEN READY " :
041        INPUT ANYTHING
042     CASE OPTION = "C"                        ; * TEST ECHO ON AND OFF
043        ECHO OFF                              ; * DISABLE CHARACTER ECHO
044        PRINT @(-1) : @(10,10) : "ECHO IS NOW OFF. ENTER YOUR NAME " :
045        INPUT YOUR.NAME                       ; * SHOULD NOT APPEAR ON SCREEN
046        ECHO ON                               ; * ENABLE CHARACTER ECHO
```

```
047          PRINT @(10,12) : "ECHO IS ON AGAIN.    "  :
048          PRINT  "HI THERE, " : YOUR.NAME    ; * PROVE IT'S BACK ON
049          PRINT @(10,14) : "ENTER ANYTHING "  :
050          INPUT  ANYTHING
051     CASE 1          ;  * MUST NOT BE A VALID ANSWER ANNOY OPERATOR NOW.
052          PRINT @(-1) : @(10,10) : "SORRY.   THAT WASN'T WHAT I WANTED"  :
053          PRINT @(10,12) : "PRESS <CR> TO TRY AGAIN "  :
054          INPUT  ANYTHING
055     END CASE
056     GOTO 10     ; * START WHOLE THING OVER
057     END
```

On line 17 of the example appeared the statement:

IF OPTION[1,1] = "Q" THEN STOP

This tells the program to extract only the first character of the variable called OPTION. If it is the letter "Q," then the program stops. Otherwise, the program continues at the next line.

This approach simplifies the number of possible responses that you may need to test for when asking questions of operators. For example, if the program contained these statements:

PRINT "DO YOU WANT THIS REPORT PRINTED ? (Y/N) " :
INPUT ANSWER
IF ANSWER[1,1] = "Y" THEN PRINTER ON

It would prevent having to check for all the possible derivatives of the response, "YES." For example:

IF ANSWER = "Y" OR ANSWER = "YES" OR ANSWER = "YUP" THEN PRINTER ON

Note that on Ultimate systems, the second argument in the substring function defaults to one if omitted. For instance:

ANSWER[1,1]

produces the same result as

ANSWER[1]

THE CASE CONSTRUCT

You have seen the IF-THEN and IF-THEN-ELSE construct in most of the previous examples. The CASE construct in the example program (Fig. 9-2) is similar to a series of IF statements.

```
021   BEGIN CASE
022   CASE OPTION = "A"        ; * TEST BREAK ON AND OFF
023      BREAK OFF                        ; * DISABLE BREAK KEY
024      PRINT @(-1) : @(10,10) :         ; * POSITION FOR MESSAGE
025      PRINT "YOUR BREAK KEY IS NOW DISABLED..." ; * TAUNT OPERATOR
026      PRINT @(10,12) : "GIVE IT A TRY.  PRESS <CR> WHEN READY  " :
027      INPUT ANYTHING                   ; * AWAIT RESPONSE
028      BREAK ON                         ; * ENABLE BREAK KEY
029      PRINT @(-1) : @(10,10) : "YOUR BREAK KEY IS NOW WORKING AGAIN" :
030      PRINT @(10,12) "PRESS <CR> WHEN READY " :
031      INPUT ANYTHING
```

Fig. 9-2. The first CASE condition in Program Example 7.

The CASE construct always begins with the statement **BEGIN CASE**. This statement generally appears on a line all by itself. It indicates to the system that a series of CASE statements will follow. The **END CASE** statement terminates the CASE construct.

The next executable statement after BEGIN CASE must be a CASE statement. The CASE statement has a structure somewhat similar to the IF statement, in that it is always followed by a conditional expression. When the conditional expression following a CASE statement evaluates true, all statements up to the next CASE or END CASE statement are executed.

In line 22 of this example, if the operator enters the letter ''A,'' then all of the statements up to and including line 31 are executed. Execution then resumes at line 57, which is the first executable statement following the END CASE statement.

THE BREAK ON AND BREAK OFF STATEMENTS

The terminal break key may be enabled or disabled under program control:

```
023   BREAK OFF          ; * DISABLE BREAK KEY

028   BREAK ON           ; * ENABLE BREAK KEY
```

This is sometimes very important. There are many occasions when programs update multiple files. Disabling the break key prevents the operator from interrupting the program before all of the files have been updated, which would leave some of them updated and others not updated.

To prevent the operator from interrupting program execution by using the break key, use the statement:

```
BREAK OFF
```

This turns off the break key, rendering it useless until it is reenabled with the statement:

At line 23, the break key is disabled, and the operator is then encouraged to go ahead and "give it a try." The operator may hammer the break key as long (or as hard) as he or she wants to, but it won't work. Even the "last resort" of turning the terminal off and then on again proves useless on most versions of Pick. After they have exhausted their patience and hit a carriage return to satisfy the INPUT statement on line 27, the break key is enabled again on line 28 and once again the program suggests trying it.

This time it works. The side effect of "breaking" a program is that you are left in the PICK/BASIC debugger, at the "*" prompt character.[1] For example, when the break key is pressed, this program displays:

```
(break)
*I28
*
```

At the * prompt character, enter the letter "G" and press Return. This instructs the program to "Go ahead" and resume execution exactly where it left off.

An important note about the debugger: There are two ways to get into it. One is voluntarily, as you just discovered. Under this circumstance, it is OK for you to enter a "G" and have the program continue from where it left off. The other case of entering the debugger is, of course, involuntarily. This occurs when you are running programs that encounter a "fatal" error condition, like trying to write to a diskette that is still in its jacket. A whole section is devoted to using the debugger in Appendix D. For now, you are left with your own intuitive skills for dealing with "fatal" program errors. Two other responses at the debugger prompt are END (to return control to TCL), and OFF.

GROUP LOCKS AND THE "DEADLY EMBRACE"

Everything that has a potential benefit seems to come with some strings attached. This is true when dealing with the break key. The obvious benefit achieved by disabling the break key is in the protection that it offers to interrupting multiple file updates. The disadvantage occurs in the potential phenomenon known as "deadly embrace". This situation occurs, albeit rarely, when two processes contend for information from the same group in a file.

The Pick System scatters data items "across" the file storage area in a method referred to as *hashing*. Each file is created from a contiguous *block* of *frames*. The number of contiguous frames is a function of the *modulo* that was chosen for the file by the person who created it. The modulo thus specifies the number of *groups* that are available to the file. As extra storage space is required for a group, frames are automatically *linked* to the end of each group. This technique provides for automatic file expansion, which is completely transparent to the user. Unfortunately, it has some potentially serious side effects.

---

1. On some implementations of Pick, the program "breaks" into the debugger when the break key is enabled.

The problem stems from the theory of how items are updated in a file. When a new item is placed into a file, it is always placed at the "end" of the group. When an item is updated in a group, the item is physically "pulled out" of its old location. All the remaining items in the group "shift left" to fill in the gap created by the departure of the updated item. (It's like stepping out of a line for a movie: your space is immediately filled.) The updated item then is put at the end of the group.

While the group is "in motion," that is, "shifting left," there is a danger of another process attempting to update the group. If a second process does attempt to update the group, it may result in what commonly has been called a *soft Group Format Error*. This "transient" GFE is usually self-correcting. It often displays the terror-inducing message GROUP FORMAT ERROR! and then goes away. What happened is that once the update by the first process completed, the group returns to a stable condition, where the second process can now update the group. Realizing this, the second process effectively says "Just kidding!" and then completes the update. In theory, no data is lost.

To prevent this potential problem, PICK/BASIC has a provision for avoiding "contention." It is called *group locks*. Group locks are set with any derivative of a READ statement. These are the instructions that activate group locks:

Regular (non-locking) form:	*Group-lock form:*
READ	READU
READV	READVU
MATREAD	MATREADU

Once a group lock has been "set" on a group, no other process may access that group until the lock is "released."[2] Group locks are released when the item is written with the "normal" form of the appropriate WRITE statement, or when the RELEASE statement is executed. Here are more statements which affect the locks:

Regular (unlocking) form:	*Group-lock (non-unlocking) form:*
WRITE	WRITEU
READV	WRITEVU
MATREAD	MATWRITEU

The potential scenario for disaster goes like this: Suppose there are two terminals running programs which update the same file. The first process reads an item from Group A and sets a group lock. Next, the second process reads an item from Group B, also setting a group lock. Now, without unlocking the group lock on Group A, the first process attempts to read an item from Group B, and runs into the group lock. The terminal running the first process "locks up" and starts beeping. Meanwhile, the second process—not even aware that the first process is "locked out"—attempts to read an item from Group A.

---

2. Access, in this definition, means that no other process may retrieve any item from the group through PICK/BASIC. Non-PICK/BASIC tasks, such as the SAVE process and the ACCESS retrieval language, are granted access to the data without even noticing the group locks.

The second process terminal also locks up and starts beeping. Neither process may continue until the other has released the group locks, but they have locked each other out—hence the term "deadly embrace."

If the break key happens to be disabled at this point, both processes are in deep trouble, since they cannot be interrupted and ended through the PICK/BASIC debugger. Some implementations of Pick provide a TCL verb called CLEAR-GROUP-LOCKS, which unconditionally resets all of the group locks. Without having this verb, there are still a few other resorts, one of which is trying to log the locked terminals off from a third terminal using the LOGOFF verb. This doesn't always work, especially when the terminals' break keys are disabled. The last resort is a cold start; before doing so, make sure that all the other users have completed what they are doing and have logged off. This helps to ensure that all the write-required frames in real memory have had a chance to be written to disk, thus helping to avoid the possibility of a *hard GFE*.

OPTIONS FOR OUTPUT CONTROL

PICK/BASIC offers a number of statements that allow you to specify, under program control, the destination of program output.

The PRINTER ON Statement

In the second CASE statement, the program checks to see if the letter "B" is requested as the option. If so, then program execution transfers to line 33, where the PRINTER ON statement is executed:

```
033   PRINTER ON            ; * ENABLE PRINTER OUTPUT
```

The PRINTER ON statement directs all output from subsequent PRINT statements to the printer. Actually, the output first goes to a part of the operating system called the *spooler*. Perhaps you've had some prior experience with the Pick spooler. If not, issue the command SP-ASSIGN at TCL before running this example. That sets your output assignment status to "normal." As long as you have a printer and it's ready, this works. "Ready" means that it is plugged in, turned on, and the "on-line" light is lit.

Incidentally, there is another way of directing output to the PRINTER. In Chapter 2 there was a brief discussion about the options that are available with the TCL commands used to compile and execute programs. The RUN command allows a (P) option. This has the same effect as issuing a PRINTER ON statement at the start of the program. From then on, all of the output from PRINT statements is directed to the spooler. For example:

```
>RUN BP EXAMPLE (P)<cr>
```

Or, if the program is cataloged, simply enter EXAMPLE (P) and press Return.

The CRT Statement

The CRT statement functions exactly like the PRINT statement but it always directs its output to the screen, regardless of the PRINTER ON/OFF status. Line 34 clears the screen, then positions the cursor to position 10 on line 10 and outputs the message "THE PRINTER FLAG IS NOW ON."

```
034 CRT @(-1) : @(10,10) : "THE PRINTER FLAG IS NOW ON." :
```

Line 35 issues a CHAR(12). On most printers, this causes a form feed. The first statement in a program that directs output to the printer also displays a message on the screen indicating the spooler entry (job) number. This number is assigned automatically by the spooler. In the example, after sending out the form feed, three rapid-fire PRINT statements are executed, which output several blank lines at the top of the report. These are followed by the message "PRINTER TEST IN PROGRESS," and that completes the print job.

Note for Ultimate users: The CRT statement may not compile in your program. If not, change the CRT statement(s) to DISPLAY, which may work.

The PRINTER CLOSE Statement

Once a program starts directing output to the spooler, the report doesn't actually start printing until the print job is "closed":

```
037  PRINTER CLOSE          ; * CLOSE SPOOLER ENTRY
```

Although the program has printed everything that it was told to, and even though a PRINTER OFF statement is about to be issued, the printer is not considered closed. It "closes" when one of two things happens: either a PRINTER CLOSE statement is executed, or the program stops.

The PRINTER OFF Statement

The PRINTER OFF statement resets the status of printer output. This means that the output from subsequent PRINT statements in the program are directed to the screen, rather than to the spooler:

```
038  PRINTER OFF            ; * DISABLE PRINTER OUTPUT
```

The message "THE PRINTER FLAG IS NOW OFF," is displayed and the program pauses to await input. Upon receipt of input, program execution transfers to line 57, the first executable statement after the END CASE statement.

The ECHO ON and ECHO OFF Statements

Normally, every character that is typed on the keyboard is first sent to the computer to be recognized, and then is "echoed" back to the screen. The ECHO OFF statement turns off the echo function. Although the program accepts all the characters that are entered, they are not displayed on the screen.

```
043 ECHO OFF                        ; * DISABLE CHARACTER ECHO
044 PRINT @(-1) : @(10,10)  : "ECHO IS NOW OFF. ENTER YOUR NAME " :
045 INPUT YOUR.NAME                 ; * SHOULD NOT APPEAR ON SCREEN
046 ECHO ON                         ; * ENABLE CHARACTER ECHO
```

Typically this feature is used when requesting passwords.

At line 44, terminal echo is disabled with the ECHO OFF statement, and you are then asked to enter your name. You will not be able to see the characters that you type as they are entered. On line 47, the terminal echo is reenabled with the ECHO ON statement and you are asked to enter something else. The characters that you type will appear as they are entered.

THE CASE 1 STATEMENT

At this point in the logic of the program, it has been determined that the response received is not the letter "A," nor "B," nor "C." If it had been one of these letters, then the series of statements following the appropriate CASE statement would have been executed and program execution would have then resumed at the first executable statement after the END CASE statement. Since the first executable statement after the END CASE is the statement GOTO 10, it causes program execution to go back to the top of the program, where the menu is displayed.

The CASE 1 statement is the catch-all case. It is generally used as the last CASE statement in a BEGIN CASE statement. This statement is executed if none of the other conditional expressions in the other CASE statements evaluate to true. If this statement is executed, a message is displayed indicating that there is a faulty operator at the keyboard, who should please try again.

THE CASE CONSTRUCT VS. IF-THEN

You may be wondering when to use a series of CASE statements rather than a series of IF-THEN statements. Good question. Some people feel that the CASE construct is more visually appealing than the IF-THEN construct—but then, some people like Hawaiian music in elevators and some don't. Generally, CASE statements are used for "n-way" branches. There is at least one provable efficiency in the CASE statement over the IF-THEN statement.

Consider the examples shown in Fig. 9-3. The first example (A) illustrates "fall-through" IF-THEN logic, while the second shows the CASE construct.

These two examples effectively do the same thing. They assign the variable NAME based on the single letter entered into INITIAL. This kind of logic appears frequently in programs. The CASE form is much more efficient than the IF-THEN example, because once any of the conditional expressions evaluate true, then program execution transfers immediately to the next executable statement after the END CASE statement. In the first example, even after any one of the conditional expressions evaluates true, all of the other IF statements are still evaluated, even though they cannot possibly be true.

```
Ⓐ  PRINT "ENTER CHARACTER'S INITIAL " :
    INPUT INITIAL
    IF INITIAL = "F" THEN NAME = "FRED FLINTSTONE"
    IF INITIAL = "W" THEN NAME = "WILMA FLINTSTONE"
    IF INITIAL = "P" THEN NAME = "PEBBLES FLINTSTONE"
    IF INITIAL = "D" THEN NAME = "DINO FLINTSTONE"
    IF INITIAL # "F" AND INITIAL # "W" AND INITIAL # "P"...
       ... AND INITIAL # "D" THEN NAME = "UNKNOWN"
    PRINT NAME




Ⓑ  PRINT "ENTER CHARACTER'S INITIAL " :
    INPUT INITIAL
    BEGIN CASE
      CASE INITIAL = "F"
        NAME = "FRED FLINTSTONE"
      CASE INITIAL = "W"
        NAME = "WILMA FLINTSTONE"
      CASE INITIAL = "P"
        NAME = "PEBBLES FLINTSTONE"
      CASE INITIAL = "D"
        NAME = "DINO FLINTSTONE"
      CASE 1
        NAME = "UNKNOWN"
    END CASE
    PRINT NAME
```

Fig. 9-3. "Fall-through" IF-THEN logic vs. the CASE statement.

Additionally, the catch-all logic on line 7 of the first example is clumsy, where the CASE 1 portion of the second example is a much more elegant way of handling the "otherwise" situation.

REVIEW QUIZ 7

1) What is the significance of the "[" and "]" characters? Give an example of how they are used:

2) What does the BEGIN CASE statement do?

3) What is the general form of the CASE statement?

4) What do BREAK OFF and BREAK ON do?

5) What does PRINTER OFF do?

6) What impact does the PRINTER ON statement have on PRINT statements? On CRT statements?

7) What other method, besides PRINTER ON, is available for activating printer output?

8) What does PRINTER CLOSE do? When is it used?

9) What do ECHO OFF and ECHO ON do?

10

Looping with the
FOR-NEXT Statement

IN EXAMPLE 8, ITERATIVE LOOP FUNCTIONS ARE COVERED, SPECIFICALLY, THE FOR-NEXT. Additionally, the FIELD, INDEX, COL1( ), AND COL2( ) functions are discussed. Now enter Program Example 8, shown in Fig. 10-1.

ABOUT THE FOR-NEXT CONSTRUCT

In previous examples, several forms of "looping" constructs have been examined. To reiterate, a loop is a construct in which a series of instructions are repeated a certain number of times. In this example, the FOR-NEXT statement is introduced. This particular structure comes straight from standard Dartmouth BASIC, but a few twists have been added.

The basic premise of a FOR-NEXT construct is that the number of iterations to perform is defined in the FOR declaration statement, which has the general form:

FOR *counter.variable* = *starting.expression* TO *ending.expression*

The *counter.variable* is simply a variable which contains a numeric value. The first time that the FOR statement is evaluated and executed, the result of the *starting.expression* is assigned to the *counter.variable.* All of the statements up to the NEXT *counter.variable* statement are repeated until the value of the *counter.variable* is greater than or equal to the value of the *ending.expression.* The *ending.expression* also contains a numeric value which indicates the maximum number of times that the loop is performed.

A (possibly apocryphal) historical note: Virtually everyone uses the variable name I as the counter.variable. This is deeply rooted in history and comes to us from the old

Fig. 10-1. Program Example 8.

```
>ED BP EX.008
TOP
.I
001 * EX.008
002 * LOOPING WITH FOR/NEXT, THE FIELD AND INDEX FUNCTIONS
003 * mm/dd/yy : date last modified
004 * JES : author's initials
005 *
006    PROMPT ":"
007    STRING = ""      ; * SET WORK STRING TO NULL
008 *
009 * FORMAT SCREEN
010 *
011    PRINT @(-1) : @(20,0) : "EXAMPLE 8" : @(58,0) : TIMEDATE()
012 *
013 * GET NUMBER OF NAMES FOR UPPER END OF FOR ... NEXT
014 *
015    LOOP
016       PRINT @(3,3) : "ENTER A NUMBER BETWEEN 5 AND 9 " : @(-4) :
017       INPUT NUMBER
018    UNTIL (NUMBER >= 5 AND NUMBER <= 9) DO REPEAT
019    IF NUMBER = "QUIT" THEN STOP
020 *
021    FOR I = 1 TO NUMBER
022       LOOP
023          PRINT @(3,3+I) : "ENTER NAME NUMBER " : I "L#5" :
024          INPUT NAME
025       UNTIL NAME # "" DO REPEAT
026       IF NAME = "QUIT" THEN STOP
027 *
028       IF I # NUMBER THEN          ; * IF NOT LAST TIME THEN APPEND "*"
029          STRING = STRING : NAME : "*"
030       END ELSE                    ; * IF LAST TIME JUST APPEND NAME
031          STRING = STRING : NAME
032       END
033    NEXT I
034 *
035 * DISPLAY THE STRING
036 *
037    PRINT @(3,13) : "HERE'S WHAT THE NAME STRING LOOKS LIKE : "
038    PRINT @(3,14) : STRING
039 *
040 * GET THE NUMBER OF THE NAME TO RETRIEVE
041 *
042    LOOP
043       PRINT @(3,16) : "ENTER THE NUMBER OF THE NAME TO RETRIEVE " :
044       INPUT NUMBER
045    UNTIL (NUMBER >= 1 AND NUMBER <= 9) DO REPEAT
046    IF NUMBER = "QUIT" THEN STOP
```

```
047  *
048  * GET NAME FROM STRING AND SHOW BEGINNING AND ENDING COLUMNS
049  *
050     PRINT @(3,17) :"NAME " : NUMBER : " IS " :FIELD(STRING,"*",NUMBER)
051     PRINT @(3,18) : "IT BEGINS IN POSITION " : COL1() + 1
052     PRINT @(3,19) : "AND ENDS IN POSITION " : COL2() - 1
053     PRINT @(3,21) : "PRESS <cr> WHEN READY TO TEST INDEX FUNCTION " :
054     INPUT PAUSE
055  *
056  * NOW LET'S CLEAR SCREEN FOR SECOND HALF OF PROGRAM
057  *
058     PRINT @(-1) :
059     PRINT @(3,2) : "AGAIN, HERE IS WHAT THE NAME STRING LOOKS LIKE : "
060     PRINT @(3,3) : STRING
061  *
062  * GET VOWEL
063  *
064     LOOP
065        PRINT @(3,5) : "I'LL NEED A VOWEL (A,E,I,O, OR U) " : @(-4) :
066        INPUT LETTER
067     UNTIL INDEX("AEIOU",LETTER,1) OR LETTER = "QUIT" DO
068        PRINT @(3,6) : "SORRY. " : LETTER : " IS NOT A VOWEL "
069     REPEAT
070     IF LETTER = "QUIT" THEN STOP
071  *
072  * COUNT THAT VOWEL AND SHOW HOW MANY WERE FOUND
073  *
074     NUMBER.VOWELS = COUNT(STRING,LETTER)
075     PRINT @(3,6) : "THERE ARE " : NUMBER.VOWELS : " OCCURRENCES OF " :
076     PRINT LETTER
077  *
078  * NOW, SHOW EXACTLY WHERE THEY WERE FOUND
079  *
080     PRINT @(3,7) : "HERE ARE THE POSITIONS WHERE THEY WERE FOUND " :
081     FOR I = 1 TO NUMBER.VOWELS
082        POSITION = INDEX(STRING,LETTER,I)     ; * FIND NEXT OCCURRENCE
083        PRINT @(2+POSITION,4) : "^"           ; * PUT 'ARROWS' UNDERNEATH
084        PRINT @(3,8+I) : "LETTER # " : I : " IS IN POSITION " :POSITION
085     NEXT I
086  *
087  * ALL DONE
088  *
089     PRINT
090     END
```

Fortran[1] programming days. In Fortran, I was the first of the predeclared integer variable types. Old habits die hard. There is no rule that you must use I as your counter variable. Rather, I suggest you try to use descriptive variable names instead.

---

1. Fortran derives its name from FORmula TRANslator, a programming language developed by IBM primarily for scientific applications, but subsequently adapted to commercial applications as well.

Statements between the FOR and the NEXT *counter.variable* statement are executed, and when program execution reaches the NEXT *counter.variable*, the *counter.variable* is automatically incremented by 1 (one). Program execution then transfers back to the start of the loop, where the FOR statement is found.

After going back to the start of the loop and incrementing the *ending.expression*, the current value of *counter.variable* is checked to see if it is greater than or equal to the value of *ending.expression*. If *counter.variable* is greater than or equal to the *ending.expression*, then the loop is considered done, and program execution transfers to the first executable statement after the NEXT *counter.variable* statement. Otherwise (if they are not equal) the loop executes again and the pattern continues.

The following example illustrates how the computer could be instructed to count from 1 to 10 and print the numbers along the way:

```
FOR I = 1 TO 10
    PRINT I
NEXT I
```

LOOPS WITHIN LOOPS

Before continuing with the explanation about the FOR-NEXT in Example 7, an important side trip needs to be taken to introduce the concept of loops within loops. Invariably, you will discover these in your programs and you will eventually find a need to include them yourself.

When a FOR-NEXT construct occurs within another FOR-NEXT construct, the ''interior'' loop acts almost like a single statement or function, meaning, that it will perform its designated number of iterations in each iteration of the exterior loop. For example, the following ''nested'' loop executes 100 times:

```
FOR I = 1 TO 10
    FOR J = 1 TO 10
        PRINT "I = " : I : " " : "J = " : J
    NEXT J
NEXT I
```

Notice that the interior loop, which is referred to as the ''J-loop'' in this explanation, is entirely contained within the ''I-loop.'' When this code executes, the variable I, initially is set to 1. Then the ''J-loop'' begins, and J is set to 1. The next line of code prints the current value of I and J, and then J is incremented automatically by 1. Again, the current values of I (which has not changed), and J (which is now 2) are printed. The J-loop continues until J reaches 10. Just as soon as J-loop terminates, the I-loop increments I by 1, then checks to determine if I is 10. If I is 10 then both loops are done and the program continues at the next executable statement. Otherwise, ''J-loop'' happens again. And again. And again.

I suggest that you indent source programs to assist in visually identifying ''levels'' of logic. The FOR-NEXT constructs are excellent examples of why this is so important. Without indenting the ''levels'' of logic, it becomes increasingly trickier to maintain programs.

FOR-NEXT IN CONTEXT

On line 21 of our example program (see Fig. 10-2), I is assigned the value of 1. Program execution then picks up on line 22, where a LOOP statement is started. Line 23 positions the cursor at position 3 on line 4 (which was calculated by adding the current value of I, which is still 1, to 3). The prompt "ENTER NAME NUMBER" is then followed by the current value of I (still the number 1), which is "masked" left-justified in a field of five blanks. The cursor is then held next to this prompt and the program awaits input on line 24. You have two choices, as usual. You may either enter a name for testing the example (use the seven dwarves' names if you can't think of any) or you may enter "QUIT," which means that you are ready to bail out.

The purpose of the exterior loop is to build a string of names, each of which is delimited by an asterisk. For example:

SLEEPY*DOPEY*GRUMPY*HAPPY*DOC*SNEEZY*BASHFUL

The number of names you are asked for depends upon the number you entered on line 16, when you were asked to enter a number between 5 and 9.

Consequently, on line 28 the program compares the current value of I to NUMBER (your number), to determine if this is the last time through the loop. If it is not the last time through, then, on line 29, the name you entered is concatenated to the end of STRING, followed by an asterisk. Otherwise, if it is the last time through, then on line 31 the last name you entered is concatenated to the end of STRING, without being followed by an asterisk.

On line 33, I is incremented by 1, and the program checks to see if I is equal to NUMBER. If they are equal, then the program "falls out" of the loop and continues execution on line 37 (the next executable statement). If they are not equal, then program execution transfers back to the top of the loop, in this case, back to line 21, where the process repeats.

```
021     FOR I = 1 TO NUMBER
022         LOOP
023             PRINT @(3,3+I) : "ENTER NAME NUMBER " : I "L#5" :
024             INPUT NAME
025         UNTIL NAME # "" DO REPEAT
026     IF NAME = "QUIT" THEN STOP
027 *
028     IF I # NUMBER THEN          ; * IF NOT LAST TIME THEN APPEND "*"
029         STRING = STRING : NAME : "*"
030     END ELSE                    ; * IF LAST TIME JUST APPEND NAME
031         STRING = STRING : NAME
032     END
033     NEXT I
```

Fig. 10-2. Main input loop of Program Example 8.

THE FIELD FUNCTION

There are many occasions (in programs) where you need to manipulate strings of characters that are delimited by known, yet *unreserved* delimiters.[2] Our example program demonstrates one such occasion:

```
050 PRINT @(3,17) :"NAME " :NUMBER :" IS " :FIELD(STRING,"*",
NUMBER)
```

The *reserved delimiters* are the *attribute mark, value mark,* and *subvalue mark.* They are the special characters used to accommodate the Pick item structure. There are a handful of intrinsic functions used exclusively for dealing with attributes, values, and subvalues, which are discussed in Example 11.

The first portion of this program constructs a string of names, each of which is separated from the others by an asterisk. This string is stored in the variable STRING. The example provided was:

SLEEPY*DOPEY*GRUMPY*HAPPY*DOC*SNEEZY*BASHFUL

The string may now be manipulated with a special intrinsic function called FIELD. The FIELD function is used to locate and extract a string of characters from within another string of characters. Before the string may be extracted, however, two things must be known: the character that is being used as the "field" (or group) delimiter, and the relative number of the field to retrieve. The term "group" is used as a reference to the individual strings of characters, which happen to be names in this example. Note that the group, or field, delimiter may not be one of the reserved delimiters (attribute, value, or subvalue mark).

This example has seven groups, or "fields," each of which is separated from the others by an asterisk:

```
STRING = "SLEEPY*DOPEY*GRUMPY*HAPPY*DOC*SNEEZY*BASHFUL"
Group number =    1      2       3       4     5     6       7
```

Given that these two pieces of information are known, any individual group may now be retrieved with the FIELD function which has the general form:

FIELD(*string.variable,group.delimiter,occurrence*)

The *string.variable* is the variable which contains the groups, or fields, of strings to search through. The *group.delimiter* is the character (sometimes characters) that constitutes a group delimiter. The *occurrence* is a variable which evaluates to a number to indicate the number of the group to retrieve. As with most intrinsic functions, the FIELD statement

---

2. The reserved delimiters could actually be used in this function, but this rarely occurs. A special set of intrinsic functions are provided for dealing with the reserved delimiters. These are: INSERT, REPLACE, DELETE, EXTRACT, LOCATE, and the special "dynamic array" functions which use the < and > characters.

always appears in either an assignment statement (on the right side of an equals sign), or may be immediately printed or displayed with a PRINT or CRT statement.

Line 50 positions the cursor to position 3 on line 17, where it then displays the word NAME, followed by a space, followed by the number that you entered into the variable NUMBER on line 44. After another space, the word "IS" is displayed, followed by yet another forced space. Finally, the last thing done on line 50 is the FIELD function, which takes your number and searches through STRING until it finds that particular group. The name that corresponds with the group number you requested then displays on the screen.

This program required you to enter five to nine groups, and then required you to pick a number between 5 and 9 to extract that particular group. Things are not always this cut and dried. To further expand on this, suppose there were a variable called NAME that contained the value:

```
NAME = "LINCOLN, ABRAHAM"
```

To extract the last name seems pretty elementary. This could be done with the statement:

```
LAST.NAME = FIELD(NAME,",",1)
```

Executing this statement results in the string LINCOLN being assigned to the variable LAST.NAME. This statement literally reads: Search through the variable called NAME until you find the first delimiter (a comma) and extract all the characters up to that point in the string, not including the delimiter itself. The FIELD function never retrieves the group delimiter.

Getting the first name out of the string is a little trickier. Certainly, it requires using the FIELD function, but there will still be a "problem" remaining, i.e., how to get rid of the space before the first name. Consider the following statement:

```
FIRST.NAME = FIELD(NAME,",",2)
```

This statement literally reads: Search through the variable called NAME until you find the second comma delimiter, and extract all the characters from the first comma to the second. Executing this statement results in the string " ABRAHAM" (note the space) being assigned to the variable called FIRST.NAME. Since there is no second delimiter in the string, the FIELD function extracted all the remaining characters after the first comma, and placed the extracted string into FIRST.NAME.

Now, how might the extra space be removed? The answer is: Lots of ways. Remember the TRIM function? It is used to "trim" off extra leading and/or trailing spaces (as well as two or more embedded spaces). It could easily be used here, as in the following example:

```
FIRST.NAME = FIELD(NAME,",",2)
FIRST.NAME = TRIM(FIRST.NAME)
```

That's one way. These two functions actually could have been combined into one more powerful, if a little more obscure, statement:

```
FIRST.NAME = TRIM(FIELD(NAME,",",2))
```

As we learned earlier, when introducing the concept of functions and expressions, functions may be nested within other functions. When this combination format is used, the program works outward from the innermost set of parentheses. As each successive function completes, the results that it produces is passed along to the next successive function.

Another method for extracting the first name requires the use of multiple FIELD functions, as in the following examples:

```
FIRST.NAME = FIELD(NAME,",",2)
FIRST.NAME = FIELD(FIRST.NAME," ",2)
```

Again, these two functions could be combined into one statement:

```
FIRST.NAME = FIELD(FIELD(NAME,",",2)," ",2)
```

Fortunately, good sense steps in every once in a while and shouts in your ear, "Hey! Do you *really* want to have to support this later? So what if you trim 3 milliseconds off the processing time if it takes you 15 minutes to figure it out next year when you wander back through this code?"

There are at least two additional ways that the first name could have been extracted, but these previous methods are probably the most effective and efficient. One of the two additional ways available is to not store the space, which removes the extra processing time to remove it. Finally, the ACCESS "MCA" conversion could have been used in the form:

```
FIRST.NAME = FIELD(NAME,",",2)
FIRST.NAME = OCONV(FIRST.NAME,"MCA")
```

Or they could have been combined into one statement:

```
FIRST.NAME = OCONV(FIELD(NAME,",",2),"MCA")
```

The MCA conversion code retrieves all of the alphabetic characters from a string. This means just the letters A-Z, in either the upper or lower cases.

THE COL1 AND COL2 FUNCTIONS

Each time a FIELD statement is executed, two special system functions, called COL1( ) and COL2( ), are updated. These functions retrieve the current values of special system variables.

```
051 PRINT @(3,18) :"IT BEGINS IN POSITION " :COL1()+1
```

COL1( ) contains the character position at which the beginning group delimiter was found in the last FIELD statement; COL2( ) contains the ending position where the group delimiter was found.

Observe the example string again, along with the columnar display of the character positions:

```
Character                 1         2         3         4
Position        12345678901234567890123456789012345678901234
STRING          SLEEPY*DOPEY*GRUMPY*HAPPY*DOC*SNEEZY*BASHFUL
```

Suppose that you had requested the third group from this string in the FIELD function. Afterward, COL1( ) contains 13, because the asterisk that precedes the "third" group was found in the 13th character position of the string. COL2( ) contains 20, since that is the position in which the terminating group delimiter was found.

Both the COL1( ) and COL2( ) may be used in calculations or may be assigned to another variable. An important note: Each time the FIELD function is executed, the values in COL1( ) and COL2( ) change.

For instance if you wanted to remove the third group, and its delimiter, the following statement could be used:

```
STRING = STRING[1,COL1()] : STRING[COL2()+1,LEN(STRING)]
```

This reads: Extract from the first position of the string all of the characters up to the current value of COL1( ), which is 13 in the example. Consequently, this takes the string "SLEEPY*DOPEY*" and holds it in a temporary work area. The second portion of the statement tells the program to extract all of the characters after COL2( ), using the LEN function, which determines how many characters there are in a string. This effectively extracts the string:

HAPPY*DOC*SNEEZY*BASHFUL

and joins it to the end of the former string in the temporary work area so that the string ends up as:

SLEEPY*DOPEY*HAPPY*DOC*SNEEZY*BASHFUL

It might seem like a lot of work, but this is the way to manipulate strings of characters that are delimited by non-reserved delimiters. (Note that in most implementations of Pick, the "[" and "]" text extraction characters must be on the right side of an = symbol or in a PRINT statement.)

On line 51 of Example 8, the program moves the cursor to position 3 on line 18 of the screen and outputs the message, "IT BEGINS IN POSITION". The program then calculates the actual starting columnar position at which the string was found by taking the current value of COL1( ) and adding 1 to it. Remember that the COL1( ) function returns the position where the delimiter was found, not the position where the string began. Similarly, On line 52 the ending position of the string is calculated by taking the current value of COL2( ) and subtracting 1 from it.

ABOUT THE INDEX FUNCTION

The INDEX function is closely related to the FIELD function. It, too, is used to locate a string of characters within another string of characters, when the string being searched through is not delimited by reserved system delimiters.[3] The main difference between the FIELD and the INDEX function, however, is that the FIELD function relies upon knowing the character that is being used as the delimiter and the "group" number to retrieve. Conversely, the INDEX function does not need to know which character is being used as the string delimiter. That's because the INDEX function is used to find a string of characters within another string of characters and to report the actual starting position of the desired string.

The INDEX function has the following general form:

INDEX(*string.variable,search.string,occurrence*)

The *string.variable* is the variable which contains a string of characters to search through. The *search.string* is the character (or characters) to be located within the *string.variable*. The *occurrence* is a variable that evaluates to a number to indicate which occurrence of the *search.string* of the group to retrieve. As with most intrinsic functions, the INDEX statement always appears in either an assignment statement (on the right side of an equals sign), or may be immediately printed or displayed with a PRINT or CRT statement. The INDEX function may also appear in a conditional expression (IF, CASE, LOOP). It is also capable of being used in calculated GOTO and GOSUB statements, referred to as ON-GOTO and ON-GOSUB.

Before explaining the mechanics of the INDEX functions provided in Example 8, study the following example which illustrates the general use of the function by finding DOPEY in the Seven Dwarves string:

```
001 STRING = "SLEEPY*DOPEY*GRUMPY*HAPPY*DOC*SNEEZY*BASHFUL"
002 SEARCH.STRING = "DOPEY"
003 POSITION.FOUND = INDEX(STRING,SEARCH.STRING,1)
```

In line 1 of this example, a string of characters is assigned to the variable, STRING. Line 2 assigns a variable called SEARCH.STRING, which is the string of characters to find within STRING. Line 3 is where the variable, POSITION.FOUND is assigned by using the INDEX function to find the first occurrence of DOPEY in the variable, STRING.

---

3. Again, the reserved system delimiters could be used in the INDEX function, but additional intrinsic functions have been added specifically to deal with the system delimiters.

The effect of line 3 is that the value 8 is stored in the variable POSITION.FOUND, since the string DOPEY is found beginning in the eighth character position of the string.

INDEX in Program Example 8

Remember that conditional expressions return a value that represents either a true or false answer. "False" is always 0 (zero) or null. "True," however, may be any numeric non-zero. This example demonstrates the use of the INDEX function as a conditional expression in line 67:

```
067 UNTIL INDEX("AEIOU",LETTER,1) OR LETTER = "QUIT" DO
```

To illustrate this principle as a self-standing example, observe the following:

```
001 ALPHABET.STRING = "ABCDEFGHIJKLMNOPQRSTUVWXYZ"
002 CHARACTER = "M"
003 POSITION.FOUND = INDEX(ALPHABET.STRING,CHARACTER,1)
```

In this example, after execution of line 3, the variable called POSITION.FOUND contains the value 13, since the letter M is found in the 13th character position of ALPHA-BET.STRING.

Suppose, however, that the object of the search is not located within the string, as in the following example where the INDEX function fails:

```
001 ALPHABET.STRING = "ABCDEFGHIJKLMNOPQRSTUVWXYZ"
002 CHARACTER = "@"
003 POSITION.FOUND = INDEX(ALPHABET.STRING,CHARACTER,1)
```

In this example, after execution of line 3, the variable called POSITION.FOUND contains the value 0 (zero), since the @ character is not found in any position of ALPHABET.STRING.

On line 66 of Example 8, you are asked to enter a vowel. The character (or characters) that you enter is stored in the variable called LETTER. Line 67 lists two conditional expressions, connected with an OR, which means either conditional expression may evaluate true to satisfy the UNTIL portion of the loop. There are, however, six possible responses that qualify as "true." As always, the "QUIT" bail-out mechanism is provided. The other five possible true responses are determined by the following INDEX function:

```
INDEX("AEIOU",LETTER,1)
```

This reads: If the variable called LETTER contains a letter that is found in the string "AEIOU," then the program returns the position number at which it is found. The resulting value is a numeric non-zero, or "true." If the letter is not found, the program returns a 0 (zero), or false, value. Regardless of the outcome, the result is returned to the UNTIL clause as the result of a conditional expression.

Note that the null string is always considered present in a string. This is illustrated in the following statements:

```
INDEX("AEIOU","",1)
```

This function retrieves the value 1, since the null is "found" at the beginning of the string.

Using Multiple INDEX Functions

The loop of statements between lines 64 and 69 effectively forced you to enter a vowel or to bail out. Line 74 takes the vowel you just entered into LETTER and counts the number of occurrences of that particular vowel within the string of names that you entered earlier into STRING.

Suppose, for example, that STRING contained the names:

```
STRING = "SLEEPY*DOPEY*GRUMPY*HAPPY*DOC*SNEEZY*BASHFUL"
```

Suppose further that you wanted to know how many occurrences of the letter E there were. This could be done with the statement:

```
NUMBER.VOWELS = COUNT(STRING,"E")
```

After execution, NUMBER.VOWELS contains the value 5, since there are five occurrences of the letter E in the string. Line 75 reports the number of occurrences of the specified vowel in your string.

On line 81, a FOR-NEXT construct is initiated, and the NUMBER.VOWELS variable is "set" as the upper boundary of the loop with the number calculated on line 74. This determines how many times the FOR-NEXT construct is to be executed. The loop counter variable, I, is assigned the initial value of 1.

On line 82, the INDEX function is called upon to determine the character position of the vowel, based upon the occurrence number determined by the current value of I. The first time through the loop, I is 1. The second time through, I is 2, and so on. If the vowel is found, then its corresponding character position is assigned to the variable called POSITION.

Line 83 calculates where the cursor is to be placed on the screen by adding the value of POSITION to the constant 2 (remember that the string display began in position 3), and then adding the value of POSITION. When the cursor position is calculated, an up-arrow (^) is placed at that spot on the screen.

Line 84 does more or less the same thing, but calculates the screen line number rather than the position number. Additionally, it prints the number of each occurrence of the vowel, along with the corresponding character positions.

Line 85 causes I to be incremented by 1 and then checks to see if I has become greater than or equal to NUMBER.VOWELS. If they are equal, then execution continues on line 89, where a PRINT statement issues a blank line on the screen and the program stops. If they are not equal, then program execution transfers back to the top of the loop, on line 81.

REVIEW QUIZ

1) What does the FIELD function do?

2) Study the following assignment statement:

   `DESTINATIONS = "NEW YORK,ZURICH,PARIS,SINGAPORE,SYDNEY"`

   What statement determines how many destinations there are, and assigns the result to a variable called NUMBER.DESTINATIONS? What statement, or statements, would extract the fifth destination and assign it to a variable called LAST.STOP?

3) What is the INDEX function used for?

4) Study the following statement:

   `ALPHABET = "ABCDEFGHIJKLMNOPQRSTUVWXYZ"`

   What statement determines the character position of the letter S in the variable called ALPHABET?

11

Extending the
FOR-NEXT Construct

PROGRAM EXAMPLE 8 IN THE LAST CHAPTER INTRODUCED THE FOR-NEXT CONSTRUCT. This chapter's example illustrates the various extensions that are available to this loop construct. The principal statement covered is FOR-NEXT-STEP.

Now enter Program Example 9, shown in Fig. 11-1.

THE STEP FUNCTION IN FOR-NEXT

The FOR-NEXT construct, in its simplest form, has the general format:

FOR *counter.variable* = *starting.expression* **TO** *ending.expression*

For example:

```
FOR I = 1 TO 10
```

Several additional features may be included in the FOR-NEXT construct. These features are the STEP function, and WHILE or UNTIL conditional expressions.

Normally, when the FOR-NEXT construct reaches the bottom of the loop, where the NEXT *counter.variable* statement is encountered, the *counter.variable* is incremented by 1. The STEP feature is used to change the value by which the counter variable is

Fig. 11-1. Program Example 9.

```
>ED BP EX.009
TOP
.I
001 * EX.009
002 * USING "STEP" IN THE FOR ... NEXT FUNCTION
003 * mm/dd/yy : date last modified
004 * JES : author's initials
005 *
006    PROMPT ":"
007 *
008 * GET BEGINNING RANGE NUMBER
009 *
010    LOOP
011       PRINT "ENTER A NUMBER BETWEEN 1 AND 10 " :
012       INPUT START
013    UNTIL (START > 0 AND START < 11) DO REPEAT
014    IF START = "QUIT" THEN STOP
015 *
016 * GET ENDING RANGE NUMBER
017 *
018    LOOP
019       PRINT "ENTER A NUMBER BETWEEN 100 AND 200 " :
020       INPUT FINISH
021    UNTIL (FINISH > 99 AND FINISH < 201) DO REPEAT
022    IF FINISH = "QUIT" THEN STOP
023 *
024 * GET STEP FACTOR
025 *
026    LOOP
027       PRINT "ENTER A NUMBER BETWEEN 1 AND 5 " :
028    INPUT FACTOR
029    UNTIL (FACTOR > 0 AND FACTOR < 6) DO REPEAT
030 *
031 * HAVE ALL DATA. SHOW INSTRUCTION TO BE EXECUTED.
032 *
033    PRINT
034    PRINT "HERE'S WHAT HAPPENS WHEN WE ISSUE THE INSTRUCTION : "
035    PRINT "FOR I = " : START : " TO " : FINISH : " STEP " : FACTOR
036 *
037 * NOW DO IT
038 *
039    FOR I = START TO FINISH STEP FACTOR
040       PRINT I "L#4" :
041    NEXT I
042    PRINT
043    PRINT
044 *
045 * NOW, DO IT BACKWARDS.
046 *
```

```
047     PRINT
048     PRINT "AND HERE'S WHAT HAPPENS WHEN WE ISSUE THE INSTRUCTION "
049     PRINT "FOR I = " : FINISH : " TO " : START :
050     PRINT " STEP " : (FACTOR * (-1))        ; * NEGATE FACTOR
051 *
052 * READY. GO.
053 *
054     FOR I = FINISH TO START STEP -FACTOR
055         PRINT I "L#4" :
056     NEXT I
057 *
058 * ALL DONE
059 *
060     PRINT
061     PRINT
062     END
```

incremented. For instance, if the following loop were executed:

```
FOR I = 1 TO 10 STEP 2
NEXT I
```

The loop would iterate five times. The first time through the loop, I is 1. When the NEXT I instruction is executed, I is incremented by 2, so its value becomes 3. The next time, I is 5, then 7, then 9, then 11, where the loop is terminated.

The first portion of this chapter's example program simply captures the value for three variables. START is the variable which serves as the *starting.expression*, a number between 1 and 9. The variable FINISH functions as the *ending.expression*, which in this case is a number between 100 and 200. The FACTOR variable is then captured, which is a number between 1 and 5.

```
035 PRINT "FOR I = " :START :" TO " :FINISH :" STEP " :FACTOR
```

Line 35 displays the instruction to be executed on line 39. Suppose you entered 1 into START, 150 into FINISH, and 5 into FACTOR. Line 35 then displays:

```
FOR I = 1 TO 150 STEP 5
```

Line 40 simply displays the current value of I, left-justified in a field of four blanks. Using the previous variables and values, the following output appears:

```
1    6    11   16   21   26   31   36   41   46   51   56
61   66   71   76   81   86   91   96   101  106  111  116
121  126  131  136  141  146
```

113

DOING BACKWARD LOOPS

There are occasions where the loop may need to be decremented. This is accomplished when the STEP factor appears as a negative number. Line 50 displays the effect of having taken the previous STEP factor and multiplying it by −1, which effectively negates the previous contents of FACTOR:

```
050 PRINT " STEP " : (FACTOR * (-1))    ; * NEGATE FACTOR
```

Lines 54 through 56 are where the decrementing loop is performed. Again using the previous variables, the following values display:

```
146  141  136  131  126  121  116  111  106  101  96   91
86   81   76   71   66   61   56   51   46   41   36   31
26   21   16   11   6    1
```

A note on FOR-NEXT efficiency. Each argument in this example was entered from the keyboard, so the character is stored in its ASCII value. Under this circumstance, or when the arguments originate from a file, a binary conversion takes place with each reference to any of the arguments. This slows down program execution. It is actually more efficient to add zero (0) to the original ASCII value of each argument and store it. This forces the conversion to numeric values prior to using the arguments in the FOR-NEXT construct.

REVIEW QUIZ 9

1) What function does the STEP factor serve in the FOR-NEXT statement?

2) Write a FOR-NEXT loop that counts from 1 TO 100, in increments of 2:

3) Write a FOR-NEXT loop that counts backwards from 100 to 1, in increments of 3:

An Introduction
to File I/O

THERE ARE THREE MAIN OPERATIONS THAT PROGRAMS PERFORM: INPUT, PROCESS, AND output. Up to this point, the examples have demonstrated various techniques for processing data and directing the output to the screen or printer. Data may also be output to a file, or input from a file. This is commonly called *file input* and *file output*—or more simply, *file I/O*. Data items from a file are input to a program, processed (modified), and output to a file.

The Pick System offers several methods of processing data items within programs. Dynamic arrays are perhaps the easiest and most straightforward approach to manipulating and storing items in a file.

In order to get the full benefit of this discussion, enter the example program in Fig. 12-1 before proceeding to the explanations of the new topics covered. Before executing the program, create the STAFF file. The data items from Appendix B must be present in the file.

HANDLING FILES : THE OPEN STATEMENT

Before items may be read from or written to a file, the file must be opened:

```
010 OPEN "STAFF" TO STAFF.FILE ELSE STOP 201,"STAFF"
```

Opening the file simply means that the operating system must establish a connection to the physical location of the file on the disk. The OPEN statement directs the system to

Fig. 12-1. Program Example 10.

```
>ED BP EX.010
TOP
.I
001 * EX.010
002 * File Input and Dynamic Arrays
003 * mm/dd/yy : date last modified
004 * JES : author's initials
005 *
006   PROMPT ":"
007 *
008   STAFF.ITEM = ""              ; * INITIALIZE STAFF ARRAY
009 *
010   OPEN "STAFF" TO STAFF.FILE ELSE STOP 201,"STAFF"
011 *
012   LOOP
013     PRINT "ENTER STAFF NUMBER TO DISPLAY OR 'QUIT' TO STOP " :
014     INPUT STAFF.ID
015   UNTIL STAFF.ID = "QUIT" DO
016     READ STAFF.ITEM FROM STAFF.FILE,STAFF.ID THEN
017       PRINT
018       PRINT "NAME"        "L#16" : STAFF.ITEM<1>
019       PRINT "ADDRESS1"     "L#16" : STAFF.ITEM<2,1>
020       PRINT "ADDRESS2"     "L#16" : STAFF.ITEM<2,2>
021       PRINT "CITY"        "L#16" : STAFF.ITEM<3>
022       PRINT "STATE"       "L#16" : STAFF.ITEM<4>
023       PRINT "ZIP"         "L#16" : STAFF.ITEM<5>
024       PRINT "HIRE DATE"    "L#16" : OCONV(STAFF.ITEM<7>,"D2-")
025       PRINT "HOURLY RATE" "L#16" : OCONV(STAFF.ITEM<9>,"MR2,$")
026       PRINT
027     END ELSE
028       PRINT
029       PRINT "ITEM " : STAFF.ID : " NOT FOUND."
030     END
031   REPEAT
032 *
033   END
```

establish this connection automatically. Line 10 opens the file.

The general form of the OPEN statement is:

OPEN *"filename"* TO *filevariable* {THEN...} ELSE . . .

The *filename* argument typically is enclosed in quotes, in which case the filename must be spelled exactly as it is found in the MD of the current account. The filename also may be contained in a variable, with the same exact spelling restrictions. The TO *filevariable* specification is optional, but recommended. The file variable is the name by which the file will be referred to throughout the rest of the program for all subsequent READ and WRITE statements.

Not assigning the opened file to a file variable is called "opening the file as the default file variable." Using the default file variable form is a shortcut that affects subsequent READ and WRITE operations. Normally, each READ and WRITE statement includes the file variable from which the item is to be read or to which the item is to be written. In the default file variable form, the file variable does not have to be specified. This technique is acceptable when only one file is being used.

The THEN initiator is allowed, but not required. Any statement, or statements, following the THEN initiator are executed when *filename* is found in the MD of the current account. The ELSE clause is required. Any statements following the ELSE clause are executed when the filename is not found in the current MD. Usually, the code after ELSE advises the user that *filename* was not found and terminates the program.

Error Message Numbers with the STOP Statement

In earlier examples of the STOP statement, it most often was used in an IF-THEN or an IF-THEN-ELSE construct. None of these examples particularly required any subsequent explanation of the reason why the program was stopped, since it was most likely terminated voluntarily.

In this example, however, the STOP statement is followed by the item-id "201."

```
010 OPEN "STAFF" TO STAFF.FILE ELSE STOP 201,"STAFF"
```

This extension to the STOP statement allows any error message from the ERRMSG file to be displayed upon execution of the STOP statement. This message happened to be error message 201, which, if examined, appears as follows:

```
Filename : ERRMSG
Item-id  : 201

001 H'
002 A
003 H' IS NOT A FILE NAME
```

Upon activation of this error message, the literal "STAFF" is inserted ("passed") into the text of the message where the letter A appears. This means that if this executes, it displays:

```
'STAFF' IS NOT A FILE NAME
```

STOP vs. ABORT

The error message extension also applies to the ABORT statement. The difference between the STOP and ABORT statements is that the STOP statement terminates a program, but if the program had been activated from a PROC, the PROC will not be terminated.

The ABORT statement terminates the program and any PROC from which it may have been activated.

For instance, suppose this program had been activated from a PROC menu—a very common situation. Normally the PROC menu clears the screen and offers a number of different menu options. If this program executed the STOP statement and displayed the error message about the file not being found, and then control returned to the menu, the message would display so quickly on the screen that it could be noticed only by graduates of speed-reading classes.

On the other hand, if the STOP statement had been replaced with the ABORT statement, the message would display on the screen and the program and menu would be terminated. The disadvantage of the ABORT statement is that the bewildered operator is left at the TCL prompt. That's when the programmer gets the phone call announcing that something is wrong with the program. One frequent cause of this problem is that the program is being run from the wrong account.

One popular method of tackling this problem is by adding a few lines of code to the ELSE clause that issues the STOP statement. For example:

```
OPEN "STAFF" TO STAFF.FILE ELSE
    PRINT "STAFF IS NOT A FILENAME!" :
    INPUT RESPONSE
    STOP
END
```

This technique is not quite as slick as using the error message extension illustrated in Example 10, but it has the added advantage of pausing the program long enough to advise the operator about the error condition and awaiting their response.

Some programmers prefer to keep the operators on their toes by putting the message up on the screen for a certain amount of time. This involves the use of the SLEEP statement, as illustrated in the following example:

```
OPEN "STAFF-FILE" TO STAFF.FILE ELSE
    PRINT "STAFF-FILE IS NOT A FILENAME!" :
    SLEEP 5
    STOP
END
```

When this code is executed, and the ELSE clause is executed, the message appears on the screen for 5 seconds before resuming the menu. For added fun, the number of seconds may be randomized, so that the program's naptime varies each time it is executed. (Operators tend not to find this technique amusing.)

OBTAINING THE ITEM-ID

Before reading an item from a file, the item-id must be obtained. There are a number of methods of obtaining the item-id. This particular method prompts the operator to enter it:

```
013 PRINT "ENTER STAFF NUMBER TO DISPLAY OR 'QUIT' TO STOP " :
014 INPUT STAFF.ID
```

Use one of the data items from the STAFF file for this example. This program stores
the item-id in the variable STAFF.ID.

READING DYNAMIC ARRAYS FROM FILES

An *array* is a data structure which contains multiple data elements. Each element may
be referenced by a numeric *subscript*, which indicates its position in the array. A dynamic
array is generally used to hold an item (record) while it is being processed in a PICK/BA-
SIC program.

Once the item-id is entered, and after checking the response to see if the operator
wants to quit, the item may be read from the file and placed into the dynamic array.

The READ statement is used to retrieve an item from a file. It has the following general
format:

> READ *array.variable* FROM *file variable,id.expression* . . .
> . . . {THEN *statement(s)*} ELSE *statement(s)*

Like the OPEN statement, the THEN clause is optional in a READ statement, and the
ELSE clause is required. The statement, or statements, following the ELSE clause instruct
the program how to behave if the requested item-id is not found.

In Example 10, both the THEN and the ELSE initiators were used (Fig. 12-2). Line
16 performs the READ statement. If the item-id is found, the statements from lines 17
through 26 are executed. These statements display some of the attributes from the item.
After line 26 is executed, control returns to the top of the loop, where the operator is
again prompted to enter an item-id.

```
016     READ STAFF.ITEM FROM STAFF.FILE,STAFF.ID THEN
017         PRINT
018         PRINT "NAME"          "L#16" : STAFF.ITEM<1>
019         PRINT "ADDRESS1"      "L#16" : STAFF.ITEM<2,1>
020         PRINT "ADDRESS2"      "L#16" : STAFF.ITEM<2,2>
021         PRINT "CITY"          "L#16" : STAFF.ITEM<3>
022         PRINT "STATE"         "L#16" : STAFF.ITEM<4>
023         PRINT "ZIP"           "L#16" : STAFF.ITEM<5>
024         PRINT "HIRE DATE"     "L#16" : OCONV(STAFF.ITEM<7>,"D2-")
025         PRINT "HOURLY RATE" "L#16" : OCONV(STAFF.ITEM<9>,"MR2,$")
026         PRINT
027     END ELSE
028         PRINT
029         PRINT "ITEM " : STAFF.ID : " NOT FOUND."
030     END
```

Fig. 12-2. The THEN and ELSE clauses in the READ statement.

ENTER STAFF NUMBER TO DISPLAY OR 'QUIT' TO STOP :**100**<cr>

NAME	THOMPSON, HUNTER
ADDRESS1	C/O STARDUST HOTEL
ADDRESS2	
CITY	LAS VEGAS
STATE	NV
ZIP	77777
HIRE DATE	05-01-92
HOURLY RATE	$150.00

Fig. 12-3. Sample output from Program Example 10.

If the item-id is not found, then the statements after the ELSE clause on line 27 are executed. Line 28 issues a blank line on the screen, and line 29 advises the operator that the just-entered item-id was not found. Execution then passes back to the top of the loop.

Suppose you entered the item-id 100, and you had entered the data from the sample data in Appendix D. The information shown in Fig. 12-3 then displays on the screen:

REFERENCING DYNAMIC ARRAYS

In referring to any element within a dynamic array, such as STAFF.ITEM in our example (Fig. 12-4), the angle brackets < and > are used to specify subscript locations. A subscript is simply a number that corresponds to an attribute, value, or subvalue location within an array. Dynamic arrays may be referenced in several different ways.

Referencing Attributes with Array Reference Symbols

The general syntax for referencing attributes with array reference symbols is:

array.variable<amc.expression>

```
018        PRINT "NAME"         "L#16" : STAFF.ITEM<1>
019        PRINT "ADDRESS1"     "L#16" : STAFF.ITEM<2,1>
020        PRINT "ADDRESS2"     "L#16" : STAFF.ITEM<2,2>
021        PRINT "CITY"         "L#16" : STAFF.ITEM<3>
022        PRINT "STATE"        "L#16" : STAFF.ITEM<4>
023        PRINT "ZIP"          "L#16" : STAFF.ITEM<5>
024        PRINT "HIRE DATE"    "L#16" : OCONV(STAFF.ITEM<7>,"D2-")
025        PRINT "HOURLY RATE"  "L#16" : OCONV(STAFF.ITEM<9>,"MR2,$")
```

Fig. 12-4. Referencing the fields of the STAFF.ITEM dynamic array.

The *amc. expression* is a number which refers to the Attribute Mark Count (AMC). For example:

```
018 PRINT "NAME"          "L#16" : STAFF.ITEM<1>
```

This displays the literal ''NAME,'' left-justified in a field of 16 spaces, and then outputs the entire contents of attribute 1.

Referencing with the EXTRACT Function

Before the dynamic array reference symbols were added to the PICK/BASIC language, locations from within a dynamic array were extracted using the intrinsic function EXTRACT. This function has the general format:

EXTRACT(*array. variable,amc. expression,vmc. expression,svmc. expression***)**

Line 18 could have been replaced with the statement:

```
018 PRINT "NAME"          "L#16" : EXTRACT(STAFF.ITEM,1,0,0)
```

This produces the same result as using the dynamic array reference symbols. The manner you choose to retrieve locations from dynamic arrays is up to you. There is not a great deal of difference in execution efficiency between the two methods. Additionally, both methods are fully implemented across all implementations of Pick, so compatibility is not an issue.

One consideration of the dynamic array reference symbols versus the EXTRACT function is that the EXTRACT function needs a little more code, due to syntax requirements. The general format of the EXTRACT function requires all four of the arguments within the parentheses. This is how the function was originally designed to be used. As you recall, in the previous illustration the code read:

```
... EXTRACT(STAFF.ITEM,1,0,0)
```

Zero (0) was substituted for the *vmc. expression* and *svmc. expression*, since they are required by the syntax of the EXTRACT function.

Referencing Values

The general syntax for referencing values is:

array. variable < *amc. expression,vmc. expression* >

The *vmc. expression* derives a number which refers to the Value Mark Count (VMC) within an attribute. For example:

```
019 PRINT "ADDRESS1"      "L#16" : STAFF.ITEM<2,1>
```

This displays the literal "ADDRESS1," left-justified in a field of 16 spaces, and then outputs the contents of the first value in the second attribute.

The dynamic array reference symbol form of this instruction has an alternative in the EXTRACT function. Line 19 also could have been replaced with the statement:

```
019 PRINT "ADDRESS1"    "L#16" : EXTRACT(STAFF.ITEM,2,1,0)
```

Referencing Subvalues

Expressions referencing subvalues have the following general form:

array.variable < amc.expression,vmc.expression,svmc.expression >

The *svmc.expression* derives a number which refers to the Subvalue Mark Count (SVMC) within a value.

A subvalue also may be retrieved with the EXTRACT function using the same general format as illustrated before:

EXTRACT(*array.variable,amc.expression,vmc.expression,svmc.expression*)

THE "LOGICAL" AND "PHYSICAL" VIEWS OF DATA

The way you see data within a process such as the Editor is not at all the way the operating system sees it. For the most part, this is not particularly important and will remain transparent to the majority of the people who actually use the system. For you, as the programmer, it is important to know how the system deals with data.

For example, take an array called CUSTOMER.ITEM, which, in its "logical" view, looks like this:

```
ITEM-ID :       100
Attribute       Content

   001          YUPPIE HAVEN RESORT
   002          PO BOX 7]ROUTE 17
   003          BEDFORD
   004          VA
   005          24505
```

This is its "logical" form, because this is how it is typically displayed by the Editor, with the line numbers on the left corresponding to attribute mark numbers.

The "physical" form, on the other hand is the way the item is actually handled and stored by the operating system:

```
100^YUPPIE HAVEN RESORT^PO BOX 7]ROUTE 17^BEDFORD^VA^24505^_
```

To the program, a dynamic array simply appears as one long string of characters, delimited by attribute marks (^), value marks (]), and occasionally, subvalue marks (\ ), which are not shown in this example.

Since the system treats dynamic arrays as string variables, if the statement:

    PRINT CUSTOMER.ITEM

were issued, the entire item displays, along with all of its embedded delimiters—the attribute, value, and subvalue marks.

Important note: Any time that any of the reserved delimiters are displayed by a PICK/BASIC program, a metamorphosis occurs. This is due to the fact that PICK/BASIC strips the high-order bit on characters above decimal 127. The program thus subtracts 127 from the actual decimal value of the delimiter and prints the corresponding character. This means that the attribute mark, which normally displays as a caret (^), appears when printed by a PICK/BASIC program as a tilde (~). Value marks, which normally appear as a left bracket (]), instead appear as a brace (}). And finally, subvalue marks, which normally appear as a backslash (\ ), appear as a vertical bar (|).

Normally, the entire item is not printed in one PRINT statement, since the display of the extra characters which serve as delimiters might be confusing. Rather, specific locations, such as an attribute or value locations, are requested, as in either of the following statements:

    PRINT CUSTOMER.ITEM<1>

or

    PRINT EXTRACT(CUSTOMER.ITEM,1,0,0)

This prints the contents of the first attribute. Using the physical view of our item, the following displays on the screen:

    YUPPIE HAVEN RESORT

If an attribute or value contains multiple values or subvalues, then additional specifications are added to the syntax, as in the following examples:

    PRINT CUSTOMER.ITEM<2,1>

or

    PRINT EXTRACT(CUSTOMER.ITEM,2,1,0)

Again using the same item, this displays:

    PO BOX 7

These statements both instructed the program to print the first value from attribute two.

To retrieve the second attribute, either of the following two statements may be issued:

    PRINT CUSTOMER.ITEM<2,2>

or

    PRINT EXTRACT(CUSTOMER.ITEM,2,2,0)

Finally, a specification to reference subvalues may be added. Using the sample data and instruction shown in Fig. 12-5, we can print the third subvalue from the second value of the first attribute. From this example, the display is "789."
The alternate instruction that could have been used in Fig. 12-5 is:

    PRINT EXTRACT(INVOICE.ITEM,1,2,3)

WHY DYNAMIC ARRAYS NEED TO BE REFERENCED

Now that you have seen how to reference a location, you now need to know why you want to. Dynamic array references are used in two ways. First, as in Example 10,

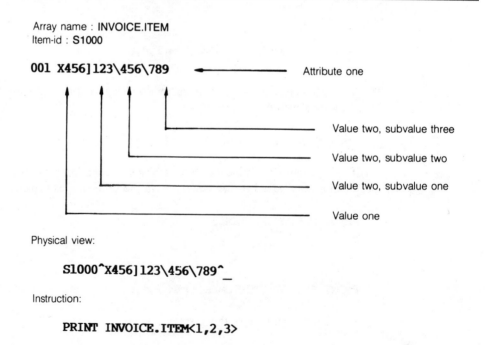

Fig. 12-5. A logical data view with values and subvalues.

they were used to output values to the screen or printer. Second, in some cases they may be used in an assignment statement. This means that they appear on the left side of a "=" symbol, like in the following example:

```
001    PRINT "ENTER NAME " :
002    INPUT NAME
003    IF NAME = "QUIT" THEN STOP
004    CUSTOMER.ITEM<1> = NAME
```

Line 1 prompts the operator to enter a name, which is assigned to the variable NAME on line 2. Line 3 checks to see if the operator wanted to quit, in which case the STOP statement is issued. If not quitting is chosen, then line 4 assigns the response to attribute "one" of the array CUSTOMER.ITEM.

While this appears to be a rather simple means of dealing with a dynamic array, there are some sneaky side effects and further implications to be discussed.

SNEAKY SIDE EFFECTS OF DYNAMIC ARRAYS

In the next example, four special intrinsic functions are discussed. These are INSERT, REPLACE, DELETE, and LOCATE. They are used to manipulate dynamic arrays and were the first methods available for this purpose. The alternate array reference symbols < and > came later to the language.

The INSERT statement is used to add a new value at a specified subscript location in an array. It does exactly what it is told to do. This means that if you INSERT a string into attribute one, then it "pushes" down any existing attributes by one attribute.

The REPLACE statement, on the other hand, replaces the contents of any subscript location. If there is no value in the specified subscript location, the REPLACE statement adds all of the necessary delimiters to accommodate the request; in this case, it acts like the INSERT function.

The dynamic array references in an assignment statement are nearly as ambiguous.

Confused? Relax. So was I at first. If you follow some simple guidelines, this gets to be quite easy.

When a dynamic array reference appears on the left side of an equal symbol, it may be interpreted as either an INSERT or a REPLACE function, depending on the existing contents of the array. For instance, suppose an array variable called VENDOR.ITEM, is currently empty, as in this example:

```
001    VENDOR.ITEM = ""
002    PRINT "ENTER VENDOR CITY " :
003    INPUT CITY
004    IF CITY = "QUIT" THEN STOP
005    VENDOR.ITEM<3> = CITY
```

Further suppose that you enter "BATON ROUGE" as the response and the array is displayed with the statement:

```
006    PRINT VENDOR.ITEM
```

125

The following appears on the screen:

```
~~BATON ROUGE
```

(Remember the "metamorphosis" note pertaining to the conversion of the delimiters when printed by a program.)

In this case, the dynamic array reference on line 5 is treated as an INSERT function. Since none of the attribute marks are already in place, the program inserted two attribute marks before the string "BATON ROUGE" to accommodate your request.

On the other hand, assume that an array had already been constructed, and appeared as follows (in its logical view):

```
Array Name : VENDOR.ITEM
Item-id    : 1000

001 U.S. COPYRIGHT OFFICE
002 LIBRARY OF CONGRESS
003 WASHINGTON
004 DC
005 20001
```

Suppose the following code were executed:

```
001    PRINT "ENTER VENDOR CITY " :
002    INPUT CITY
003    IF CITY = "QUIT" THEN STOP
004    VENDOR.ITEM<3> = CITY
```

and the response entered was "NEW YORK." Here's how the array appears after the execution of line 4:

```
001 U.S. COPYRIGHT OFFICE
002 LIBRARY OF CONGRESS
003 NEW YORK
004 DC
005 20001
```

In this case, the dynamic array reference on line 5 is treated as a REPLACE function. Since all of the attribute marks are already in place, the program did not have to insert any attribute marks before the string, "NEW YORK," to accommodate the request.

The implication of what you have just seen is that you basically need to know, with reasonable accuracy, just what you want to do to an array, based on whether the structure is already in place. If the array is not already in place, then the INSERT or REPLACE functions may be used to put strings into specific locations. If the array is in place, then the REPLACE function may be used to exchange the contents of any subscript location.

SPECIAL ARGUMENTS IN DYNAMIC ARRAY REFERENCES

In the previous illustrations of referring to subscripts within a dynamic array, each numeric expression within the array reference symbols < and > evaluate to positive numbers which corresponded to attribute, value, and subvalue locations.

A "−1" argument may be used in place of any of the numeric expressions within the dynamic array reference symbols to force the position index to the end of the appropriate array location. For instance, suppose the following statements were executed:

```
001    WORK.ITEM = ""
002    WORK.ITEM<-1> = "ATTRIBUTE ONE"
003    WORK.ITEM<-1> = "ATTRIBUTE TWO"
004    WORK.ITEM<-1> = "ATTRIBUTE THREE"
005    PRINT WORK.ITEM
```

Line 1 initializes the dynamic array WORK.ITEM. Line 2 inserts a new attribute at the end of the otherwise "null" array. This effectively creates attribute one. Similarly, line 3 also adds a new attribute to the end of the array, which results in the literal "ATTRIBUTE TWO" being placed into attribute two. Line 4 does the same thing yet again, putting the string "ATTRIBUTE THREE" into attribute three.

When line 5 is executed, the following appears:

```
ATTRIBUTE ONE˜ATTRIBUTE TWO˜ATTRIBUTE THREE
```

This approach to dealing with arrays is, at best, highly unconventional. More realistically, the "−1" argument is used to add a new value at the end of a multivalued attribute, or to add a new subvalue to the end of a value which may need to contain subvalues. The example in Fig. 12-6 illustrates this principle.

Line 1 initializes the array CUSTOMER.ITEM. On line 2, the operator is prompted to enter the first line of the address, which is stored in the variable RESPONSE on line 3. Line 4 checks to see if he or she wants to quit. Line 4 adds the response to the *end* of attribute two. As a result, the array now has two attributes, the second of which has one value.

This logic is repeated in lines 6 through 8 and on line 9, the second line of the address is added to the end of attribute two. After execution of line 9, the array has two attributes, the second of which contains two values. These two values are displayed on lines 10 and 11.

CHOOSING THE ITEM-ID

Each item-id in the Pick System is *hashed* to determine the group in which it will reside. The process of hashing effectively takes each character in the item-id and converts it to its decimal equivalent. The result of each of these decimal conversions are added together to form the *hash total*. This hash total is then divided by the *modulo* of the file, which is the number that indicates the number of groups in a file. The *remainder* of this division is then added to the *base fid* of the file, and that effectively becomes the group to which the item hashes.

```
001    CUSTOMER.ITEM = ""
002    PRINT "ENTER ADDRESS LINE 1 " :
003    INPUT RESPONSE
004    IF RESPONSE = "QUIT" THEN STOP
005    CUSTOMER.ITEM<2,-1> = RESPONSE
006    PRINT "ENTER ADDRESS LINE 2 " :
007    INPUT RESPONSE
008    IF RESPONSE = "QUIT" THEN STOP
009    CUSTOMER.ITEM<2,-1> = RESPONSE
010    PRINT "ADDRESS 1 : " : CUSTOMER.ITEM<2,1>
011    PRINT "ADDRESS 2 : " : CUSTOMER.ITEM<2,2>
```

Fig. 12-6. An example of using −1 in dynamic array references.

Don't worry too much about understanding the mechanics of this process. Just remember this one simple fact about item-ids: When item-ids are sequentially assigned numbers, all of which are the same length, you get a nearly perfect "distribution" of items in a file. Item-ids that are random length, or composed of random characters, tend to distribute unevenly in a file. This means that some groups may contain items, while other groups remain empty. In this case, the file will never be able to be sized properly.

Discussing file sizing with a Pick technician is not unlike discussing religion with a television evangelist. They tend to have very strong opinions about their respective beliefs.

Several verbs allow you to analyze the distribution of items in a file. They are ISTAT, which shows the current distribution statistics, and HASH-TEST, which allows a hypothetical modulo to be tested to see how the distribution of items in the file would be if the modulo were to change. But rather than devote the next 100 pages of this book to the topic, just remember the suggestion: When you have a choice of item-ids for a file, use sequential numbers that are all the same length. Note also that the modulo for a file should always be a prime number (one that is divisible only by itself and one).

REVIEW QUIZ 10

1) What purpose does the OPEN statement serve? When is it used?

2) What purpose do attribute marks, value marks, and subvalue marks serve?

3) Using the dynamic array reference symbols, fill in the program instructions which are needed to construct an item which appears as follows:

Attribute	Contents
001	BARNEY RUBBLE
002	PO BOX 77]141 BEDROCK

	PLACE
003	BEDROCK
004	PA
005	19104

4) Write a routine to print the above array out in this form:

BARNEY RUBBLE
PO BOX 77
141 BEDROCK PLACE
BEDROCK, PA 19104

5) Suppose you have an array called INVOICE.ITEM that was currently "null." How does the array appear in its physical form after executing the following instructions?

```
INVOICE.ITEM<6,-1> = ICONV("03-04-93","D")

INVOICE.ITEM<2,3> = ICONV("100","MR2")
```

6) What statement is used to retrieve an item from a file?

7) What statement, or statements, are needed to retrieve an item called S1000 from a file called INVOICE-FILE?

8) What purpose does the THEN clause serve in a READ statement?

9) What purpose does the ELSE clause serve in a READ statement?

Manipulating Dynamic Arrays

PROGRAM EXAMPLE 11 ILLUSTRATES MORE VARIATIONS ON HANDLING DYNAMIC ARRAYS. The functions introduced in this example include the ON-GOSUB statement, the INSERT function, the REPLACE function, the DELETE function, and the powerful LOCATE statement.

The basic premise of Example 11 is that it permits the user to build and display a dynamic array. This is an example of processing an item before writing it to a file. The main difference between this and a practical example is that, in this example, the positions in which you place data are generalized. In a real-world program, each position is predetermined.

Now enter Program 11 from the example shown in Fig. 13-1.

THE GOSUB STATEMENT AND LOCAL SUBROUTINES

The GOSUB statement is used in PICK/BASIC programs to transfer execution to a section of code called a *local subroutine*. Often this section of code performs a series of instructions that need to be repeated many times. This is more efficient, obviously, than coding the same series of instructions over and over in a program.

```
030 ON INDEX("IRDLC",OPTION,1) GOSUB 100,200,300,400,500
```

The reason that it is called a local subroutine is that the program instructions that comprise the subroutine are physically contained in the same program, and consequently, any program variables may be shared. Subroutines normally are gathered together near

Fig. 13-1. Program Example 11.

```
    EX.011
001 * EX.011
002 * HANDLING ARRAYS AND LOCAL SUBROUTINES
003 * mm/dd/yy : date last modified
004 * JES : author's initials
005 *
006     PROMPT ":"
007 *
008     EQU TRUE TO 1
009     EQU FALSE TO 0
010     WORK.ARRAY = ""           ; * INITIALIZE 'DYNAMIC' ARRAY
011 *
012 10 * FORMAT SCREEN
013 *
014     LOOP
015        PRINT @(-1) : @(20,0) : "HANDLING ARRAYS" :
016        PRINT @(3,2) : "WORK ARRAY : " : WORK.ARRAY :
017        PRINT @(3,5) : "HERE ARE THE AVAILABLE MENU OPTIONS :" :
018        PRINT @(3,7)  : "I --> INSERT STRING INTO ARRAY" :
019        PRINT @(3,8)  : "R --> REPLACE STRING IN ARRAY" :
020        PRINT @(3,9)  : "D --> DELETE STRING FROM ARRAY" :
021        PRINT @(3,10) : "L --> LOCATE (ATTRIBUTE) STRING IN ARRAY" :
022        PRINT @(3,11) : "C --> CLEAR ARRAY AND START OVER" :
023        PRINT @(3,13) : "ENTER OPTION OR 'QUIT' " :
024        INPUT OPTION
025     UNTIL OPTION # "" DO REPEAT
026 *
027 * EVALUATE RESPONSE TO OPTION REQUEST
028 *
029        IF OPTION = "QUIT" THEN STOP
030        ON INDEX("IRDLC",OPTION,1) GOSUB 100,200,300,400,500
031 *
032 *  RETURN TO TOP OF PROGRAM
033 *
034     GOTO 10
035 *
036 100 * INSERT STRING
037 *
038     PRINT @(3,16) : "ENTER STRING TO INSERT " :
039     INPUT STRING
040     IF STRING = "QUIT" THEN STOP
041     GOSUB 700    ; * GET AMC NUMBER
042     GOSUB 800    ; * GET VMC NUMBER
043     GOSUB 900    ; * GET SVMC NUMBER
044     WORK.ARRAY = INSERT(WORK.ARRAY,AMC,VMC,SVMC,STRING)
045     RETURN
046 *
047 200 * REPLACE STRING
048 *
```

```
049     PRINT @(3,16) : "ENTER STRING TO USE IN REPLACE " :
050     INPUT STRING
051     IF STRING = "QUIT" THEN STOP
052     GOSUB 700   ; * GET AMC NUMBER
053     GOSUB 800   ; * GET VMC NUMBER
054     GOSUB 900   ; * GET SVMC NUMBER
055     WORK.ARRAY = REPLACE(WORK.ARRAY,AMC,VMC,SVMC,STRING)
056     RETURN
057 *
058 300 * DELETE STRING
059 *
060     PRINT @(3,16) : "DELETE ELEMENT FROM ARRAY..."
061     GOSUB 700   ; * GET AMC NUMBER
062     GOSUB 800   ; * GET VMC NUMBER
063     GOSUB 900   ; * GET SVMC NUMBER
064     WORK.ARRAY = DELETE(WORK.ARRAY,AMC,VMC,SVMC)
065     RETURN
066 *
067 400 * LOCATE STRING
068 *
069     LOOP
070         PRINT @(3,15) : "ENTER STRING TO LOCATE " :
071         INPUT STRING
072     UNTIL STRING # "" DO REPEAT
073     IF STRING = "QUIT" THEN STOP
074 *
075     LOOP
076         PRINT @(3,16) : "(A)TTRIBUTE, (V)ALUE OR (S)UB-VALUE ?":
077         INPUT TYPE
078     UNTIL TYPE # "" DO REPEAT
079     IF TYPE = "QUIT" THEN STOP
080 *
081 * NOW USE APPROPRIATE LOCATE STATEMENT
082 *
083     BEGIN CASE
084         CASE TYPE = "A"
085             LOCATE(STRING,WORK.ARRAY;AMC.POSITION) THEN
086                 FOUND = TRUE
087             END ELSE
088                 FOUND = FALSE
089             END
090             VMC.POSITION = 0
091             SVMC.POSITION = 0
092         CASE TYPE = "V"
093             GOSUB 700       ; * GET AMC TO SEARCH FOR VALUE
094             LOCATE(STRING,WORK.ARRAY,AMC;VMC.POSITION) THEN
095                 FOUND = TRUE
096             END ELSE
097                 FOUND = FALSE
098             END
099             SVMC.POSITION = 0
```

```
100        CASE TYPE = "S"
101           GOSUB 700     ; * GET AMC TO SEARCH FOR VALUE
102           GOSUB 800     ; * GET VMC TO SEARCH FOR SUB-VALUE
103           LOCATE(STRING,WORK.ARRAY,AMC,VMC;SVMC.POSITION) THEN
104              FOUND = TRUE
105           END ELSE
106              FOUND = FALSE
107           END
108        CASE 1
109           PRINT @(3,18) : "THAT WASN'T A VALID OPTION "
110           GOSUB 1000    ; * WAIT FOR RESPONSE
111     END CASE
112 *
113     IF FOUND THEN
114        PRINT @(3,18) : @(-3) ; * CLEAR TO END OF SCREEN
115        PRINT @(3,18) : STRING : " WAS FOUND. "
116        PRINT @(3,19) : "ATTRIBUTE" : @(15,19) : AMC.POSITION
117        PRINT @(3,20) : "VALUE" : @(15,20) : VMC.POSITION
118        PRINT @(3,21) : "SUB-VALUE " : @(15,21) : SVMC.POSITION
119     END ELSE
120        PRINT @(3,18) : @(-3) : STRING : " NOT FOUND "
121     END
122 *
123     GOSUB 1000    ; * "PAUSE..."
124     RETURN
125 *
126 500 * CLEAR ARRAY
127 *
128     PRINT @(3,16) : "ARRAY CLEARED"
129     WORK.ARRAY = ""
130     GOSUB 1000    ; * "PAUSE..."
131     RETURN
132 *
133 700 * GET AMC NUMBER
134 *
135     LOOP
136        PRINT @(3,18) : "ENTER ATTRIBUTE NUMBER " :
137        INPUT AMC
138     UNTIL NUM(AMC) OR AMC = "QUIT" DO REPEAT
139     IF AMC = "QUIT" THEN STOP
140     IF AMC = "" THEN AMC = 0      ; * FORCE NULL TO ZERO
141     RETURN
142 *
143 800 * GET VMC NUMBER
144 *
145     LOOP
146        PRINT @(3,19) : "ENTER VALUE NUMBER " :
147        INPUT VMC
148     UNTIL NUM(VMC) OR VMC = "QUIT" DO REPEAT
149     IF VMC = "QUIT" THEN STOP
150     IF VMC = "" THEN VMC = 0      ; * FORCE NULL TO ZERO
151     RETURN
```

```
152 *
153 900 * GET SVMC NUMBER
154 *
155     LOOP
156         PRINT @(3,20) : "ENTER SUB-VALUE NUMBER " :
157         INPUT SVMC
158     UNTIL NUM(SVMC) OR SVMC = "QUIT" DO REPEAT
159     IF SVMC = "QUIT" THEN STOP
160     IF SVMC = "" THEN SVMC = 0      ; * FORCE NULL TO ZERO
161     RETURN
162 *
163 1000 * PAUSE AND AWAIT RESPONSE
164 *
165     PRINT @(3,22) : "PRESS <CR> TO CONTINUE " :
166     INPUT RESPONSE
167     IF RESPONSE = "QUIT" THEN STOP
168     RETURN
169 *
170 * ALL DONE
171 *
172     END
```

the physical end of the program. Local subroutines are the opposite of *external subroutines,* in which the program instructions are physically located in a separate program (item), with its own unique program name (item-id). In external subroutines, shared variables are specifically "passed into" the subroutine when it is activated.

The GOSUB has the same general format as the GOTO statement discussed in Example 2. This general format is:

GOSUB *statement.label*

The local subroutines are often gathered together near the bottom of a program. In most versions of the Pick System, the *statement.label* must be a number; some versions now also allow alphanumeric statement labels.

When the GOSUB statement is executed, execution immediately transfers to the line number that begins with the statement label. Any number of statements may be executed in the subroutine. The subroutine must have a RETURN statement as the last executable statement in the routine. When the RETURN statement is executed, execution returns to the next line after the line on which the GOSUB statement was found.

Study the general example of using the GOSUB statement shown in Fig. 13-2. On line one, the program immediately transfers execution to local subroutine 1000, which is found on line 5 of the program. On line 7, the current system time is displayed in external format. Upon executing line 8, execution returns to line 2, the first line after the GOSUB 1000 statement.

On line 2, execution passes immediately to local subroutine 2000, which occurs on line 10 of the program. At line 12, the current system date is displayed in external format. Line 13 returns execution back to line 3, where the program immediately stops.

```
001    GOSUB 1000 ; * transfer control to subroutine 1000
002    GOSUB 2000 ; * transfer control to subroutine 2000
003    STOP        ; * terminate program execution
004 *
005 1000 * DISPLAY THE CURRENT TIME
006 *
007    PRINT "THE CURRENT TIME IS " : OCONV(TIME(),"MTHS")
008    RETURN              ; * all done. return to next statement
009 *
010 2000 * DISPLAY THE CURRENT DATE
011 *
012    PRINT "THE CURRENT DATE IS " : OCONV(DATE(),"D2-")
013    RETURN
014 *
```

Fig. 13-2. An example of the GOSUB statement.

THE ON-GOSUB STATEMENT

Line 30 introduces the ON-GOSUB statement, which is a *computed* GOSUB statement. This means that the actual GOSUB is selected based on the value of the INDEX expression:

```
030 ON INDEX("IRDLC",OPTION,1) GOSUB 100,200,300,400,500
```

Suppose there were five menu choices in a program, each of which performs a separate local routine within a program. This may be coded as shown in Fig. 13-3. In lines 3 through 7, each possible response to the question is individually tested to determine which subroutine will be activated. This is exactly what Program Example 11 did. There are five possible responses to the question.

The ON-GOSUB statement has the general format:

ON *numeric.expression* **GOSUB** *statement.label,statement.label* . . .

The value of *numeric.expression* determines which *statement.label* program execution is transferred to upon evaluation.

For example, examine the use of a calculated GOSUB statement in Fig. 13-4. If you enter the number "3," the statement at line 8 is executed. The message "SUBROUTINE THREE" is displayed. Program execution then immediately returns to line 4, where the program stops.

The nature of the problem here is how to turn the alphabetic menu choices into numbers. Enter the INDEX function, stage left. The INDEX function, as discussed earlier in Example 8, is used to return the numeric position of a string within another string. Observe line 30 one more time:

```
030 ON INDEX("IRDLC",OPTION,1) GOSUB 100,200,300,400,500
```

```
001    PRINT "ENTER OPTION (A,B,C,D OR E) " :
002    INPUT OPTION
003    IF OPTION = "A" THEN GOSUB 100
004    IF OPTION = "B" THEN GOSUB 200
005    IF OPTION = "C" THEN GOSUB 300
006    IF OPTION = "D" THEN GOSUB 400
007    IF OPTION = "E" THEN GOSUB 500
008    STOP
009 *
010 100 * "A" ROUTINE
011 *
013    RETURN
014 *
015 200 * "B" ROUTINE
016 *
017    RETURN
018 *
019 300 * "C" ROUTINE
020 *
021    RETURN
022 *
023 400 * "D" ROUTINE
024 *
025    RETURN
026 *
027 500 * "E" ROUTINE
028 *
029    RETURN
```

Fig. 13-3. "Fall-through" logic using GOSUB statements.

The embedded INDEX function searches for the first occurrence of the response you entered into OPTION within the string of characters, "IRDLC." If you entered the letter "R," for example, the INDEX function returns the number 2 to the ON-GOSUB statement,

```
001    PRINT "ENTER A NUMBER BETWEEN 1 AND 5 ":
002    INPUT RESPONSE
003    ON RESPONSE GOSUB 1000,2000,3000,4000,5000
004    STOP
005 *
006 1000 PRINT "SUBROUTINE ONE"    ; RETURN
007 2000 PRINT "SUBROUTINE TWO"    ; RETURN
008 3000 PRINT "SUBROUTINE THREE" ; RETURN
009 4000 PRINT "SUBROUTINE FOUR"   ; RETURN
010 5000 PRINT "SUBROUTINE FIVE"   ; RETURN
```

Fig. 13-4. Calculated GOSUB statements.

which then transfers execution to local subroutine 200, the second statement label in the list of labels.

ABOUT THE INSERT FUNCTION

The INSERT function, briefly introduced in Example 10, is used to place a string at a specific location in a dynamic array. If the necessary delimiters are not in place to accommodate your request, then the INSERT function automatically puts them in to ensure that the string ends up in the position you requested.

The general form of the INSERT function is:

array.variable = **INSERT**(*array.variable, amc.expression,. . .*
. . .vmc.expression, svmc.expression, string.expression)

Note that the ". . ." ellipsis in the above general format—and throughout this text—means that the statement has been broken up into multiple lines for explanation purposes only. The ellipsis is *not* part of the syntax.

This function requires all five of the arguments within the parentheses and always appears on the right side of an equals operator, meaning that it is always the source of an assignment.

The *array.variable* on the left side of the "=" assignment operator is the same as the *array.variable* on the right side of the operator. The *amc.expression* is an expression which contains a number indicating the attribute position where the string is to be placed. The *vmc.expression* is an expression which contains a number indicating the value position within the specified attribute. The *svmc.expression* is an expression which contains a number indicating the subvalue position within a specified value.

The *string.expression* is the expression which contains the string of characters to be inserted at some specific location within the dynamic array. Any statement or function which produces output may be used here. Note that the special argument "−1" may be used interchangeably with any of the numeric expressions within the list of arguments to append the string to the end of the item, the end of an attribute, or to the end of a value, as illustrated in Example 10.

The "Shortcut" Method of INSERTing

Some implementations of Pick allow a shortcut method, which effectively allows certain unnecessary arguments to be omitted. The syntax changes a bit, to the general forms listed in the next two sections.

Omitting the VMC and SVMC Expressions. This form may be used when you simply want to insert a new attribute at some location within a dynamic array:

array.variable = **INSERT**(*array.variable, amc.expression*; *string.expression*)

Note the first appearance of a semicolon (;) between the *amc.expression* and the *string.expression* being inserted. On machines that allow the shortcut method, this means that the expression following the semicolon is the actual string to be inserted into the attribute specified by the *amc.expression*.

Omitting the SVMC Expression. This form may be used to insert a new value within a particular attribute:

array.variable = INSERT(*array.variable*, *amc.expression*,. . .
. . .*vmc.expression*; *string.expression*)

Once again the semicolon appears in the syntax, indicating that the argument following is the string expression which is to be inserted into the array at the specified attribute and value locations.

The INSERT Function in Context

On lines 38 and 39 of the example program (Fig. 13-5) you are prompted to enter the string of characters you want to insert. The response you provide is stored in the variable STRING. After checking to see if you entered "QUIT," the program transfers execution to local subroutine 700 (Fig. 13-6), which is used to input a number—which is, in turn, used as the attribute position.

At line 138 the loop begins. On lines 139 and 140 you are requested to enter the attribute number, which is subsequently stored in the variable, AMC. Line 141 checks to make sure that the response you entered was either a numeric value or the word "QUIT." Line 142 deals with your response to quit, or falls through if you choose not to quit.

Line 143 exists as a protective mechanism. Some implementations of Pick treat the null string as though it were numeric, meaning that it passes through the NUM function as true. Unfortunately, the INSERT function is not quite as sympathetic with null strings. If the INSERT function tries to insert a string into a location indicated by a null string, it often will report the message, "NON-NUMERIC DATA WHERE NUMERIC DATA REQUIRED!"

Line 143 checks the contents of AMC to determine if it is null. If it is null, then AMC is assigned the value 0 (zero). On line 144 the RETURN statement is issued. This causes program execution to return to line 42, where the statement GOSUB 800 is issued. This again sends execution off to another local subroutine (Fig. 13-7).

The logic is identical to that of local subroutine 700, which requested the AMC numeric value. Coincidentally, this is also the same logic for local subroutine 900, which requests the subvalue mark count, SVMC.

```
036 100 * INSERT STRING
037 *
038     PRINT @(3,16) : "ENTER STRING TO INSERT " :
039     INPUT STRING
040     IF STRING = "QUIT" THEN STOP
041     GOSUB 700    ; * GET AMC NUMBER
042     GOSUB 800    ; * GET VMC NUMBER
043     GOSUB 900    ; * GET SVMC NUMBER
044     WORK.ARRAY = INSERT(WORK.ARRAY,AMC,VMC,SVMC,STRING)
```

Fig. 13-5. Use of the INSERT function n Program Example 11.

```
133 700 * GET AMC NUMBER
134 *
135    LOOP
136       PRINT @(3,18) : "ENTER ATTRIBUTE NUMBER " :
137       INPUT AMC
138    UNTIL NUM(AMC) OR AMC = "QUIT" DO REPEAT
139    IF AMC = "QUIT" THEN STOP
140    IF AMC = "" THEN AMC = 0       ; * FORCE NULL TO ZERO
141    RETURN
```

Fig. 13-6. The logic behind local subroutine 700.

Once subroutines 700, 800, and 900 have completed their tasks, execution returns to line 44, where the following INSERT function is performed on WORK.ARRAY:

```
044 WORK.ARRAY = INSERT(WORK.ARRAY,AMC,VMC,SVMC,STRING)
```

After execution of line 44, the RETURN statement transfers execution back to line 31, the first line after the GOSUB statement that initially transferred execution to subroutine 100. Since there is no executable code on line 31, the next line which causes the program to do anything is line 34, which executes the statement "GOTO 10." This unconditionally transfers execution back to the starting point of the program, where the menu of choices is displayed and WORK.ARRAY is displayed.

ABOUT THE REPLACE FUNCTION

The REPLACE function was also briefly introduced in Example 10. It is typically used to exchange the contents of a specific location within a dynamic array. Like the INSERT function, it too may add the appropriate delimiters to accommodate your request.

This is the general form of the REPLACE function:

array.variable = **REPLACE**(*array.variable, amc.expression,. . .*
. . .vmc.expression, svmc.expression, string.expression)

```
143 800 * GET VMC NUMBER
144 *
145    LOOP
146       PRINT @(3,19) : "ENTER VALUE NUMBER " :
147       INPUT VMC
148    UNTIL NUM(VMC) OR VMC = "QUIT" DO REPEAT
149    IF VMC = "QUIT" THEN STOP
150    IF VMC = "" THEN VMC = 0       ; * FORCE NULL TO ZERO
151    RETURN
```

Fig. 13-7. The logic behind local subroutine 800.

The REPLACE function, like the INSERT function, requires all five of the arguments within the parentheses; some versions of Pick do allow the "shortcut" method discussed earlier in this chapter.

The *array.variable* on the left side of the "=" assignment operator is the same as the array.variable on the right side of the sign. The *amc.expression* is an expression which derives a number indicating the attribute position where the string is to be placed. The *vmc.expression* is an expression which derives a number indicating the value position within the specified attribute. The *svmc.expression* is an expression which contains a number indicating the subvalue position within a specified value.

The *string.expression* is the expression which contains the string of characters to be replaced at some specific location within the dynamic array. Any statement or function which produces output may be used here. Note that the special argument, −1, may be used interchangeably with any of the numeric expressions within the list of arguments to append the string to the end of the item, the end of an attribute, or to the end of a value, as illustrated in Example 10.

The "Shortcut" Method of Replacement

Some implementations of Pick allow a "shortcut" method, which effectively allows certain unnecessary arguments to be omitted. The syntax changes a bit, to the following general forms.

Omitting the VMC and SVMC Expressions. This form may be used when you simply need to replace the contents of an entire attribute at some location within a dynamic array:

array.variable = **REPLACE**(*array.variable, amc.expression*; *string.expression*)

Note the appearance of a semicolon between the *amc.expression* and the *string.expression* being replaced. On machines that allow the shortcut method, this means that the expression following the semicolon is the actual string to be replaced in the attribute specified by the *amc.expression*.

Omitting the SVMC Expression. This form may be used to replace a value within a particular attribute:

array.variable = **REPLACE**(*array.variable, amc.expression,. . .*
. . .vmc.expression; *string.expression*)

Once again the semicolon appears in the syntax, indicating that the following argument is the string expression which is to be replaced in the array at the specified attribute and value locations.

The REPLACE Function in Context

On lines 49 and 50 of Example 11 (Fig. 13-8), you are asked to enter the string of characters you want to use to replace an existing string. The response that you provide is stored in the variable STRING. After checking to see if you entered "QUIT," the

```
047 200 * REPLACE STRING
048 *
049     PRINT @(3,16) : "ENTER STRING TO USE IN REPLACE " :
050     INPUT STRING
051     IF STRING = "QUIT" THEN STOP
052     GOSUB 700    ; * GET AMC NUMBER
053     GOSUB 800    ; * GET VMC NUMBER
054     GOSUB 900   ·; * GET SVMC NUMBER
055     WORK.ARRAY = REPLACE(WORK.ARRAY,AMC,VMC,SVMC,STRING)
```

Fig. 13-8. Use of the REPLACE function in Program Example 11.

program transfers execution to local subroutines 700, 800, and 900 to request AMC, VMC, and SVMC, respectively.

Line 55 performs the REPLACE function. After replacing the new string into the array, execution is then returned to line 34, where the GOTO 10 statement is executed, causing execution to transfer to the top of the program.

THE DELETE FUNCTION

The DELETE function is used to remove an attribute, value, or subvalue from a dynamic array. In deleting a location, the corresponding delimiters that accompanied the contents of the location are also deleted. This means, for example, that if you delete attribute two from an array, all of the following attributes effectively move "up" by one position. If you simply want to "null out" a location in an array, this may be done with the RE-PLACE function, which does not remove the delimiters.

Here is the general form of the DELETE function:

array.variable = **DELETE**(*array.variable, amc.expression,. . .
. . .vmc.expression, svmc.expression*)

Unlike the INSERT and REPLACE functions mentioned earlier, this function requires only four arguments. The contents of the string being deleted do not have to be known, meaning that you may delete a string from within the array simply by indicating the element location you wish deleted.

The DELETE function produces a string. It is loaded, or stored, in the variable on the left side of the assignment operator. Therefore, the *array.variable* on the left side of the "=" generally (but not always) is the same as the *array.variable* on the right side. The *amc.expression* is an expression which contains a number indicating the attribute position to be deleted. The *vmc.expression* is an expression which contains a number indicating the value position within the specified attribute. The *svmc.expression* is an expression which contains a number indicating the subvalue position within a specified value.

Note that the special argument "−1" may not be used in this function. Also, the shortcut method is not available. This means that each argument must be provided in the expression.

141

Now let's look at the DELETE function as it is used in Example 11:

```
058 300 * DELETE STRING
059 *
060     PRINT @(3,16) : "DELETE ELEMENT FROM ARRAY..."
061     GOSUB 700    ; * GET AMC NUMBER
062     GOSUB 800    ; * GET VMC NUMBER
063     GOSUB 900    ; * GET SVMC NUMBER
064     WORK.ARRAY = DELETE(WORK.ARRAY,AMC,VMC,SVMC)
```

In subroutine 300, execution is sent to local subroutines 700, 800, and 900 to request the AMC, VMC, and SVMC. These three variables are then used in the DELETE function on line 64. After returning execution to the top of the program, the array reflects the change made by the DELETE function.

HOW TO TEST THE PROGRAM

By this point, you have probably experimented with Example 11. Before covering the LOCATE statement, take a moment to perform the following steps, which will make it easier to explain and understand this function.

1) Clear the Work Array. An option is provided on the menu to clear, or initialize, the variable WORK.ARRAY. This is accomplished by choosing the letter C from the menu. Choosing this option causes execution to be transferred to local subroutine 500:

```
126 500 * CLEAR ARRAY
127 *
128     PRINT @(3,16) : "ARRAY CLEARED"
129     WORK.ARRAY = ""
130     GOSUB 1000   ; * "PAUSE..."
131     RETURN
```

Line 131 simply announces the fact that the array has been cleared. Line 132 assigns a null to the variable WORK.ARRAY, instantly replacing its former contents. Line 133 sends execution to local subroutine 1000, which simply pauses the program and awaits a response. After the response is received, execution returns to the top of the program.

2) Choose the I Option. This is how you elect to INSERT a string into the dynamic array.

3) Enter FRED at the prompt for you to enter the string.

4) Enter the attribute, value, and subvalue. At the appropriate prompt, enter these numbers, which are 1, 1, and 0, respectively. Upon displaying the work array again, the string FRED appears. This is the first value of the first attribute.

5) Choose the I Option. This begins the process of inserting a second string.

6) Enter BARNEY. at the prompt for you to enter the string.

7) Enter the attribute, value, and subvalue. At the appropriate prompt, enter 1, 2, and 0, respectively. Upon displaying the work array again, the string BARNEY appears in the second value of the first attribute.

8) Enter the Remaining Data. Following the same steps as above, enter:

WILMA
    Attribute: 1
    Value: 2
    Subvalue: 0

BETTY
    Attribute: 1
    Value: −1
    Subvalue: 0

DINO
    Attribute: 2
    Value: 0
    Subvalue: 0

Note that when you displayed the work array after WILMA was inserted into the second value of the first attribute, BARNEY was "pushed down" into the third value and the work array appeared as:

```
FRED]WILMA]BARNEY
```

Then the string BETTY appeared as the fourth, or last, value in attribute one. Finally the string DINO appeared as the first (and only) value in attribute two.

The work array now appears as:

```
FRED]WILMA]BARNEY]BETTY^DINO
```

and you are now ready to meet the LOCATE statement. Fasten your seat belts. This may be a rough ride.

THE LOCATE STATEMENT

The LOCATE statement searches for strings within a dynamic array. The string it searches for may represent an entire attribute, value, or subvalue, and the statement indicates if the string was located. The LOCATE statement has several general forms, depending on where and how it is being applied.

For example, to retrieve an attribute requires the following general form:

LOCATE(*string.expression,array.variable;setting.variable*). . .
. . .{**THEN** *statement(s)*} **ELSE** *statement(s)*

This form is illustrated in Example 11 in the following section of code:

```
084 CASE TYPE = "A"
085    LOCATE(STRING,WORK.ARRAY;AMC.POSITION) THEN
086       FOUND = TRUE
087    END ELSE
088       FOUND = FALSE
089    END
```

In the CASE construct, responding with the letter A indicates that you are attempting to locate an attribute; this CASE statement evaluates true and the LOCATE statement on line 85 is executed.

Using the test array you just constructed with the names that were provided, the work array appears as:

FRED]WILMA]BARNEY]BETTY~DINO

Consequently, it has only two attributes.

To test this function, choose the L option to locate a string. At the prompt to ENTER A STRING, enter "DINO" and press Return. The next prompt is:

IS IT AN (A)TTRIBUTE, (V)ALUE OR (S)UB–VALUE?

Enter an A and press Return.

The program now performs the LOCATE statement listed on line 85. At the time of execution, the variable STRING contains DINO. The variable WORK.ARRAY contains

FRED]WILMA]BARNEY]BETTY^DINO

The variable POSITION is determined by the LOCATE statement. Since the string DINO matches exactly the contents of attribute two of the array, the LOCATE statement stores the number 2 in the variable POSITION. Had the string not been found, POSITION would have remained unchanged.

Notice that the LOCATE statement must have the ELSE condition. This means that it also allows the THEN clause. The statements following the ELSE initiator are executed when the string being located is not found. The statements following the THEN clause are executed when the string being located is found.

Since the string you requested was found, and the attribute position at which it was found was stored in the variable POSITION, then the THEN clause on line 86 is executed. This assigns the value TRUE to the variable FOUND.

After execution falls out of the CASE construct, the next block of code displays the string and locations:

```
113 IF FOUND THEN
114    PRINT @(3,18) : @(-3) ; * CLEAR TO END OF SCREEN
```

```
115    PRINT @(3,18) : STRING : " WAS FOUND. "
116    PRINT @(3,19) : "ATTRIBUTE" : @(15,19) : AMC.POSITION
117    PRINT @(3,20) : "VALUE" : @(15,20) : VMC.POSITION
118    PRINT @(3,21) : "SUB-VALUE " : @(15,21) : SVMC.POSITION
119 END ELSE
120    PRINT @(3,18) : @(-3) : STRING : " NOT FOUND "
121 END
```

This section does one of two things: If the string was found, then it is displayed by the statement on line 115. The attribute, value, and subvalue positions at which it was found are displayed by lines 116, 117, and 118. If it was not found, then line 120 displays the string along with the message that it was not found.

Locating Values within Attributes

To retrieve a value from within an attribute requires the following general form of the LOCATE statement:

LOCATE(*string.expression,array.variable,amc.expression;. . .*
. . .*setting.variable*) {**THEN** *statement(s)*} **ELSE** *statement(s)*

This form is illustrated in Example 11 in the following section of code:

```
092 CASE TYPE = "V"
093    GOSUB 700    ; * GET AMC TO SEARCH FOR VALUE
094    LOCATE(STRING,WORK.ARRAY,AMC;VMC.POSITION) THEN
095       FOUND = TRUE
096    END ELSE
097       FOUND = FALSE
098    END
099    SVMC.POSITION = 0
```

If you respond with the letter V, which indicates that you are attempting to locate a value, then this CASE statement evaluates true and the LOCATE statement on line 94 is executed.

Using the test array you just constructed, you can see that attribute one has four values:

FRED]WILMA]BARNEY]BETTY

To test this function, choose the L option to locate a string. At the prompt to enter a string, enter "BARNEY" and press Return. The next prompt is:

IS IT AN (A)TTRIBUTE, (V)ALUE OR (S)UB-VALUE?

Enter V and press Return.

The program now performs the LOCATE statement listed on line 94. At the time of execution, the variable STRING contains BARNEY. The variable WORK.ARRAY contains:

```
FRED]WILMA]BARNEY]BETTY^DINO
```

The variable POSITION is determined by the LOCATE statement. Since the string BARNEY matches exactly the contents of value three of attribute one in the array, the LOCATE statement stores the number 3 in the variable POSITION. Had the string not been found, POSITION would have remained unchanged.

Since the string you requested was found, and the value position at which it was found was stored in the variable POSITION, then the THEN clause on line 95 is executed. This assigns the value TRUE to the variable FOUND.

After execution falls out of the CASE construct, the next block of code spans lines 116-124 and is the routine to display the string and its location in the work array:

```
113 IF FOUND THEN
114    PRINT @(3,18) : @(-3) ; * CLEAR TO END OF SCREEN
115    PRINT @(3,18) : STRING : " WAS FOUND. "
116    PRINT @(3,19) : "ATTRIBUTE" : @(15,19) : AMC.POSITION
117    PRINT @(3,20) : "VALUE" : @(15,20) : VMC.POSITION
118    PRINT @(3,21) : "SUB-VALUE " : @(15,21) : SVMC.POSITION
119 END ELSE
120    PRINT @(3,18) : @(-3) : STRING : " NOT FOUND "
121 END
```

Since the string was found, it is displayed by the statement on line 115. The attribute, value, and subvalue positions at which it was found are displayed by lines 116, 117, and 118.

Locating Subvalues within Values

To retrieve a subvalue from within a value requires the following general form of the LOCATE statement:

LOCATE(*string.expression,array.variable,amc.expression,*. . .
. . .*vmc.expression;setting.variable*) {**THEN** *statement(s)*}. . .
. . .**ELSE** *statement(s)*

This form is illustrated in Example 11 in the following section of code:

```
100 CASE TYPE = "S"
101    GOSUB 700  ; * GET AMC TO SEARCH FOR VALUE
102    GOSUB 800  ; * GET VMC TO SEARCH FOR SUB-VALUE
103    LOCATE(STRING,WORK.ARRAY,AMC,VMC;SVMC.POSITION) THEN
104        FOUND = TRUE
105    END ELSE
106        FOUND = FALSE
107    END
```

146

There were no subvalues in the array that you constructed. If you feel adventurous, reconstruct the array with one or more subvalues and test this function.

As an aside here, I would like to interject a controversial point: *Avoid using subvalues.* Now it's out in the open. The PICK/BASIC language is well suited to manipulating the three-dimensional record structure of attributes, values, and subvalues. If you plan to write report programs in PICK/BASIC, then using subvalues is acceptable. The ACCESS retrieval language does not deal well with subvalues, however—and that's putting it politely. Subvalues may seem like a convenient method of structuring data items, but if you plan to use ACCESS to produce reports on subvalued data, be prepared for some very strange output.

USING LOCATE TO SORT STRINGS

The LOCATE statement, as introduced in this example, is typically used to search for a string within an item, and to report the position at which it was found. The ELSE clause is executed when the string being searched for is not found.

The LOCATE statement has the added ability to determine the position at which a string *would belong* within an attribute or value. This involves the use of *sequencing parameters*:

Code	Meaning
'AL'	Ascending, left-justified.
'DL'	Descending, left-justified.
'AR'	Ascending, right-justified.
'DR'	Descending, right-justified.

These sequencing parameters appear in the LOCATE statement immediately after the *setting.variable*.

The sequencing parameter you choose is a function of two things: whether the data is to be in ascending (lowest to highest) or descending (highest to lowest) order, and whether the data contains any alphabetic characters. Left justification must be used on data that contains alphabetic characters, while right justification is used exclusively on purely numeric data. This is extremely important, because it has drastic effects on the sorting of data.

The various forms of the LOCATE statement, using the sequencing parameters, are illustrated in the following general formats.

Sorting Attributes within Items

This is the general form of sequencing parameters in the LOCATE statement for sorting attributes within items:

LOCATE(*string.expression,array.variable;setting.variable;. . .*
. . .*'sequence.parameter'*) {THEN *statement(s)*} ELSE *statement(s)*

For example, suppose the array looked like this:

```
ARRAY = BARNEY^FRED^WILMA
```

This indicates that there are three attributes, currently in alphabetical order. Consider the following statement:

```
LOCATE("BETTY",ARRAY;POSITION;'AL') ELSE FOUND = FALSE
```

When this statement is executed, the string "BETTY" is not found. Since the sequence parameter "AL" is in effect, POSITION is assigned the value 2, since that is the position at which the string belongs. (BETTY is "higher" than BARNEY, and "less than" FRED.) As a side effect, the ELSE clause is also executed, since BETTY was "not" found.

Sorting Values within Attributes

This is the general form of sequencing parameters in the LOCATE statement for sorting values within attributes:

LOCATE(*string.expression,array.variable,amc.expression;. . .*
. . .setting.variable;'sequence.parameter') {**THEN** *statement(s)*}. . .
. . ..**ELSE** *statement(s)*

For example, suppose the array looked like this:

```
ARRAY<13> = 6666]7777]8888
```

This indicates that in attribute 13 of the array there are three values, which currently are in ascending numeric order. If the following statement were executed:

```
LOCATE("8010",ARRAY,13;POSITION;'AR') ELSE FOUND = FALSE
```

the string 8010 would not be found. Since the sequence parameter 'AR' is in effect, POSITION is assigned the value 3, since that is the position at which the string belongs. (8010 is "greater than" 7777, and "less than" 8888.) As a side effect, the ELSE clause is also executed, since 8010 was "not" found.

Sorting values within attributes is much more common than the former example of sorting attributes within items. This is useful, for example, when a list of dates or money amounts is to be stored in ascending or descending order.

WHY YOU DON'T WANT TO SORT STRINGS WITH LOCATE

Although the power of the LOCATE statement to sort strings is tempting, it is used very infrequently because attributes which contain multivalues often have a relationship with other multivalued attributes in the same item. This is very common in applications.

```
File name  =  ORDER-FILE
Array name  =  ORDER.ITEM
Item-id  =  4678
```

Attribute	Contents	Purpose
001	7777	Date of order.
002	13	Salesman code.
003	W101]J336]T807	Multivalued list of inventory parts that were ordered.
004	12]4]36	Multivalued list of quantities ordered.
005	0]4]0	Multivalued list of quantities backordered.
006	1345]677]1898	Multivalued list of prices of each part ordered.

Fig. 13-9. Sample use of multivalues in items.

For instance, consider the proverbial "order" item shown in Fig. 13-9. This type of design is very common in applications. The phenomenon illustrated by attributes three through six goes by several names. Some people call these *parallel multivalues*; others call them *correlated sets*. Some people call them *bad design*.

The point is this: The values in each attribute have a positional correspondence with the values in the other attributes. For instance, this hypothetical order item indicates that the customer ordered a product whose inventory part number is W101 (the first value of attribute three). It further appears that they ordered 12 of these products (the first value of attribute four) and that 0 (zero) were backordered (the first value of attribute five) and finally, the cost per unit is $13.45 (the first value of attribute six, which is stored in its internal format). Although this type of item structure is popular among programmers and analysts, it has some serious potential side effects.

POTENTIAL SIDE EFFECTS OF PARALLEL MULTIVALUES

All but a few implementations of Pick currently have an item size restriction. This means (at the moment) that no single item may exceed 32K (about 32,000) bytes. For the most part, this is not a problem—but it can be. Suppose, for example, that the structure of items in the order file were like the one just illustrated. This structure works fine for the majority of the items in the file, but what happens when you get an order that has 4000 or 5000 line items? Yes, this is exceptional, but that's the kind of problem you must anticipate. This structure has no provision for dealing with such a case. Eventually, the item gets so large that an "INSUFFICIENT WORKSPACE" message appears on the screen of the operator who is entering the order, and the program enters the PICK/BASIC debugger. The operator is not amused. At this point, there is no way to recover the item.

File name = ORDER-HEADER-FILE
Array name = ORDER.HEADER.ITEM
Item-id = 4678

Attribute	Contents	Purpose
001	7777	Date of order.
002	13	Salesman code.
003	3	Number of line items.

Fig. 13-10. Alternate item design without multivalues.

File name = ORDER-DETAIL-FILE
Array name = ORDER.DETAIL.ITEM

Item-ID	Attribute	Contents	Purpose
4678*1			(the "first" line item)
	001	W101	Single-valued item-id of inventory part ordered.
	002	12	Single-valued quantity ordered.
	003	0	Single-valued quantity backordered.
	004	1345	Single-valued price of part ordered.
4678*2			(the "second" line item)
	001	J336	Single-valued item-id of inventory part ordered.
	002	4	Single-valued quantity ordered.
	003	4	Single-valued quantity backordered.
	004	677	Single-valued price of part ordered.
4678*3			(the "third" line item)
	001	T807	Single-valued item-id of inventory part ordered.
	004	36	Single-valued quantity ordered
	005	0	Single-valued quantity backordered.
	006	1898	Single-valued price of part ordered.

Fig. 13-11. Second half of an alternate item design without multivalues.

Another popular method of designing items is through the use of multiple items, rather than multiple values within an item. Instead of keeping all of the order information in one file, the information could be spread out into two files, such as a "order header" and "order detail" file. The "order header" file contains just the "static," single-valued attributes. Using the former example, this appears as shown in Fig. 13-10.

The "order detail" file contains single-valued items that represent the line items of the order. Using the data from the previous example, there would be three separate items in this file, which would appear as shown in Fig. 13-11. Using this technique not only removes the potential item size problem, but it also makes it easier for ACCESS to deal with this file. Remember, ACCESS is only moderately friendly to multivalues, and hates subvalues.

14

A Generalized
Data Entry Program

PROGRAM EXAMPLE 12 EMPLOYS NEARLY ALL OF THE TECHNIQUES DISCUSSED IN THE previous exercises. This is a full-blown data entry program which may be used to add data to the STAFF file, correct existing data, and remove unwanted data.

Enter the example program from the listing in Fig. 14-1. As you do, remember that the logic of the program is nearly as important as the program instructions used.

SETTING UP WORK ARRAYS: THE DIM STATEMENT

In Example 11, the concept of dynamic arrays was discussed in depth. The other type of array that is available in PICK/BASIC is referred to as a *dimensioned array*. The work arrays used in our data entry program example are of this type:

```
007 * SETUP WORK ARRAYS
008 *
009    DIM SCREEN.LABELS(10)
010    DIM LABEL.COLUMN(10)
011    DIM LABEL.ROW(10)
012    DIM DATA.COLUMN(10)
013    DIM DATA.ROW(10)
014    DIM INPUT.CONVERSIONS(10)
015    DIM OUTPUT.CONVERSIONS(10)
016    DIM LENGTH(10)
017    DIM STAFF.ITEM(10)
```

Fig. 14-1. Program Example 12.

```
    EX.012
001 * FILE.IO
002 * UPDATING FILES AND ITEMS
003 * mm/dd/yy : date last modified
004 * JES : author's initials
005 *
006 *
007 * SETUP WORK ARRAYS
008 *
009    DIM SCREEN.LABELS(10)
010    DIM LABEL.COLUMN(10)
011    DIM LABEL.ROW(10)
012    DIM DATA.COLUMN(10)
013    DIM DATA.ROW(10)
014    DIM INPUT.CONVERSIONS(10)
015    DIM OUTPUT.CONVERSIONS(10)
016    DIM LENGTH(10)
017    DIM STAFF.ITEM(10)
018 *
019 * DEFINE CONSTANTS
020 *
021    PROMPT ""
022    EQUATE TRUE TO 1
023    EQUATE FALSE TO 0
024    LAST.FIELD = 7
025 *
026 * DEFINE VARIABLES
027 *
028    EXIT.FLAG = FALSE
029    ERROR.FLAG = FALSE
030    CURRENT.FIELD = 1
031 *
032 * OPEN FILES
033 *
034    OPEN "STAFF" TO STAFF.FILE ELSE
035       PRINT "STAFF IS NOT A FILE NAME " :
036       INPUT ANYTHING
037       STOP
038    END
039 *
040 * DEFINE SCREEN.LABELS
041 *
042    SCREEN.LABELS(1) = "1 NAME"
043    SCREEN.LABELS(2) = "2 ADDRESS"
044    SCREEN.LABELS(3) = "3 CITY"
045    SCREEN.LABELS(4) = "4 STATE"
046    SCREEN.LABELS(5) = "5 ZIP"
047    SCREEN.LABELS(6) = "6 PHONE"
048    SCREEN.LABELS(7) = "7 BIRTHDAY"
```

```
049 *
050 * DEFINE LABEL.COLUMN
051 *
052     LABEL.COLUMN(1) = 3
053     LABEL.COLUMN(2) = 3
054     LABEL.COLUMN(3) = 3
055     LABEL.COLUMN(4) = 3
056     LABEL.COLUMN(5) = 3
057     LABEL.COLUMN(6) = 3
058     LABEL.COLUMN(7) = 3
059 *
060 * DEFINE LABEL.ROW
061 *
062     LABEL.ROW(1) = 4
063     LABEL.ROW(2) = 5
064     LABEL.ROW(3) = 6
065     LABEL.ROW(4) = 7
066     LABEL.ROW(5) = 8
067     LABEL.ROW(6) = 9
068     LABEL.ROW(7) = 10
069 *
070 * DEFINE DATA.COLUMN
071 *
072     DATA.COLUMN(1) = 20
073     DATA.COLUMN(2) = 20
074     DATA.COLUMN(3) = 20
075     DATA.COLUMN(4) = 20
076     DATA.COLUMN(5) = 20
077     DATA.COLUMN(6) = 20
078     DATA.COLUMN(7) = 20
079 *
080 * DEFINE DATA.ROW
081 *
082     DATA.ROW(1) = 4
083     DATA.ROW(2) = 5
084     DATA.ROW(3) = 6
085     DATA.ROW(4) = 7
086     DATA.ROW(5) = 8
087     DATA.ROW(6) = 9
088     DATA.ROW(7) = 10
089 *
090 * DEFINE INPUT.CONVERSIONS
091 *
092     INPUT.CONVERSIONS(1) = ""
093     INPUT.CONVERSIONS(2) = ""
094     INPUT.CONVERSIONS(3) = ""
095     INPUT.CONVERSIONS(4) = "P(2A)"
096     INPUT.CONVERSIONS(5) = "P(5N)"
097     INPUT.CONVERSIONS(6) = ""
098     INPUT.CONVERSIONS(7) = "D"
099 *
100 * DEFINE OUTPUT.CONVERSIONS
```

```
101 *
102     OUTPUT.CONVERSIONS(1) = ""
103     OUTPUT.CONVERSIONS(2) = ""
104     OUTPUT.CONVERSIONS(3) = ""
105     OUTPUT.CONVERSIONS(4) = ""
106     OUTPUT.CONVERSIONS(5) = ""
107     OUTPUT.CONVERSIONS(6) = ""
108     OUTPUT.CONVERSIONS(7) = "D2/"
109 *
110 * DEFINE LENGTH
111 *
112     LENGTH(1) = 30
113     LENGTH(2) = 30
114     LENGTH(3) = 30
115     LENGTH(4) = 30
116     LENGTH(5) = 30
117     LENGTH(6) = 30
118     LENGTH(7) = 30
119 *
120 * MAIN POINT OF PROGRAM
121 *
122     LOOP
123        GOSUB 1000    ; * ENTER ID AND READ ITEM
124     UNTIL EXIT.FLAG DO
125        GOSUB 2000    ; * EDIT ITEM
126     REPEAT
127     STOP   ; * END OF PROGRAM
128 *
129 1000 * ENTER ID AND READ ITEM
130 *
131     PRINT @(-1) :   ; * CLEAR SCREEN
132     LOOP
133        PRINT @(3,2) : "ENTER ITEM-ID OR 'QUIT' TO STOP " :
134        INPUT STAFF.ID
135     UNTIL STAFF.ID > '' DO REPEAT
136     IF STAFF.ID = "QUIT" THEN EXIT.FLAG = TRUE ELSE EXIT.FLAG = FALSE
137 *
138 * READ ITEM
139 *
140     NEW.ITEM.FLAG = FALSE
141     MATREAD STAFF.ITEM FROM STAFF.FILE, STAFF.ID ELSE
142        MAT STAFF.ITEM = ''
143        NEW.ITEM.FLAG = TRUE
144     END
145     RETURN   ; * DONE WITH ENTER ID AND READ ITEM
146 *
147 2000 * EDIT ITEM
148 *
149     GOSUB 10000    ; * PRINT LABELS
150     GOSUB 20000    ; * PRINT DATA
151     IF NEW.ITEM.FLAG THEN
```

```
152        GOSUB 30000   ; * ENTER NEW ITEM
153      END
154      GOSUB 40000   ; * UPDATE OLD ITEM
155      RETURN
156 *
157 10000 * PRINT LABELS
158 *
159      FOR I = 1 TO LAST.FIELD
160         PRINT @(LABEL.COLUMN(I),LABEL.ROW(I)) : SCREEN.LABELS(I) :
161      NEXT I
162      RETURN
163 *
164 20000 * PRINT DATA
165 *
166      FOR I = 1 TO LAST.FIELD
167         GOSUB 25000; * PRINT ONE DATUM
168      NEXT I
169      RETURN
170 *
171 25000 * PRINT ONE DATUM
172 *
173      IF OUTPUT.CONVERSIONS(I) # "" THEN
174         PRINT.VALUE = OCONV(STAFF.ITEM(I),OUTPUT.CONVERSIONS(I))
175      END ELSE
176         PRINT.VALUE = STAFF.ITEM(I)
177      END
178      PRINT @(DATA.COLUMN(I),DATA.ROW(I)):(PRINT.VALUE) ('L#':LENGTH(I)):
179      RETURN
180 *
181 30000 * ENTER NEW ITEM
182 *
183      CURRENT.FIELD = 1
184      LOOP
185         PRINT @(DATA.COLUMN(CURRENT.FIELD),DATA.ROW(CURRENT.FIELD)) :
186         INPUT ANS, LENGTH(CURRENT.FIELD)
187         BEGIN CASE
188            CASE ANS = "QUIT"
189               EXIT.FLAG = TRUE
190            CASE ANS = ''
191               CURRENT.FIELD = CURRENT.FIELD + 1
192            CASE ANS = "^"
193               I = CURRENT.FIELD; GOSUB 25000; * PRINT ONE DATUM
194               IF CURRENT.FIELD >= 2 THEN CURRENT.FIELD=CURRENT.FIELD-1
195            CASE 1
196               GOSUB 35000 ; * GET VALIDATED DATUM, STORE IN STAFF.ITEM
197               IF NOT(ERROR.FLAG) THEN CURRENT.FIELD = CURRENT.FIELD + 1
198         END CASE
199      UNTIL CURRENT.FIELD > LAST.FIELD OR EXIT.FLAG = TRUE DO REPEAT
200      RETURN
201 *
202 35000 * GET VALIDATED DATUM, STORE IN STAFF.ITEM, REPRINT
```

```
203 * INPUT = ANS > ''.  OUTPUT = ANS, ERROR.FLAG
204 *
205     IF ERROR.FLAG THEN PRINT @(3,21) : @(-4) :
206     ERROR.FLAG = FALSE
207     IF INPUT.CONVERSIONS(CURRENT.FIELD) > '' THEN
208         TEMP = ICONV(ANS,INPUT.CONVERSIONS(CURRENT.FIELD))
209         IF TEMP = "" THEN    ; * NOT GOOD
210             PRINT @(3,21) : "UNEXPECTED FORMAT.  PLEASE TRY AGAIN"
211             ERROR.FLAG = TRUE
212         END ELSE
213             ANS = TEMP
214         END
215     END
216     IF NOT(ERROR.FLAG) THEN STAFF.ITEM(CURRENT.FIELD) = ANS
217     I = CURRENT.FIELD; GOSUB 25000; * PRINT ONE DATUM
218     RETURN
219 *
220 40000 * UPDATE OLD ITEM
221 *
222     LOOP
223         PRINT @(3,20) :
224         PRINT "ENTER FIELD # TO CHANGE, E(X)IT, (D)ELETE, (F)ILE " :
225         INPUT OPTION
226         BEGIN CASE
227             CASE NUM(OPTION)
228                 IF OPTION >= 1 AND OPTION <= LAST.FIELD THEN
229                     CURRENT.FIELD = OPTION
230                     PRINT @(DATA.COLUMN(CURRENT.FIELD),DATA.ROW(CURRENT.FIELD)):
231                     INPUT ANS, LENGTH(CURRENT.FIELD)
232                     IF ANS > '' THEN GOSUB 35000; * VALIDATE, STORE
233                 END
234             CASE OPTION = "X" OR OPTION = "QUIT"
235                 EXIT.FLAG = TRUE
236             CASE OPTION = "D"
237                 DELETE STAFF.FILE,STAFF.ID
238                 PRINT "ITEM DELETED"
239             CASE OPTION = "F"
240                 MATWRITE STAFF.ITEM ON STAFF.FILE,STAFF.ID
241         END CASE
242     UNTIL INDEX("XDF",OPTION,1) AND OPTION > '' DO REPEAT
243     RETURN
244 *
245 END
```

A dimensioned array is very different from a dynamic array. No DIM (dimension) statement is required for dynamic arrays. An item read in with the READ statement is treated as one long string of characters, each of which is delimited by the special reserved delimiters: attribute marks, value marks, and subvalue marks. When an element from a dynamic array is referenced, the computer starts at the beginning of the string and scans through the delimiters until the requested element is found.

For example, suppose there were a dynamic array called INVOICE.ITEM, and attribute 17 of this array contains the following string:

```
W227]W338]T456]X889
```

If you were to reference the third value from attribute 17 with either of the following statements:

```
PRINT EXTRACT(INVOICE.ITEM,17,3,0)
```

or

```
PRINT INVOICE.ITEM<17,3>
```

Here's how the process would work.

The computer starts from the beginning of the array and searches for attribute marks. Once it counts 17 attribute marks, it determines that the 17th attribute has been located, and then starts to search for value marks, until the second one is located. This might not seem like such a bad way of handling arrays, but there's a catch. Suppose the next line of code requested the fourth value from the same attribute. Rather than remembering where it was, the computer starts all the way back at the beginning of the item and again searches through all of the delimiters. On small items this doesn't have a significant impact on throughput, but when it comes to dealing with large items—such as those with several or more dozen attributes, many of which contain many values and subvalues—the throughput time is a big factor.

Dynamic arrays certainly have their place in PICK/BASIC programs. They are relatively easy to manipulate using the dynamic array reference symbols; they don't eat much (processing time) when dealing with small items; they don't require any previous declaration; and they don't take up much room.

Dimensioned arrays, by contrast, are a little less flexible, but the tradeoff is that they are generally much more efficient. As an aside here, many Pick technical types have strong opinions about this issue of dynamic versus dimensioned arrays, much as they do with regards to modulo and separation. Be advised that it may be less potentially dangerous to discuss religion or politics if you are looking for light conversation at a user group meeting.

Recall from Chapter 7 that an array is simply a data structure which contains data elements, each of which may be referenced by a numeric subscript. A *dimensioned array* simply means that rather than allowing an item with a variable number of array elements, as was the case with dynamic arrays, the program is told to preassign space for a fixed number of attributes before the array (item) is read with the MATREAD statement. This preassignment occurs through the DIM statement, which has the general form:

DIM *array.variable(number.of.subscripts)*

For example:

```
DIM STAFF.ITEM(10)
```

This statement tells PICK/BASIC to set aside ten storage locations for this array. When the array is read with a subsequent MATREAD statement, each attribute is loaded into its corresponding array location. This makes it much faster to find attributes, as their locations are calculated, rather than scanned for, each time an attribute is requested.

Some Notes on Dimensioned Arrays

Once defined as a dimensioned array, each reference to the array must be followed by a subscript indicator; otherwise an unpleasant—and fatal—error message is displayed.

Two other problems occur from time to time in dealing with dimensioned arrays. The first, most common problem occurs when a reference is made to a dimensioned array subscript that is less than one, or greater than the "last" subscript location. Here's an example:

```
001  DIM STAFF.ITEM(10)
002  STAFF.ITEM(12) = DATE()
```

Upon execution of line 2, the program immediately breaks into the debugger and displays a message that an attempt has been made to reference an invalid subscript location. This normally occurs when the subscript specification is made using a variable that accidentally contains the wrong value. Note that the "problem" of accidentally using the wrong subscript is just as big a problem with dynamic arrays. With dimensioned arrays, however, the system is able to tell us we screwed up—a problem which may go undetected with dynamic arrays.

The second problem with dimensioned arrays occurs when the array is *under-dimensioned*. Suppose, for example, that the program contains the statement:

```
DIM STAFF.ITEM(10)
```

and later in the program the following statement is executed:

```
MATREAD STAFF.ITEM FROM STAFF.FILE,STAFF.ID ELSE ...
```

If the item just read with the MATREAD statement contains more than ten attributes, you have a problem. Each attribute from one through nine loads into the corresponding array location. Attributes ten through the "end" of the item are stored in the "last" array location of the dimensioned array, with each attribute being delimited by an attribute mark (just like in a dynamic array). The scheme behind this logic is that the item will at least survive the MATWRITE statement without truncating all the "extra" array elements. The real problem occurs when you try to reference attribute ten.

I suggest that you "over-dimension" your dimensioned arrays by about five elements. This has the added benefit of providing growth space. This means that you won't have to change all of your programs that refer to this array when you add a new attribute to the file.

Referencing Dimensioned Arrays

In referring to any element within a dimensioned array, the left and right parenthesis symbols are reserved to specify array elements. They have the following general format:

array.variable(amc.expression)

The *amc.expression* is an expression which derives a number to be treated as an Attribute Mark Count (AMC).

For example, suppose there were a dimensioned array called STAFF.ITEM, and the following statement were issued:

```
PRINT STAFF.ITEM
```

The program would immediately crash and burn, leaving you the message

```
VARIABLE HAS BEEN DIMENSIONED AND USED WITHOUT SUBSCRIPTS
```

If, however, the following statement were issued:

```
PRINT STAFF.ITEM(1)
```

The contents of the first array element would be printed. If it contains multiple values and/or subvalues, these too are printed, along with their corresponding delimiters, just as in dynamic arrays. That's the end of the similarities, however.

Two-Dimensional Arrays

Dimensioned arrays additionally allow *two-dimensional* DIM statements. These are rarely necessary for business applications, but to be thorough, here is an example:

```
DIM TABLE(10,10)
```

This tells PICK/BASIC to set up space for a table consisting of 10 rows and 10 columns. And remember:

- *The first dimension has nothing to do with attributes.*

- *The second dimension has nothing to do with multivalues!*

Consequently, I don't recommend MATREAD with two-dimensional arrays, unless you are prepared for the pain and agony of trying to make them work with the Pick record structure.

You may be wondering: "If dimensioned arrays have no syntactical provision for dealing with the three-dimensional record structure, then how are we going to reference multivalues and subvalues within the dimensioned arrays?" Good question. This has bothered the best philosophical minds since the beginning of time (about 1974). The answer is (hold your breath):

- *You combine both dynamic and dimensioned array reference symbols!*

OK, you're confused. Remember the standard syntactical form of dynamic arrays?

array.variable<amc.expression>

or

array.variable<amc.expression,vmc.expression>

or

array.variable<amc.expression,vmc.expression,svmc.expression>

Remember the standard syntactical form of dimensioned arrays?

array.variable(amc.expression)

To combine dynamic array references with dimensioned array references, you first indicate the *amc.expression*, then follow it with the dynamic array symbols. For example:

```
PRINT STAFF.ITEM(1)<1,2>
```

This tells PICK/BASIC to display the second value of the first attribute in the dimensioned array, STAFF.ITEM.

Now you may be wondering, "Why did we redundantly repeat the 1, which referred to the attribute number?" The answer is: Because we have to. Feel better?

We're told that we "have to" because of potential syntactical ambiguities. This is a fancy way of asking how the program would know the difference between what you just examined and this statement:

```
PRINT STAFF.ITEM(1)<2>
```

The 1 obviously means attribute one. Yet the 2 could mean either attribute two or value two, hence the requirement to repeat the *amc.expression*.

The bottom line is that when you are referring to multivalues or subvalues of a single attribute within a dimensioned array, the first dynamic array subscript must be the number 1 (one).

The following examples are similar to the exercises that were covered earlier in the explanation of dynamic arrays. If the following statement were executed:

```
PRINT STAFF.ITEM(1)<1,2>
```

161

The second value from the first attribute would be printed. And finally, if you were to issue the statement:

```
PRINT STAFF.ITEM(1)<1,2,3>
```

The third subvalue from the second value of the first attribute would be displayed.

DEFINING THE CONSTANTS AND VARIABLES

Now that the arrays have been dimensioned, the next step that the program takes is to assign values to each of the constants that will be required throughout the program:

```
019 * DEFINE CONSTANTS
020 *
021    PROMPT ""
022    EQUATE TRUE TO 1
023    EQUATE FALSE TO 0
024    LAST.FIELD = 7
```

Line 21 assigns a "null" as the prompt character, line 22 equates the value of 1 to the constant TRUE, and line 23 equates the value of 0 to the constant FALSE. Line 24 assigns the value of 7 to the constant LAST.FIELD, which is the number of fields in the data entry program, and is used later as the upper boundary of a FOR-NEXT statement.

The next step is to assign initial values to some critical variables that are used throughout the program:

```
026 * DEFINE VARIABLES
027 *
028    EXIT.FLAG = FALSE
029    ERROR.FLAG = FALSE
030    CURRENT.FIELD = 1
```

Line 28 assigns the value FALSE, which was equated to 0 (zero), to the variable EXIT.FLAG. This variable is used as a flag to determine when to terminate the program. Line 29 assigns the value FALSE to the variable, ERROR.FLAG. This variable is used to indicate whether a problem occurred in the format of data entry. Finally, line 30 assigns the value 1 (one), to the variable CURRENT.FIELD. This variable keeps track of the current field (or attribute) number being processed during program execution.

OPENING THE FILES

Line 34 executes the statement to open the STAFF file for input and/or output:

```
032 * OPEN FILES
033 *
```

```
034    OPEN "STAFF" TO STAFF.FILE ELSE
035      PRINT "STAFF IS NOT A FILE NAME " :
036      INPUT ANYTHING
037      STOP
038    END
```

If the file is not found, the statements on lines 35 through 37 are executed, which advises the operator that the file was not found, awaits a response, and then stops the program. If the file is found, execution continues at line 39.

DEFINING PARAMETER SETS: THE DATA LABELS

Our example program illustrates an important principle in program design. It is called *parameterized code*. This means that the program contains a series of "tables," in this case, dimensioned arrays. These tables contain data (parameters) pertinent to each of the fields that will be input during data entry:

```
039 *
040 * DEFINE SCREEN.LABELS
041 *
042    SCREEN.LABELS(1) = "1 NAME"
043    SCREEN.LABELS(2) = "2 ADDRESS"
044    SCREEN.LABELS(3) = "3 CITY"
045    SCREEN.LABELS(4) = "4 STATE"
046    SCREEN.LABELS(5) = "5 ZIP"
047    SCREEN.LABELS(6) = "6 PHONE"
048    SCREEN.LABELS(7) = "7 BIRTHDAY"
```

This first table being defined is called SCREEN.LABELS. These are the data labels that appear on the screen to let the operator know what is being requested. Rather than "hard coding" the data labels into a series of PRINT statements later in the program, they are gathered together in this one array. This technique tends to make program maintenance much easier. The tables could even be kept in a file to make the code more parameterized. Lines 42 through 48 assign the data labels to the appropriate locations in the SCREEN.LABELS array.

Defining Data Label Column and Row Positions

Lines 52 through 58 each assign the value 3 to the corresponding position in the LABEL.COLUMN array. This table is used later to determine the column coordinate at which to place the data labels on the screen:

```
050 * DEFINE LABEL.COLUMN
051 *
052    LABEL.COLUMN(1) = 3
053    LABEL.COLUMN(2) = 3
054    LABEL.COLUMN(3) = 3
```

```
055    LABEL.COLUMN(4) = 3
056    LABEL.COLUMN(5) = 3
057    LABEL.COLUMN(6) = 3
058    LABEL.COLUMN(7) = 3
```

Lines 62 through 68 assign the row positions to the corresponding positions in the array LABEL.ROW. This table is used later to determine the row coordinate at which to place the data labels on the screen:

```
060 * DEFINE LABEL.ROW
061 *
062    LABEL.ROW(1) = 4
063    LABEL.ROW(2) = 5
064    LABEL.ROW(3) = 6
065    LABEL.ROW(4) = 7
066    LABEL.ROW(5) = 8
067    LABEL.ROW(6) = 9
068    LABEL.ROW(7) = 10
```

Defining Display Column and Row Positions

Lines 72 through 78 assign the value 20 to the corresponding positions in the array DATA.COLUMN. This table is used later to determine the column coordinate at which to display (and enter) the actual data for each field on the screen:

```
070 * DEFINE DATA.COLUMN
071 *
072    DATA.COLUMN(1) = 20
073    DATA.COLUMN(2) = 20
074    DATA.COLUMN(3) = 20
075    DATA.COLUMN(4) = 20
076    DATA.COLUMN(5) = 20
077    DATA.COLUMN(6) = 20
078    DATA.COLUMN(7) = 20
```

Lines 82 through 88 assign the row positions to the corresponding positions in the array DATA.ROW. This table is used later to determine the row coordinate at which to display (and enter) the actual data for each field on the screen:

```
080 * DEFINE DATA.ROW
081 *
082    DATA.ROW(1) = 4
083    DATA.ROW(2) = 5
084    DATA.ROW(3) = 6
085    DATA.ROW(4) = 7
086    DATA.ROW(5) = 8
087    DATA.ROW(6) = 9
088    DATA.ROW(7) = 10
```

DEFINING THE INPUT AND OUTPUT CONVERSIONS

Lines 92 through 98 assign various (ACCESS) input conversion codes to the corresponding positions of the variable INPUT.CONVERSIONS. These are used later in the program, after the data for the field is entered.

```
090 * DEFINE INPUT.CONVERSIONS
091 *
092    INPUT.CONVERSIONS(1) = ""
093    INPUT.CONVERSIONS(2) = ""
094    INPUT.CONVERSIONS(3) = ""
095    INPUT.CONVERSIONS(4) = "P(2A)"
096    INPUT.CONVERSIONS(5) = "P(5N)"
097    INPUT.CONVERSIONS(6) = ""
098    INPUT.CONVERSIONS(7) = "D"
```

The first three fields—NAME, ADDRESS, and CITY—require no special input conversions, so they are assigned a null. Field 4, which is the STATE field, is assigned the input conversion P(2A). This "pattern match" conversion allows only two alphabetic characters. Field 5, the ZIP field, is assigned the input conversion P(5N), which accepts only 5-digit numbers. Field 7, the BIRTHDAY, is assigned the D conversion, which does the external-to-internal date conversion discussed earlier.

All of these conversions are used later to ensure that the data received is in a valid format.

Lines 102 through 107 assign null output conversions to the corresponding positions in the table.

```
100 * DEFINE OUTPUT.CONVERSIONS
101 *
102    OUTPUT.CONVERSIONS(1) = ""
103    OUTPUT.CONVERSIONS(2) = ""
104    OUTPUT.CONVERSIONS(3) = ""
105    OUTPUT.CONVERSIONS(4) = ""
106    OUTPUT.CONVERSIONS(5) = ""
107    OUTPUT.CONVERSIONS(6) = ""
108    OUTPUT.CONVERSIONS(7) = "D2/"
```

Field 7, the BIRTHDAY, is the only field which actually requires an output conversion. It is assigned the ACCESS conversion D2/, which outputs the birthday in the form MM/DD/YY—except in Europe, where it is DD/MM/YY.

DEFINING FIELD LENGTHS

This is the last of our parameter table definitions. Lines 112 through 118 assign the value 30 to each of the fields in the array LENGTH. This is used later to prevent data from exceeding the suggested length:

```
110 * DEFINE LENGTH
111 *
112    LENGTH(1) = 30
113    LENGTH(2) = 30
114    LENGTH(3) = 30
115    LENGTH(4) = 30
116    LENGTH(5) = 30
117    LENGTH(6) = 30
118    LENGTH(7) = 30
```

THE MAIN PROGRAM AND SUBROUTINES

Incredibly, the six lines from 122 through 127 represent the basic logic of the program:

```
120 * MAIN POINT OF PROGRAM
121 *
122    LOOP
123       GOSUB 1000   ; * ENTER ID AND READ ITEM
124    UNTIL EXIT.FLAG DO
125       GOSUB 2000   ; * EDIT ITEM
126    REPEAT
127    STOP            ; * END OF PROGRAM
```

Line 122 establishes the top of the loop. Line 123 executes local subroutine 1000, which is used to request the item-id or the word QUIT. Line 124 tests the condition of EXIT.FLAG to determine if it is 0 (zero) or 1 (one). If EXIT.FLAG evaluates to 1 ("true"), then execution falls out of the loop and executes the STOP statement on line 127. If EXIT.FLAG evaluates to 0 ("false"), then line 125 executes local subroutine 2000, which allows the item to be constructed or modified.

Pretty simple, isn't it? The good news is that this program is generalized and may easily be modified to fit your files. All you need to do is modify this program by filling in the tables at the top of the program.

Subroutine 1000: Enter Item-ID and Read Item from File

The data entry process begins by requesting an item-id from the operator; once it is obtained, the appropriate file is opened for modification (Fig. 14-2).

Line 131 clears the screen with the $@(-1)$ function. Line 132 defines the top of the loop. The loop is used to request either an item-id or the word QUIT. The data is then stored in the variable, STAFF.ID.

Line 135 defines the conditional logic, which repeats the loop until the response received is greater than "null." Line 136 tests the response to determine if the operator entered the word QUIT. If QUIT was entered, then EXIT.FLAG is assigned the value TRUE (set to 1). If QUIT was not entered, then EXIT.FLAG is assigned the value FALSE (set to zero).

166

```
129 1000 * ENTER ID AND READ ITEM
130 *
131    PRINT @(-1) :    ; * CLEAR SCREEN
132    LOOP
133      PRINT @(3,2) : "ENTER ITEM-ID OR 'QUIT' TO STOP " :
134      INPUT STAFF.ID
135    UNTIL STAFF.ID > '' DO REPEAT
136    IF STAFF.ID = "QUIT" THEN EXIT.FLAG=TRUE ELSE EXIT.FLAG=FALSE

138 * READ ITEM
139 *
140    NEW.ITEM.FLAG = FALSE
141    MATREAD STAFF.ITEM FROM STAFF.FILE,STAFF.ID ELSE
142      MAT STAFF.ITEM = ''
143      NEW.ITEM.FLAG = TRUE
144    END
145    RETURN   ; * DONE WITH ENTER ID AND READ ITEM
```

Fig. 14-2. Subroutine to obtain a value for STAFF.ID and retrieve the item from a file.

Line 140 sets the value of the variable NEW.ITEM.FLAG to false (zero). This happens before the item is read, for two reasons: to ensure that the variable has been assigned a value before it is referred to later, and to reset it after it has been set to TRUE.

Line 141 reads in the item with the MATREAD statement, which has the following general form:

MATREAD *array.variable* FROM *file.variable,id.expression*. . .
. . . {THEN *statement(s)*} ELSE *statement(s)*

The MATREAD statement is used to retrieve an item into a dimensioned array. The THEN clause is optional, and when it is used, any statements following it are executed when the item being read is found. The ELSE clause is required; any statements following the ELSE clause are executed when the requested item-id is not found in the file. (If you had entered the item-id 1234567, which is not currently in the file, the statements on lines 142 and 143 would be executed.)

Matrix Assignment with the MAT Statement

It is generally a good practice to initialize a dimensioned array to ensure that there are no "leftovers" from a former use. This is accomplished with the MAT statement, which has the general form:

MAT *array.variable* = *value*

For example:

```
142   MAT STAFF.ITEM = ''
```

This statement assigns a null to each element of the dimensioned array, clearing each element of any former contents.

Incidentally, one array may be assigned to another, provided they are the same size. This operation has the general form:

MAT *array.variable* = **MAT** *array.variable*

If the two arrays are not the same size, however, one of two possible events is likely to happen. If the destination array (the array on the left side of the assignment operator) is larger than the source array, then the assignment is successful; if the destination array is smaller than the source array, then the program crashes and burns.

In the program example, if the item isn't found, the STAFF.ITEM array is initialized on line 142. Then line 143 assigns the value TRUE (1), to the variable NEW.ITEM.FLAG, since the item was not found.

Whether the item was found or not, line 145 executes a RETURN statement, sending execution back to line 124, which checks the status of the EXIT.FLAG variable. If EXIT.FLAG is not TRUE, then line 125 is executed, which transfers execution to local subroutine 2000:

```
124   UNTIL EXIT.FLAG DO
125      GOSUB 2000      ; * EDIT ITEM
```

Subroutine 2000: Edit Item

Local subroutine 2000 (Fig. 14-3) is a "dispatch center" which manages the disposition of the entered item. On line 149, the first executable statement, a GOSUB 10000 statement executes local subroutine 10000, which appears in the lower portion of the figure.

```
147 2000 * EDIT ITEM
148 *
149  GOSUB 10000      ; * PRINT LABELS
150  GOSUB 20000      ; * PRINT DATA
151  IF NEW.ITEM.FLAG THEN
152     GOSUB 30000   ; * ENTER NEW ITEM
153  END
154  GOSUB 40000      ; * UPDATE OLD ITEM
155  RETURN

157 10000 * PRINT LABELS
158 *
159  FOR I = 1 TO LAST.FIELD
160    PRINT @(LABEL.COLUMN(I),LABEL.ROW(I)) :SCREEN.LABELS(I) :
161  NEXT I
162  RETURN
```

Fig. 14-3. Subroutines to edit the item and print data labels.

This routine is used to print the data labels at the predefined cursor coordinates on the screen. Line 159 establishes the loop boundaries by setting the initial value of I to 1 (one) and the upper boundary to LAST.FIELD (which is currently 7).

Then line 160 positions the cursor to the coordinates derived from the arrays LABEL.COLUMN and LABEL.ROW. Since the current value of I is 1 (one), when this statement is executed the value of LABEL.COLUMN(1) is retrieved. This value is used as the column coordinate, or the number of character positions from the left-hand side of the screen. The value of LABEL.ROW(1) is used to determine the row, or number of lines from the top of the screen. LABEL.COLUMN(1) was assigned the value 3, and LABEL.COLUMN(1) was assigned the value 4. Consequently, the cursor is placed at position 3 on line 4 of the screen.

Finally, the current contents of SCREEN.LABELS(1), which was assigned the value "1 NAME," is displayed at the current cursor position.

Each time through the FOR-NEXT loop, I is incremented by 1 (one), until all seven of the data labels have been displayed at their appropriate screen positions. Upon completing the display of the data labels, the RETURN statement on line 162 is executed, transferring execution to line 150, where another GOSUB statement is executed. This time, local subroutine 20000 is executed, which is the routine to print the data elements.

Subroutine 20000: Print Data Elements

Subroutine 20000 coordinates the printing of data elements. (Fig. 14-4). To print the data elements, another loop is established, just as before. Each time through this loop, however, execution is transferred to local subroutine 25000, which prints the data element corresponding to the value of I.

```
164 20000 * PRINT DATA
165 *
166  FOR I = 1 TO LAST.FIELD
167     GOSUB 25000; * PRINT ONE DATUM
168  NEXT I
169  RETURN

171 25000 * PRINT ONE DATUM
172 *
173  IF OUTPUT.CONVERSIONS(I) # "" THEN
174     PRINT.VALUE = OCONV(STAFF.ITEM(I),OUTPUT.CONVERSIONS(I))
175  END ELSE
176     PRINT.VALUE = STAFF.ITEM(I)
177  END
178  PRINT @(DATA.COLUMN(I),DATA.ROW(I)) :(PRINT.VALUE) ('L#':LENGTH(I)):
179  RETURN
```

Fig. 14-4. Subroutines to select and print data items.

Subroutine 25000: Print One Data Element

Subroutine 25000 (Fig. 14-4, lower portion) actually does the printing. On line 173, the current value of I is used to test the contents of the array OUTPUT.CONVERSIONS, to determine if there is an output conversion to apply to the data element being printed. The logic of line 173 reads, "If there is a conversion code for this field, then execute the statement on line 174, which converts the value of the current field with the appropriate conversion and assigns the result to the variable PRINT.VALUE. If, on the other hand, there is no conversion code present for this field, then the statement on line 176 is executed, which assigns the value of the current field—unconverted—to PRINT.VALUE."

The first part of line 178 positions the cursor to the data location using the tables DATA.COLUMN and DATA.ROW. This is done exactly as it was done before for the placement of the data labels. The second part of line 178, which reads:

```
... : (PRINT.VALUE) ('L#':LENGTH(I)) :
```

outputs the current value of PRINT.VALUE, using the mask expression derived from the LENGTH table for the current field.

In this example, all of the values of the array LENGTH were set to 30. Thus, this statement is the same as issuing the statement:

```
... : (PRINT.VALUE) ("L#30") :
```

which outputs the current value of PRINT.VALUE, left-justified in a field of 30 blanks.

Checking the NEW.ITEM.FLAG

After local subroutine 20000 finishes executing, which printed the items on the screen, the RETURN statement is encountered. This returns execution to line 151, which checks the status of the variable NEW.ITEM.FLAG. This variable was set earlier during program execution at lines 140 (before the MATREAD), and optionally at line 143 (if the item was not on file):

```
151   IF NEW.ITEM.FLAG THEN
152     GOSUB 30000   ; * ENTER NEW ITEM
153   END
```

Subroutine 30000: Enter New Item

Subroutine 30000 (Fig. 14-5) is where most of the editing logic takes place. At line 183, the variable CURRENT.FIELD is assigned the value 1 (one). This occurs if the item is "new." This routine, incidentally, is only executed if NEW.ITEM.FLAG evaluates to true.

At line 184, a loop is started. Line 185, which reads:

```
185   PRINT @(DATA.COLUMN(CURRENT.FIELD),DATA.ROW(CURRENT.FIELD)) :
```

```
181 30000 * ENTER NEW ITEM
182 *
183   CURRENT.FIELD = 1
184   LOOP
185     PRINT @(DATA.COLUMN(CURRENT.FIELD),DATA.ROW(CURRENT.FIELD)) :
186     INPUT ANS, LENGTH(CURRENT.FIELD)
187     BEGIN CASE
188       CASE ANS = "QUIT"
189         EXIT.FLAG = TRUE
190       CASE ANS = ''
191         CURRENT.FIELD = CURRENT.FIELD + 1
192       CASE ANS = "^"
193         I = CURRENT.FIELD; GOSUB 25000; * PRINT ONE DATUM
194         IF CURRENT.FIELD >=2 THEN CURRENT.FIELD = CURRENT.FIELD-1
195       CASE 1
196         GOSUB 35000 ; * GET VALIDATED DATUM,STORE IN STAFF.ITEM
197         IF NOT(ERROR.FLAG) THEN CURRENT.FIELD = CURRENT.FIELD + 1
198     END CASE
199   UNTIL CURRENT.FIELD > LAST.FIELD OR EXIT.FLAG = TRUE DO REPEAT
200   RETURN
```

Fig. 14-5. New-item entry subroutine.

positions the cursor to the appropriate input field location, based upon the value of CURRENT.FIELD. Then line 186 executes the INPUT statement to request the value for the array location indicated by CURRENT.FIELD. The length of the input is restricted to the corresponding value of the LENGTH array for the current field.

After receiving the input from the operator, line 187 starts a CASE construct with a BEGIN CASE statement to determine how to handle the operator's response. The CASE statement on line 188 checks for the presence of the response, QUIT. If this response is received, the EXIT.FLAG variable is assigned the value TRUE, and execution leaves the CASE construct, unconditionally executing the statement at line 199.

Line 199 defines the "until" portion of the loop. It appears as:

```
199   UNTIL CURRENT.FIELD > LAST.FIELD OR EXIT.FLAG = TRUE DO REPEAT
```

This specifies that either of two conditions which will terminate the loop may occur. The first condition is if the current value of CURRENT.FIELD is greater than LAST.FIELD. If this is true, then it means that all of the fields have been entered. The second condition is based upon the value of EXIT.FLAG. If EXIT.FLAG is 1 (true), then it means that the operator typed "QUIT." If either condition is true, the loop terminates.

The next CASE statement, at line 190, checks the response to determine if no response was provided (the operator entered a Return <cr>. If this is the case, then the value of CURRENT.FIELD is incremented by 1 (one), and execution falls out of the CASE construct. None of the fields in this program are required to have input, other than the item-id.

Line 192 executes a CASE statement to determine if the response is an up-arrow or caret ("^"). This is provided as a data entry convention to allow the operator to "back up" one field. Suppose, for example, that the NAME entry had been misspelled and that the program is now requesting the ADDRESS field. By entering a caret, the program repositions the cursor back to the (previous) field—in this case, the "NAME" field—and allows the operator to reenter the name.

If a caret is entered, the statement at line 193 is executed. This assigns the value of the current field to the variable I and then immediately executes subroutine 25000, which reprints the value of the current field. Upon returning from subroutine 25000, a test is performed to determine if the current value of CURRENT.FIELD is greater than or equal to 2. If it is, then the value of CURRENT.FIELD is decremented by 1. This means that the "^" character backs up a field at any field other than the first field.

Line 195 performs the "otherwise" case. This is executed upon receiving anything that was not already detected in any of the previous CASE statements, meaning, that it is not QUIT, null or "^". In other words, data was entered.

When line 196 is executed, subroutine 35000 is called, which validates the response. Upon returning from subroutine 35000, the value of ERROR.FLAG is checked. Line 197 appears as:

```
197   IF NOT(ERROR.FLAG) THEN CURRENT.FIELD = CURRENT.FIELD + 1
```

The NOT Statement

Conditional expressions normally evaluate to 1 (one), when they evaluate true and to 0 (zero) if false. The NOT function reverses the effect of the conditional expression embedded within its parentheses.

For example, consider the following source line:

```
IF NUM(RESPONSE) THEN PRINT "NUMERIC" ELSE PRINT "NON-NUMERIC"
```

This means that if the value of RESPONSE is numeric, then the program executes the THEN clause; otherwise, if RESPONSE is not numeric, the statement after the ELSE initiator is executed.

Now examine the exact same statement using the NOT function:

```
IF NOT(NUM(RESPONSE)) THEN PRINT "NOT-NUMERIC" ELSE PRINT "NUMERIC"
```

This line means that if the value of RESPONSE is not numeric, then the program executes the instruction after the THEN initiator; otherwise, if RESPONSE is numeric, the statement after the ELSE initiator is executed.

Consequently, line 197 of this program reads, "If ERROR.FLAG is not true (meaning that it must be 0), then increment the value of CURRENT.FIELD by 1 (one)." Whether ERROR.FLAG is true or not, the CASE construct is terminated at line 198, and the program unconditionally executes line 199. Again, this is the point at which the current value of CURRENT.FIELD is checked to determine if it is greater than LAST.FIELD, or to determine if EXIT.FLAG is true (1)—either of which means that it is time to leave the loop.

Subroutine 35000: Get Validated Datum

In subroutine 35000 (Fig. 14-6), validation of the input field takes place. The first statement in the subroutine is line 205, which is:

```
205   IF ERROR.FLAG THEN PRINT @(3,21) : @(-4) :
```

This line checks the status of ERROR.FLAG to determine if it is true (1). If ERROR.FLAG is true, then the cursor is positioned to position 3 on line 21 and the @(-4) function is issued, which clears the display from the current cursor position to the end of the current line. Then line 206 "resets" the current value of ERROR.FLAG to false (0).

Line 207 tests for the presence of an input conversion for the current field. If there is an input conversion to be applied against the input, the statement on line 208 is executed; otherwise, execution falls through to line 216, which will be discussed shortly.

Assuming that there is an input conversion, line 208 is executed. This is:

```
208   TEMP = ICONV(ANS,INPUT.CONVERSIONS(CURRENT.FIELD))
```

The input conversion for the current field is applied to the value of ANS. The result of the conversion is then assigned to the temporary variable TEMP. The easiest way to determine if the input conversion worked properly is to check the value of TEMP after the conversion. Input conversions that validate data produce a null if they fail. For instance, if the attempted conversion was D (for "Date") and the response entered was "NEW YORK CITY," then the date conversion fails, storing a null in the TEMP variable.

Line 209 is where the test on TEMP takes place. It means: If TEMP is null, then the operator blew it, in which case the statements on lines 210 and 211 are executed. The statement on line 210 displays the message "UNEXPECTED FORMAT. PLEASE TRY

```
202 35000 * GET VALIDATED DATUM, STORE IN STAFF.ITEM, REPRINT
203 * INPUT = ANS > ''.  OUTPUT = ANS, ERROR.FLAG
204 *
205     IF ERROR.FLAG THEN PRINT @(3,21) : @(-4) :
206     ERROR.FLAG = FALSE
207     IF INPUT.CONVERSIONS(CURRENT.FIELD) > '' THEN
208       TEMP = ICONV(ANS,INPUT.CONVERSIONS(CURRENT.FIELD))
209       IF TEMP = "" THEN    ; * NOT GOOD
210         PRINT @(3,21) :"UNEXPECTED FORMAT.  PLEASE TRY AGAIN"
211         ERROR.FLAG = TRUE
212       END ELSE
213         ANS = TEMP
214       END
215     END
216     IF NOT(ERROR.FLAG) THEN STAFF.ITEM(CURRENT.FIELD) = ANS
217     I = CURRENT.FIELD; GOSUB 25000; * PRINT ONE DATUM
218     RETURN
```

Fig. 14-6. Input validation subroutine.

AGAIN'' at position 3 on line 21. Line 211 sets the value of ERROR.FLAG to true (1), and then falls out of the IF statement to execute line 216.

The second possibility after testing TEMP is that it is not null, meaning that the input conversion ''worked.'' If this is the case, then the statement on line 213 is executed. Line 213 assigns the value of the variable TEMP to the variable ANS and then falls out of the IF statement.

Line 216 checks the status of ERROR.FLAG. If ERROR.FLAG is not true (meaning that it is 0), the received input is valid and the current value of ANS is assigned to the appropriate location within the array variable STAFF.ARRAY. If ERROR.FLAG is true (1), no assignment takes place. (After all, you don't want to stuff garbage into the array.)

Line 217 assigns the value of CURRENT.FIELD to the variable I and then executes subroutine 25000, which displays the data for field ''I.''

This concludes subroutine 30000, which returns execution to line 154. (Don't panic; we're almost done.) Line 154 executes subroutine 40000, which allows any field in the item to be updated.

Subroutine 40000: Update ''Old'' Item

Whether the item is ''new'' or not, program execution always passes through subroutine 40000 (Fig. 14-7). This code block allows changing an individual field in the item, as

```
220 40000 * UPDATE OLD ITEM
221 *
222    LOOP
223      PRINT @(3,20) :
224      PRINT "ENTER FIELD # TO CHANGE, E(X)IT, (D)ELETE, (F)ILE " :
225      INPUT OPTION
226      BEGIN CASE
227        CASE NUM(OPTION)
228          IF OPTION >= 1 AND OPTION <= LAST.FIELD THEN
229            CURRENT.FIELD = OPTION
230            PRINT @(DATA.COLUMN(CURRENT.FIELD),DATA.ROW(CURRENT.FIELD)):
231            INPUT ANS, LENGTH(CURRENT.FIELD)
232            IF ANS > '' THEN GOSUB 35000; * VALIDATE, STORE
233          END
234        CASE OPTION = "X" OR OPTION = "QUIT"
235          EXIT.FLAG = TRUE
236        CASE OPTION = "D"
237          DELETE STAFF.FILE,STAFF.ID
238          PRINT "ITEM DELETED"
239        CASE OPTION = "F"
240          MATWRITE STAFF.ITEM ON STAFF.FILE,STAFF.ID
241      END CASE
242    UNTIL INDEX("XDF",OPTION,1) AND OPTION > '' DO REPEAT
243    RETURN
```

Fig. 14-7. Update subroutine.

well as handling the logic for determining what to do with the item before returning to the top of the program to retrieve the next item.

Line 222 starts the loop, line 223 positions the cursor to position 3 on line 20, and line 224 displays the message;

```
ENTER FIELD # TO CHANGE, E(X)IT, (D)ELETE, (F)ILE
```

Line 225 executes the INPUT statement to request the variable OPTION.

Once the response has been provided to OPTION, a CASE construct is started on line 226. The first CASE statement checks the response to determine if it was a number. This indicates that the operator has chosen to change one of the fields. Line 228 checks the number to ensure that it is a valid field number, which means that it is greater than or equal to 1 (one) and less than the value of LAST.FIELD. If both of these conditions evaluate to true, then lines 229 through 232 are executed.

Line 229 assigns the (numeric) value of OPTION to the variable CURRENT.FIELD, line 230 positions the cursor at the appropriate position for the field being changed, and line 231 awaits the input, again restricting its length to the restriction specified for this field by the current value of the corresponding subscript in the LENGTH array.

After receiving the input, line 232 checks whether the response entered was null. If the response is not null (something was entered), then subroutine 35000 is executed, which validates and stores one datum. Next, execution falls out of the CASE construct and executes the ''until'' portion of the loop.

Line 234 executes the second CASE statement. This checks the response to determine if the operator entered ''X'' or ''QUIT,'' meaning that the operator wanted to exit without updating the file. If this is the case, then line 235 assigns the value of true to the variable EXIT.FLAG.

Line 236 executes the next CASE statement, which checks the response to determine if it is the letter ''D,'' meaning that the item is to be deleted.

THE DELETE STATEMENT

The DELETE statement is aptly named. It is used to delete an item from a file and generally has the general form:

DELETE *array.variable,item.id*

If the operator did enter the letter ''D,'' then the DELETE statement on line 237 is executed. This deletes the current item from the file and then prints the message (on line 238) that the item has been deleted. After completing this example, as an exercise you may want to add the logic to ask the operator if he or she is ''sure'' that they want to do this.

Note that with any of the file-access statements, the ''default'' file.variable option is always available, which means that the DELETE statement possibly could take the form:

DELETE *item.id*

THE MATWRITE STATEMENT

Line 239 executes the final CASE statement, which checks the response for the letter "F," meaning that the operator chose to "File" the item.

The MATREAD statement was discussed earlier in this program, noting that the statement is always used with dimensioned arrays. Its counterpart for writing an item to a file is called MATWRITE, which has the general format:

MATWRITE *array.variable* ON *file.variable,id.expression*

Notice that no THEN or ELSE clauses are required. This is because "writes" in the Pick System are unconditional. As a note for those of you who came from a COBOL environment, there is no REWRITE statement in Pick. When Pick is instructed to "write" an array, it does. Pick doesn't particularly care whether or not the item is, or was, already in the file. It adds the item if it is new, or writes over the "old" item if it was already there.

Finally, the "until" portion of the loop occurs on line 242, which is:

```
242   UNTIL INDEX("XDF",OPTION,1) AND OPTION > '' DO REPEAT
```

This means to repeat the loop until the response received from the operator is either the letter "X," "D," or "F," and the response is not null. The only way out of the loop is one of the three letters just mentioned, or the word "QUIT."

There now, that wasn't too bad, was it? Since this is a generalized data entry program, customizing it for your own particular needs is simple. You copy the item and then change the "tables" at the beginning of the program. The main logic is generalized, and thus does not have to be changed.

One more note: Play with this program! Test all of its features. Don't forget to test things like the "back up one field" feature, by entering the "^" at any field. Also try to put invalid data in the fields that have input conversions. Have fun.

Formatting Reports and Passing PROC Arguments

THE MOST IMPORTANT PRINCIPLES OF PICK/BASIC HAVE BEEN DISCUSSED IN THE PREVIOUS examples; the remaining program examples illustrate extensions to previous concepts and introduce a few new topics that you may run across in your applications.

Program Example 13, for instance, covers the concept of the PROCREAD statement, which is used to pass information from the PROC input buffer into a PICK/BASIC program. Then Example 14 shows you why you don't want to do this.

Enter Program Example 13 from the listing in Fig. 15-1.

After entering, compiling, and cataloging EX.013, you must enter the following PROCs before the program may be tested. It also is important that you have entered the data into the STAFF file before attempting to test this program.

The first PROC is called a *trigger* PROC. It goes into the MD, as follows:

```
>ED MD PROCREAD.TEST<cr>
NEW ITEM
TOP
.I<cr>
001+PQ<cr>
002+(PROCS PROCREAD.TEST)<cr>
003+<cr>
TOP
.FI<cr>
'PROCREAD.TEST' FILED.
```

Fig. 15-1. Program Example 13.

```
EX.013
001 * EX.013
002 * Using PROCREAD
003 * mm/dd/yy : date last modified
004 * JES : author's initials
005 *
006    PROCREAD BUFFER ELSE
007       PRINT "THIS MUST BE RUN FROM THE PROC CALLED PROCREAD.TEST"
008       STOP
009    END
010 *
011    BEGIN.DATE = FIELD(BUFFER," ",1)
012    END.DATE = FIELD(BUFFER," ",2)
013    PRINTER.FLAG = FIELD(BUFFER," ",3)
014 *
015    IF PRINTER.FLAG = "" OR PRINTER.FLAG = "Y" THEN PRINTER ON
016 *
017    HEADING "'LC'BIRTHDAYS FROM " : BEGIN.DATE:" TO ":END.DATE: "'L'"
018 *
019    OPEN "STAFF" TO STAFF.FILE ELSE STOP 201,"STAFF"
020    DIM STAFF.ITEM(15)
021 *
022 1 READNEXT ITEM.ID ELSE
023       PRINTER OFF
024       PRINT "REPORT COMPLETE."
025       STOP
026    END
027 *
028    MATREAD STAFF.ITEM FROM STAFF.FILE,ITEM.ID ELSE
029       CRT "ITEM " : ITEM.ID : " IS MISSING FROM THE STAFF FILE "
030       CRT "PRESS RETURN TO CONTINUE OR 'QUIT' TO STOP " :
031       INPUT RESPONSE
032       IF RESPONSE = "QUIT" THEN STOP
033       GOTO 1
034    END
035 *
036    PRINT "STAFF ID : " : ITEM.ID
037    PRINT
038    PRINT "NAME" "L#20" : STAFF.ITEM(1)
039    PRINT "ADDRESS" "L#20" : STAFF.ITEM(2)
040    PRINT "CITY" "L#20" : STAFF.ITEM(3)
041    PRINT "STATE" "L#20" : STAFF.ITEM(4)
042    PRINT "ZIP" "L#20" : STAFF.ITEM(5)
043 *
044    PRINT "PRESS ANY KEY FOR NEXT ITEM OR <CTL> X TO QUIT " :
045    PAGE
046 *
047    GOTO 1
048 *
049    END
```

This PROC, upon execution, transfers to the file called PROCS and executes a PROC called PROCREAD.TEST. Enter into the PROCS file the PROC shown in Fig. 15-2. Assuming all goes well, the program is entered and compiled, and both PROCs are present and working. Here's how you can test to see if it works.

TESTING PROGRAM EXAMPLE 13

At the TCL prompt, enter:

>**PROCREAD.TEST**<cr>

The PROC then prompts you to enter the "beginning date." Enter:

1-1-51

```
>ED PROCS PROCREAD.TEST<cr>
NEW ITEM
TOP
.I<cr>
001+PQ
002+RI
003+10 OENTER BEGINNING DATE FOR SELECT +
004+S1
005+IP:
006+IF A1 = QUIT X
007+IF # A1 GO 10
008+20 OENTER ENDING DATE FOR SELECT +
009+S2
010+IP:
011+IF A2 = QUIT X
012+IF # A2 GO 20
013+30 ODO YOU WANT THE REPORT PRINTED ? (Y/N=<CR>) +
014+S3
015+IHN
016+IP:
017+IF A3 = QUIT X
018+HSSELECT STAFF BY NAME WITH BIRTHDAY >=
019+A"1
020+H AND WITH BIRTHDAY <=
021+A"2
022+STON
023+HRUN BP EX.013
024+P
025+<cr>
TOP
.FI<cr>
'PROCREAD.TEST' FILED.
```

Fig. 15-2. The PROC called PROCREAD.TEST (install in PROCS file).

The next prompt is the "ending date." Use any date that you want.

Finally, you are prompted to answer whether you want the report printed. I suggest that you initially answer the question with "N" (as in "Nope"). This happens to be the default, anyway, in case you just hit the Return key.

After executing the SSELECT statement from the PROC, a group of one or more items may be selected. If you get the message, "NO ITEMS PRESENT," return to the first step.

THE PROCREAD STATEMENT

Back in the old days, before the EXECUTE statement was introduced into the PICK/BASIC language, whenever a "select list" of items had to be passed into a program, it had to be done from PROC. PICK/BASIC has a statement called SELECT available, but the disadvantage of using it is that it selects the entire file, and no sorting or selection criteria may be applied.

The idea here is that a subset of a file needs to be gathered. In the PROC called PROCREAD.TEST, the operator is prompted to enter the beginning and ending dates. This is applied in an "external" SELECT (in this case, SSELECT) statement, which "gathers" a list of item-ids in the requested sequence after using the selection criteria to determine which items are to be selected. Once the external select completes, the PICK/BASIC program is activated and the list is available for processing.

The PROCREAD statement is only required when one or more pieces of data have to be retrieved from the PROC *Primary Input Buffer*. It does two things: First it checks to make sure that the program was indeed activated from a PROC, and then it "reads" the contents of the Primary Input Buffer and assigns it to a variable.

The PROCREAD statement has the following general form:

PROCREAD *variable* {**THEN** *statement(s)*} **ELSE** *statement(s)*

When the PROCREAD statement is executed, the THEN clause is optional and the ELSE clause is required. The ELSE clause is executed if the program was not run from a PROC. By the way, the statement is not smart enough to know if it was the "right" PROC; it just checks to see that it was run from a PROC.

In Example 13, if the program was not executed from the PROC, the program displays an error message and then stops the program:

```
006 PROCREAD BUFFER ELSE
007 PRINT "THIS MUST BE RUN FROM THE PROC CALLED PROCREAD.TEST"
008 STOP
009 END
```

Assuming that the program was run from the right PROC, the next executable statement occurs on line 11.

PROCREADING THE PRIMARY INPUT BUFFER

When the PROCREAD statement "worked," it grabbed the entire contents of the Primary Input Buffer and assigned it to the variable called BUFFER. Any variable name could have been used, but descriptive variables do make programs easier to read.

The way data is handled in the Primary Input Buffer varies among the several implementations of Pick. "Generic" Pick systems handle the Primary Input Buffer as one long string of characters, each of which is delimited by a space. Ultimate and McDonnell Douglas systems handle the Primary Input Buffer as if it were a dynamic array.

The code in Example 13 illustrates the form that "generic" Pick systems require:

```
011   BEGIN.DATE = FIELD(BUFFER," ",1)
012   END.DATE = FIELD(BUFFER," ",2)
013   PRINTER.FLAG = FIELD(BUFFER," ",3)
```

Line 11 performs a FIELD function on the BUFFER variable, which extracts all the characters up to the first space and assigns this string to the variable BEGIN.DATE. This is the "beginning date" that you entered in the PROC.

Line 12 executes a FIELD statement, extracting all the characters between the first and second spaces in the BUFFER variable and assigning the resulting string to the variable END.DATE. Then line 13 executes one final FIELD statement to extract the "third" string from the BUFFER variable and assign it to the variable PRINTER.FLAG.

Shown below are the instructions that would be required on an Ultimate or McDonnell Douglas implementation accomplish the same end result.

```
011   BEGIN.DATE = BUFFER<1>
012   END.DATE = BUFFER<2>
013   PRINTER.FLAG = BUFFER<3>
```

The end result is the same: the variables BEGIN.DATE, END.DATE, and PRINTER.FLAG are extracted from the "dynamic" array BUFFER.

Line 15 checks PRINTER.FLAG to determine if it is null or the letter "Y." If either of these conditions apply, the the PRINTER ON statement is executed. If not, execution falls through to line 17.

THE HEADING AND FOOTING STATEMENTS

If you have ever used the HEADING or FOOTING statements in an ACCESS sentence, this statement will be familiar. The HEADING statement is used to define the text that appears at the top of each page of output. While you could write the code to handle page headings, footings, line counters, page counters, and related logic, it is much easier to use the HEADING statement.

The HEADING and FOOTING statements have the general form:

HEADING *string.expression*

or

HEADING *"text 'options'"*

Generally, the HEADING statement is followed by a string of characters enclosed in double quotes. Between these double quotes may be any text to appear at the top of each page, and any of the special "options" that are available. Figure 15-3 illustrates the "standard" available options. To distinguish "options" from "text" in the HEADING or FOOTING, the options are enclosed in single quotes. This is important to remember. Additionally, multiple options may be (and sometimes must be) enclosed in the same set of single quotes.

The statement in example 13 appears as:

```
017 HEADING "'LC'BIRTHDAYS FROM ":BEGIN.DATE:" TO ":END.DATE: "'L'"
```

This constructs the "heading" line as follows: First, the "L" option instructs the program to put a blank *L*ine at the top of each screen. Next, the heading line is to be *C*entered. Note that the "C" option was included in the same set of single quotes as the "L" option.

Next in the heading line comes the text, "BIRTHDAYS FROM." To this heading is concatenated the current value of the variable BEGIN.DATE. This is then followed by more literal text, this time the string, " TO " (note the spaces before and after the word).

Next, the current value of the variable END.DATE is concatenated to the end of the heading. Finally, an "L" option is concatenated to the end of the heading line. As mentioned earlier in this program, this "forces" a line feed between the heading line and the first line of output on each screen or page.

Line 19 opens the STAFF file for input and/or output. If the STAFF file is not found, then the program stops and executes error message 201, passing to it the string "STAFF." (See the discussion of the STOP statement for more information on this feature.)

Option	Function
'C'	Centers the text.
'D'	Retrieves the current date in the "standard" date format. For example, "12 DEC 1997".
'L'	Issues a line feed. Once you take control of the HEADING and/or FOOTING, you are responsible for everything that happens. For example, if you want a blank line between the heading text and the "top" line of data, then you must force the line feed to make it happen.
'P'	Retrieves the current report page number. Note: Consult your ACCESS reference manual on this one. Most versions of Pick have a few derivatives for handling the page number.
'T'	Retrieves the current system time and date. For example, "11:45:00 12 DEC 1997."

Fig. 15-3. The "standard" options for the HEADING and/or FOOTING statements.

Line 20 dimensions the array STAFF.ITEM in anticipation of a maximum of 15 subscripts.

THE READNEXT STATEMENT

Before executing this program, the PROC called PROCREAD.TEST externally selected a group of items, which must be dealt with one at a time. This is where the READNEXT statement comes into play:

```
022 1 READNEXT ITEM.ID ELSE
023     PRINTER OFF
024     PRINT "REPORT COMPLETE."
025     STOP
026   END
```

The READNEXT statement has the general form:

READNEXT *id.variable* {**THEN** *statement(s)*} **ELSE** *statement(s)*

When the READNEXT statement is executed, the program extracts the top item-id off the "stack" of item-ids created by the (external) SELECT or SSELECT statement. When this occurs successfully, the stack of item-ids "moves up" by one—exactly like removing a plate from one of those dispensers found in cafeterias. The item-id just "read" from the stack is assigned to the specified variable. In this program, that variable is called, creatively enough, ITEM.ID.

The READNEXT statement executes its ELSE clause when it runs out of item-ids (no more plates). In this program, when the READNEXT statement discovers that there are no more item-ids to be dealt with, it takes the ELSE clause, which causes the statements from lines 23 through 25 to be executed. Line 23 thoughtfully remembers to turn off printer output with the PRINTER OFF statement, line 24 issues the "REPORT COMPLETE" message, and line 25 terminates the program with a STOP statement.

READING THE ITEM: THE MATREAD STATEMENT

This routine attempts to retrieve the item corresponding to the current item-id via the MATREAD statement:

```
028 MATREAD STAFF.ITEM FROM STAFF.FILE,ITEM.ID ELSE
029     CRT "ITEM " :ITEM.ID :" IS MISSING FROM THE STAFF FILE"
030     CRT "PRESS RETURN TO CONTINUE OR 'QUIT' TO STOP " :
031     INPUT RESPONSE
032     IF RESPONSE = "QUIT" THEN STOP
033     GOTO 1
033 END
```

If the MATREAD statement on line 28 fails to find the item-id in the STAFF file (which is unlikely in this case), the statements from lines 29 through 33 are executed.

Line 29 executes a CRT[1] statement to route the output unconditionally to the screen. The message displays the fact that the item-id is missing from the file, and further advises the operator to press the Return key to continue or enter QUIT to stop. After requesting the response on line 31, line 32 checks to see if the operator entered QUIT. If he did, then the program stops. If he did not enter QUIT, then the program executes the GOTO statement on line 33, which transfers execution to statement label 1, which attempts to retrieve the next item-id from the list.

PRINTING THE ARRAY

The following routine handles the print tasks:

```
036   PRINT "STAFF ID : " : ITEM.ID
037   PRINT
038   PRINT "NAME" "L#20" : STAFF.ITEM(1)
039   PRINT "ADDRESS" "L#20" : STAFF.ITEM(2)
040   PRINT "CITY" "L#20" : STAFF.ITEM(3)
041   PRINT "STATE" "L#20" : STAFF.ITEM(4)
042   PRINT "ZIP" "L#20" : STAFF.ITEM(5)
```

Line 36 prints the literal "STAFF ID : " and then displays the current item-id. Line 37 issues a blank line. Line 38 prints the literal "NAME," left-justified in a field of 20 blanks, immediately followed by the contents of array location one, STAFF.ITEM(1). This logic is the same for the next four fields.

THE PAGE STATEMENT

The PAGE statement clears the screen, or issues a page eject on the printer, when a HEADING or FOOTING is in effect:

```
045   PAGE
```

When a HEADING or FOOTING is "active" in a report program, the PAGE statement is used to handle pagination control. This means several important things to you as the programmer. First, you do not have to issue CHAR(12) or "@(-1)" to clear the screen (or eject a page). Second, the standard end-of-page options are in effect; this means that pressing any key (not *the* Any key) advances to the next page. Third, at any end of page, the operator may issue a "Control-X," which immediately terminates the program. Fourth, and last, the program "figures out" the device width, based upon the current terminal or printer characteristics as defined by the TERM command. Note that the items 2 and 3 of these features are irrelevant when the report is being directed to the printer (spooler).

---

1. Don't forget, Ultimate users, that the CRT statement may have to be changed to a DISPLAY statement.

DOING IT ALL AGAIN

Line 47 unconditionally transfers execution back to statement label 1 (one) to get the next item or wrap up the program.

REVIEW QUIZ 13

This quiz is is more of an essay question than fill-in-the-blanks as before. Here is your assignment:

1) Add the logic to display the other four fields from each item in the STAFF file. These are: PHONE (attribute 6), RENEW.DATE (attribute 7), BIRTHDAY (attribute 8), and HOURLY.RATE (attribute 9). Note that each of these requires special handling to output.

2) Add an "item counter" to the program to display the number of the item being displayed (*not* the item-id).

3) Add the logic to accumulate the total hourly rates for all the staff items. At the end of the report, on a page all by themselves, print out the following:

   a) The total of all hourly rates.
   b) The number of items that were processed.
   c) The average hourly rate.

4) Assume that everyone will retire at the age of 65. Display the current age of each person and determine the number of years they have until retirement.

16

Using the
EXECUTE Statement

PROGRAM EXAMPLE 13 ILLUSTRATED THE "OLD" WAY OF PERFORMING A SELECT OR SSELECT. Almost all versions of Pick now support the EXECUTE statement. Unfortunately, they do not all have the same syntax, although they are similar in theory.

The EXECUTE statement allows (virtually) any TCL command to be executed from a PICK/BASIC program. Upon completion of the TCL process, the PICK/BASIC program resumes where it left off. The results or output from the TCL process may be "passed" into the program for processing.

Program Example 14 illustrates the "uptown" method of doing the same thing that was done with Example 13.

THE EXECUTE STATEMENT

The "generic" form of the Pick EXECUTE statement has the general format:

EXECUTE *"TCL.expression"* {**RETURNING** *return.variable*} . . . . . .
{*CAPTURING capture.variable*}

Any TCL command may be issued. Upon completion of the TCL process, execution is returned to the program at the next statement after EXECUTE. There are two commands, however, that do not return control; one, of course, is OFF, and the other is LOGTO. Effectively, Program Example 14, does exactly the same thing that Example 13 did: it generates a "select list" which is passed into the program. The means by which the

186

Fig. 16-1. Program Example 14.

```
EX.014
001 * EX.014
002 * Using EXECUTE
003 * mm/dd/yy : date last modified
004 * JES : author's initials
005 *
006    PROMPT ":"
007 *
008    PRINT "ENTER BEGINNING DATE " :
009    INPUT BEGIN.DATE
010    IF BEGIN.DATE = "QUIT" THEN STOP
011 *
012    PRINT "ENTER ENDING DATE " :
013    INPUT END.DATE
014    IF END.DATE = "QUIT" THEN STOP
015 *
016    PRINT "DO YOU WANT THE REPORT PRINTED ? (Y/N=<CR>) " :
017    INPUT PRINTER.FLAG
018    IF PRINTER.FLAG = "" OR PRINTER.FLAG = "Y" THEN PRINTER ON
019 *
020    SENTENCE = \SSELECT STAFF BY NAME WITH BIRTHDAY >= "\
021    SENTENCE = SENTENCE : BEGIN.DATE : \" AND WITH \
022    SENTENCE = SENTENCE : \BIRTHDAY <= "\ : END.DATE : \"\
023 *
024    EXECUTE SENTENCE
025 *
026    HEADING "'LC'BIRTHDAYS BETWEEN ":BEGIN.DATE:" AND ":END.DATE:"'L'"
027 *
028    OPEN "STAFF" TO STAFF.FILE ELSE STOP 201,"STAFF"
029    DIM STAFF.ITEM(15)
030 *
031 1 READNEXT ITEM.ID ELSE
032        PRINTER OFF
033        PRINT "REPORT COMPLETE."
034        STOP
035    END
036 *
037    MATREAD STAFF.ITEM FROM STAFF.FILE,ITEM.ID ELSE
038        CRT "ITEM " : ITEM.ID : " IS MISSING FROM THE STAFF FILE "
039        CRT "PRESS RETURN TO CONTINUE OR 'QUIT' TO STOP " :
040        INPUT RESPONSE
041        IF RESPONSE = "QUIT" THEN STOP
 42        GOTO 1
043    END
044 *
045    PRINT "STAFF ID : " : ITEM.ID
046    PRINT
047    PRINT "NAME" "L#20" : STAFF.ITEM(1)
048    PRINT "ADDRESS" "L#20" : STAFF.ITEM(2)
```

```
049    PRINT "CITY" "L#20" : STAFF.ITEM(3)
050    PRINT "STATE" "L#20" : STAFF.ITEM(4)
051    PRINT "ZIP" "L#20" : STAFF.ITEM(5)
052 *
053    PRINT "PRESS ANY KEY FOR NEXT ITEM OR <CTL> X TO QUIT " :
054    PAGE
055 *
056    GOTO 1
057 *
058    END
```

command was constructed for the EXECUTE statement were as follows:

```
020 SENTENCE = \SSELECT STAFF BY NAME WITH BIRTHDAY >= "\
021 SENTENCE = SENTENCE : BEGIN.DATE : \" AND WITH \
022 SENTENCE = SENTENCE : \BIRTHDAY <= "\ : END.DATE : \"\
```

The SELECT and SSELECT statements have a syntactical requirement that "value strings" used in the selection criteria must be enclosed in double quotes.

Suppose, for instance, that you wanted to issue the following sentence at the TCL prompt:

```
SSELECT STAFF WITH BIRTHDAY>="5/1/51" AND WITH BIRTHDAY<="12/1/91/"
```

The value strings in this sentence are "5/1/51" and "12/1/91."

To enclose quotes within a literal string is sometimes a little tricky. For example, attempting to print the literal:

```
JOE'S BAR & GRILL
```

by issuing the statement:

```
PRINT 'JOE'S BAR & GRILL'
```

fails the compile phase and reports the message "UNEVEN NUMBER OF DELIMITERS." This happens because of the choice of quotes in the literal string. It may be correctly stated with the statement:

```
PRINT "JOE'S BAR & GRILL"
```

or, the statement:

```
PRINT \JOE'S BAR & GRILL\
```

The "\" (backslash) character is treated just like a single or double quote when used as a literal string delimiter. The reason the backslash character was chosen instead of single quotes is that sometimes the string needs to have both single and double quotes embedded. An example of this is when you want to issue an ACCESS sentence which contains a HEADING, such as:

```
>SORT STAFF BY NAME HEADING "'LC'STAFF REPORT  PAGE 'PL'"
```

Note that the sentence contains both single and double quotes. To treat this as a literal string requires the backslash as the string delimiter. Shown below is the statement to EXECUTE this sentence:

```
EXECUTE \SORT STAFF BY NAME HEADING "'LC'STAFF REPORT  PAGE 'PL'"\
```

The CAPTURING Clause

The CAPTURING clause in an EXECUTE statement is used to direct the output from the TCL process into a variable. For example:

```
EXECUTE "WHO" CAPTURING OUTPUT
```

Upon execution of this EXECUTE statement, the output from the WHO verb is placed into the variable, OUTPUT.

Normally, the WHO verb produces output similar to the following:

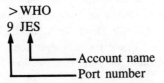

The "9" indicates the port number, and "JES" indicates the current account name. Now that this output is assigned to the variable, OUTPUT, it may be manipulated or printed. For instance, if the statement:

```
PRINT OUTPUT
```

were issued, the following displays:

```
9 JES
```

This could also be manipulated with any of the functions discussed in the earlier chapters. For example, retrieving just the port number could be accomplished with the statement:

```
PORT = FIELD(OUTPUT," ",1)
```

which retrieves all the characters up to the first space in the variable OUTPUT, and assigns it to the variable PORT.

Similarly, the account name could be extracted with the statement:

```
ACCOUNT = FIELD(OUTPUT," ",2)
```

which retrieves the string of characters from the first through the second space in the variable OUTPUT, and assigns it to the variable ACCOUNT.

When the CAPTURING clause "captures" output that has more than one line, each line feed at the end of an output line is "converted" to an attribute mark. This effectively allows the output to be treated as a dynamic array. Here's an example:

```
EXECUTE "LISTU" CAPTURING OUTPUT
```

To print each line of the output separately requires treating OUTPUT as a dynamic array. Figure 16-2 illustrates this principle.

Line 1 equates the constant ATTRIBUTE.MARK to the decimal character 254. Line 2 performs the EXECUTE statement, routing the output to the variable OUTPUT. Line 3 is used to determine how many lines of output were generated by the EXECUTE. Line 4 establishes a FOR-NEXT construct to loop through all the lines of output. Line 5 takes the current value of I and extracts the corresponding "attribute" from the dynamic array OUTPUT. After looping through all the attributes, the program stops.

The RETURNING Clause

The optional RETURNING clause in the EXECUTE statement provides a means of dealing with error messages that are generated as a result of a TCL expression. When this clause is used, all error message item-ids (from the ERRMSG file) are returned to the specified variable. When more than one error message item-id is returned, each is separated from the others by a space (much like the Primary Input Buffer). For example:

```
EXECUTE "SSELECT STAFF BY NAME" RETURNING ERROR.LIST
```

Once the statement has been issued, the program may then be instructed to examine the list of error message item-ids. Figure 16-3 illustrates one such technique for examining the error message item-id list.

```
001   EQUATE ATTRIBUTE.MARK TO CHAR(254)
002   EXECUTE "LISTU" CAPTURING OUTPUT
003   NUMBER.LINES = DCOUNT(OUTPUT,ATTRIBUTE.MARK)
004   FOR I = 1 TO NUMBER.LINES
005      PRINT OUTPUT<I>
006   NEXT I
```

Fig. 16-2. Printing the dynamic array created with the CAPTURING clause.

```
001 EXECUTE "SSELECT STAFF BY NAME" CAPTURING OUTPUT RETURNING ERROR.LIST
002   MAX = DCOUNT(ERROR.LIST," ")
003   FOR I = 1 TO MAX
004     ERROR.NUMBER = FIELD(ERROR.LIST," ",I)
005     BEGIN CASE
006       CASE ERROR.NUMBER = "210"
007         PRINT "FILE HAS ACCESS PROTECTION IMPLEMENTED"
008       CASE ERROR.NUMBER = "401"
009         PRINT "NO ITEMS WERE SELECTED"
010       CASE ERROR.NUMBER = "404"
011         NUMBER.ITEMS.SELECTED = FIELD(OUTPUT," ",1)
012     END CASE
013   NEXT I
```

Fig. 16-3. Examining the error message item-ids.

Line 1 executes the EXECUTE statement, using both the CAPTURING and RETURNING clauses. Line 2 determines the number of error message item-ids that were returned by the TCL command. Line 3 sets up a FOR-NEXT loop, using the variable MAX as the upper end of the loop.

Line 4 assigns the variable ERROR.NUMBER by issuing a FIELD function which extracts all the characters up to the position of the space indicated by the value of I. Then line 5 establishes a CASE construct, where each of the error message item-ids may be individually handled. (The three sample CASE statements just skim the tip of the iceberg in terms of error handling. Naturally, much more logic may be added for each possible error condition.)

SOME IMPORTANT NOTES ABOUT EXECUTE

The EXECUTE statement builds a new "workspace" area for each "level" of EXECUTE. For example, the first time a program executes an EXECUTE statement, a block of workspace is attached, using frames from the overflow table. If this first level of EXECUTE were to run a PICK/BASIC program that also contained an EXECUTE statement, this "second-level" EXECUTE would also attach another set of workspace frames. As a protective mechanism, most versions of Pick provide a limit to the number of levels of EXECUTE. The Pick AT implementation, for example, limits each process to five levels of EXECUTE. This preventive measure is important; without it, one process could quickly "eat up" the entire disk.

FEEDING THE EXECUTE STATEMENT

All good things come with a price tag. In the case of the EXECUTE statement, this price tag is the DATA statement. Back in the old days, all SELECTs and SSELECTs were done from the PROC language. One obscure PROC instruction, called STON and pronounced "STack ON," was used to handle cases of issuing commands that required some further input. These days, when I teach people about the STON instruction, I relate it to "the mighty Carnac," the Johnny Carson character known for his telepathic abilities. His famous shtik is to hold an envelope up to his forehead and announce, "The answer is . . . "; then he opens the envelope to reveal the "question."

This is similar to the STON statement, which activates the Secondary Output Buffer in PROC (some people call this the S.O.B. for short). When a TCL process, such as a SELECT, is executed from the Primary Output Buffer, the command to deal with the result of the process (in this case, a select list) is placed in the Secondary Output Buffer. (This is like answering the question before it is asked.)

PICK/BASIC does not have a similar requirement. You don't have to worry about any of the nefarious input or output buffers. Rather, when a process like a SELECT is executed with an EXECUTE statement, the command to deal with the result of the process is "fed" from the DATA statement. Here are two lines of code that illustrate this principle:

```
001   DATA "SAVE-LIST STAFF.LIST"
002   EXECUTE "SSELECT STAFF BY NAME"
```

Note that the DATA statement containing the "answer" must occur in the program *before* the EXECUTE statement.

A CONTROVERSIAL STATEMENT ABOUT THE PROC LANGUAGE

The EXECUTE statement is a much more elegant way of handling TCL processes than its predecessor, the PROC language. One controversial point needs to be mentioned: The EXECUTE statement could single-handedly do away with the need for the PROC language. Yes, I know, all of your reports and menus are written in PROC—but that doesn't mean that you can't start doing things in PICK/BASIC with the EXECUTE statement, rather than relying on PROC interaction. The PROC language provided a "bridge" between PICK/BASIC and the ACCESS retrieval language. Now that PICK/BASIC can "talk" to ACCESS without getting confused, PROC is really no longer needed. The most important aspect of eliminating PROCs is that everything can be done in one programming language.

REVIEW QUIZ 14

1) What function does the EXECUTE statement perform?

2) What function does the CAPTURING clause perform in an EXECUTE statement?

3) What function does the HEADING statement perform?

4) What HEADING statement is required to print the following sample heading?

```
                    (top line blank)
           Aged Trial Balance Report      Page n
                as of (dd mmm yyyy)
                    (blank line)
```

5) What function does the READNEXT function serve?

6) What function does the PAGE statement serve?

17

External Subroutines

ANOTHER TYPE OF SUBROUTINE IS AVAILABLE IN THE PICK/BASIC LANGUAGE. THIS TYPE is called an *external subroutine*. A subroutine is a program that contains the statements to perform an operation. In Chapter 13, you examined local subroutines; a local subroutine is found in the same item as the program that uses it. An external subroutine, on the other hand is a separate item which contains program statements. Consequently, an external subroutine may be "shared" by multiple programs. This principle assists in making programs more *modular*.

Enter the programs in Fig. 17-1 and Fig. 17-2. Then compile and catalog them both.

ABOUT PROGRAM EXAMPLE 15

For Program Example 15, think of EX.015 as the master program. It "calls" the external subroutine STRIP.CONTROL. Examine the logic of EX.015, as illustrated in Fig. 17-1.

Line 6 starts a loop. On line 7, the screen is cleared and the cursor is positioned to column position 3 on row 3. The operator is prompted to enter a string that contains control characters. Note: When testing this program, be careful with the control characters you use; some of them do strange things to keyboards and terminals. A <Control-G> (the "bell") usually is a safe choice. Also, it is normal to *not* see a control character on the screen when it is entered. Enter several non-control characters along with the control characters, so that you will be better able to see the effect of the routine.

```
    EX.015
001 * EX.015
002 * External subroutines
003 * mm/dd/yy : date last modified
004 * JES : author's initials
005 *
006   LOOP
007     PRINT @(-1) : @(3,3) :
008     PRINT "ENTER A STRING THAT CONTAINS CONTROL CHARACTERS"
009     INPUT STRING
010   UNTIL STRING = "" OR STRING = "QUIT" DO
011     CALL STRIP.CONTROL(STRING)
012   REPEAT
013   PRINT "EX.015 TERMINATED"
014   END
```

Fig. 17-1. Program Example 15.

```
STRIP.CONTROL
001 SUBROUTINE STRIP.CONTROL(STRING)
002 * STRIPS CONTROL CHARACTERS FROM STRING
003 * mm/dd/yy : date last modified
004 * JES : author's initials
005 *
006   STRING = OCONV(STRING,"MCP")
007   PRINT "BEFORE STRIPPING, HERE'S HOW THE STRING LOOKS :"
008   PRINT STRING
009   PRINT
010 *
011 10 * LOOP TO STRIP CHARACTERS OUT
012 *
013   NUMBER.OF.DOTS = COUNT(STRING,".")   ;* HOW MANY ARE THERE?
014 *
015   FOR I = 1 TO NUMBER.OF.DOTS
016     FOUND = INDEX(STRING,".",1)
017     IF FOUND THEN
018       STRING = STRING[1,FOUND-1] : STRING[FOUND+1,33000]
019       PRINT STRING
020     END ELSE
021       PRINT "AFTER STRIPPING, HERE'S HOW IT LOOKS :"
022       PRINT STRING
023     END
024   NEXT I
025   RETURN
```

Fig. 17-2. The STRIP.CONTROL external subroutine.

The string containing the control characters is stored in the variable STRING on line 9. Line 10 checks to see if a null or the word "QUIT" was entered, in which case the program falls out of the loop, displays the message "EX.015 TERMINATED," and then stops.

If a non-null string is received, however, line 11 is executed. This "calls" the external subroutine:

```
011      CALL STRIP.CONTROL(STRING)
```

The CALL statement is used to locate and activate an external subroutine. It has the ability to "pass" arguments and/or expressions into the external subroutine, which may then act upon them, change them, and return them to the "master" program upon termination of the external subroutine.

The CALL statement has the general format:

CALL *program.name*

or

CALL *program.name(argument{,argument. . . })*

Any optional arguments passed from the master program must be *captured* by the external subroutine. The names of the variables do not necessarily have to be the same, but they must be passed in the same order that they are received. Any number of arguments may be passed, and each must be delimited by a comma. Note that the list of arguments must be enclosed in parentheses.

In EX.015, only one argument was passed into the STRIP.CONTROL external subroutine. This was the variable STRING, which is the string that contains the control characters.

CREATING AN EXTERNAL SUBROUTINE

Every external subroutine must have the SUBROUTINE statement on the first line of the program. The SUBROUTINE statement has the general format:

SUBROUTINE *{program.name}*

or

SUBROUTINE *{program.name} (argument{,argument. . . })*

In line 1 of the subroutine, STRIP.CONTROL, the following statement appears:

```
001 SUBROUTINE STRIP.CONTROL(STRING)
```

This defines the program as an external subroutine and further indicates the argument to be received.

196

Line 6 performs an output conversion on the STRING variable, using the "MCP" conversion code:

```
006    STRING = OCONV(STRING,"MCP")
```

The "MCP" conversion code "masks" all the control characters and turns them into periods. To a PICK/BASIC program, control characters are those characters in the ASCII coding scheme which have a decimal value from 1 through 31, and all of the characters above decimal 127. Unfortunately, this happens to include the special reserved delimiters (attribute, value, and subvalue marks), so special attention must be paid when using this function.

Line 7 displays the message:

```
BEFORE STRIPPING, HERE'S HOW THE STRING LOOKS :
```

Line 8 outputs the contents of the STRING variable. All of the control characters will now appear as periods in the string of characters that you entered.

STRIPPING CONTROL CHARACTERS FROM A STRING

The heart of subroutine STRIP.CONTROL is in lines 13-24:

```
013  NUMBER.OF.DOTS = COUNT(STRING,".") ;* HOW MANY?
014  *
015  FOR I = 1 TO NUMBER.OF.DOTS
016     FOUND = INDEX(STRING,".",1)
017     IF FOUND THEN
018        STRING = STRING[1,FOUND-1] :STRING[FOUND+1,33000]
019        PRINT STRING
020     END ELSE
021        PRINT "AFTER STRIPPING, HERE'S HOW IT LOOKS :"
022        PRINT STRING
023     END
024  NEXT I
```

On line 13 of the subroutine, the COUNT function is used to determine the number of periods (control characters) present in the string. The numeric value that the COUNT function returns is stored in the variable NUMBER.OF.DOTS, which is used as the upper boundary of the FOR-NEXT statement on line 15.

On line 16, the INDEX function is called upon to search for and report the character position of the first period in the STRING variable. If the INDEX function detects a period, the corresponding character position at which it was found is stored in the variable FOUND.

Line 17 checks the FOUND variable to determine if it is true (non-zero and numeric), which indicates that a period was found. If FOUND evaluates True, then the statements on lines 18 and 19 are executed, to remove the period from the string. Line 18 is:

```
STRING = STRING[1,FOUND-1] :STRING[FOUND+1,33000]
```

The first portion of this line, which is:

```
STRING = STRING[1,FOUND-1]
```

tells the program to perform a "text extraction" (substring) function on the variable STRING, extracting all of the characters from the first character in the string to the position indicated by the value of the calculation "FOUND-1" (found minus one).

Suppose, for instance, that the string appeared as:

XXX...XXX

When the statement STRING = STRING[1,FOUND-1] is applied against this value, the number 4 is stored in the variable FOUND, since the first period appears in the fourth character position of the string. Consequently, in this example, the statement:

```
STRING = STRING[1,FOUND-1]
```

would be exactly the same as executing the statement:

```
STRING = STRING[1,3]
```

The result of this operation is temporarily held while the second half of the statement is executed. This second portion appears as:

```
STRING[FOUND+1,33000]
```

A calculated text extraction again is performed. This time, the beginning character position is calculated by taking the current value of FOUND and adding 1 to it. This means that you are starting the extraction one character past the control character (period). The number of characters to extract from this beginning point is specified by the number 33000 (since no string can be larger than 32K anyway, this assures that the entire string is affected).

Using the same sample data as before:

XXX...XXX

The second portion would extract "..XXX" as the remaining characters in the string. Now the operation can be completed. Again, the statement appeared as:

```
STRING = STRING[1,FOUND-1] :STRING[FOUND+1,33000]
```

The ":" (concatenation) symbol appears between the two expressions. This takes the result from the first portion of the statement, concatenates the result of the second portion of the statement, and then stores the result back in the STRING variable. Line 19 displays the result of the operation. There will be one less period in the resulting string.

This loop is repeated until all of the control characters have been stripped from the string. Upon removing the last period, the resulting string is displayed and the external subroutine executes the RETURN statement on line 25. This returns execution to the next executable statement after the CALL statement in the master program. Just like internal subroutines, each external subroutine must contain at least one RETURN statement to return execution to the program that activated it.

Note that if the input string that was stripped of control characters had contained any "real" periods, they too would have been stripped. This could have been prevented by storing the "original" string in a variable and adding the following logic:

```
ORIGINAL = STRING
STRING = OCONV(STRING,"MCP")
    •
    •
IF FOUND AND ORIGINAL[FOUND,1] # "." THEN ...
```

SOME NOTES ABOUT MODULAR CODE AND SUBROUTINES

Making programming more modular has some distinct advantages. The program and external subroutine in Example 15 illustrated a means of stripping control character input from the keyboard. This external subroutine could be connected to every program that receives input to perform its single task. There are many other operations that are capable of being made modular, such as verifying a date to ensure that it is a valid format and within an acceptable range.

The single largest advantage to separating a self-standing operation as a module or external subroutine is that it only has to be coded once. This way, when you want to change the program or add a feature, it only has to be changed in one place. Another advantage occurs as a side effect of the first advantage. Programs start to become smaller as sections of redundant code are removed and replaced with calls to external subroutines.

Here's an example of a modular program:

```
PROGRAM: MAINLINE
001    CALL INITIALIZE
002    CALL GET.DATA
003    CALL POST
004    CALL WRAPUP
```

This is modular code to the extreme, although the special-purpose routines are not shared.

Some experts argue that "in-line" code runs faster than using external subroutines. This is true, but the tradeoffs are enormous. Using "in-line" code means that every time an operation is needed, the code for that operation is duplicated where it is needed. True "in-line" code avoids GOTO statements like the plague.

The basis of the defense of not using external subroutines is the overhead that is involved in fetching the executable object code from disk and loading it into main memory, where it may be used. It is no secret that the more trips that you have to make to the disk, the slower things go. In the old days, when RAM was expensive, this argument had some merit. These days, RAM is cheap, cheap, cheap! Many implementations of Pick allow multiple *megabytes* of RAM.

The nature of the Pick virtual memory manager is very friendly to external subroutines. Suppose a program called an external subroutine. If the executable object code for that particular subroutine is not found in main memory, then the code is located on disk and moved to an available *buffer* in real memory. This is known as *paging* or *frame-faulting*. If another program requests the same object code, it is detected in main memory and made immediately available to the requesting program. This is known as *program re-entrancy*.

As long as the code is resident in main memory, it is there for anyone who wants to use it. This makes for a very strong argument in favor of using subroutines. Not only does breaking programs into subroutines make applications more maintainable, but with large-memory systems, it is likely that the most often used subroutines will stay in main memory, since multiple processes may be requesting them.

18

Additional
PICK/BASIC Concepts

THIS CHAPTER COVERS A VARIETY OF TOPICS WHICH WERE TOUCHED ONLY LIGHTLY, or not at all, during the tutorial portion of the book. These include structured programming and programming standards, common PICK/BASIC instructions not used in the tutorial, and dealing with the Dictionary level of your BP (Basic Programs) file.

STRUCTURED PROGRAMMING

The phrase *structured programming* has been used to mean a collection of programming techniques designed to make programs better. Programmers disagree on what constitutes "better." Does it mean faster? Easier to analyze? Or something else? Some programmers prefer the term "programming standards," which doesn't limit the concept to control structures. Some common programming standards include the following:

1) Restricting the size of program structures. The idea is that something that is smaller is easier to understand. For example:

a) Limiting the size of separately compiled programs.
b) Limiting the size of local subroutines, for instance to one printer page, so that an entire programming function may be viewed at once.
c) Limiting the size of loops. One guideline limits loops to 20 lines, thus making it possible to easily see the scope of the loop.

2) Restricting the numbers and kinds of program structures. For example the LOOP construct allows many syntactical forms; limiting the choices to one (or two) forms keeps things consistent.

3) Avoiding the GOTO statement. Some experts believe that the *real* idea behind avoiding the GOTO statement is to do the following:

   a) *Never* branch into or out of an IF statement.
   b) *Never* branch into or out of a loop.

Whether or not you are a newcomer to programming, you would do well to adopt some programming standards when you write programs.

OTHER PICK/BASIC INSTRUCTIONS

Some instructions were not discussed during the course of this book. Those instructions follow in this section, along with a short, summary explanation of how they are used. The syntax for these instructions, as well as all of those covered in the text is found in Appendix A.

The CHAIN Statement

The CHAIN statement is somewhat similar to the EXECUTE statement, in that it allows any TCL expression to be executed. The one major difference between CHAIN and EXECUTE is that the EXECUTE statement is capable of returning to the program that issued the statement, and retaining all of the program variables. The CHAIN statement does not return to the program that executes it.

The COM or COMMON Statement

The COM or COMMON statement is used to declare variables that are to be "shared" among external subroutines. This is the alternative to passing variables into an external subroutine as arguments (immediately following the program name on the line that executes the CALL statement).

The common opinion about COMMON is: Don't use it. Using it makes program maintenance much more tedious, because each time a new variable is added to one program, it must be added to all the other programs that also will use it.

READU and MATREADU

The concept of group locks was discussed earlier in the text. The statement for reading a dynamic array is, of course, the READ statement, and the dimensioned array equivalent is the MATREAD statement.

The READU and MATREADU forms of these statements cause the group in which the requested item is found to be "group locked." These group locks remain in effect until:

1) The item is written with the appropriate "write" statement. (WRITE or MATWRITE).

2) The program terminates.

3) A RELEASE statement is issued.

Note that many of the implementations are now supporting *item locks* instead of just group locks.

WRITEU and MATWRITEU

The WRITEU and MATWRITEU statements differ from their "normal" counterparts in that they keep the group lock set even after the WRITE statement.

The ON-GOTO Statement

This statement is exactly like the ON-GOSUB statement discussed earlier, but with the difference that execution does not automatically return to the next line after completion.

The PROCWRITE Statement

The PROCWRITE statement provides PICK/BASIC the ability to "write" a string of characters, each of which is delimited by a space (except on Ultimate and McDonnell Douglas systems, where it is treated as a dynamic array), over the previous contents of the Primary Input Buffer.

The READV, READVU, WRITEV, and WRITEVU Statements

The READV statement is typically used by those who don't understand it. Rather than reading an entire item in one trip to disk, like the READ or MATREAD statement did, this reads items one attribute at a time. It has the general form:

> **READV** *variable.name* **FROM** *file.variable,id.expression*, ... *amc.expression*
> {**THEN** *statement(s)*} **ELSE** *statement(s)*

Note the *amc.expression* following the *id.expression*. This tells the statement which attribute from the array to read and store in the specified variable. This tends to be extremely wasteful. The only time it is allowed is when you only need one attribute from an item.

The RELEASE Statement

The RELEASE statement is used to release one or more group locks set by the current process. It has two general forms:

RELEASE

releases all group locks set by the current process.

RELEASE *file.variable,id.expression*

to release the group lock set on the group that the specified item resides in.

The SYSTEM Function

This intrinsic function has quite a few powerful features that come in handy from time to time. Unfortunately, it is not consistent across all Pick systems, so consult your PICK/BASIC manual for more information.

To illustrate some of its features, as found in "generic" Pick, here are two of the functions of SYSTEM:

SYSTEM(2)   Returns the current page width as defined by
the TERM statement:

```
IF SYSTEM(2) > 80 THEN ...
```

SYSTEM(14)   Returns the number of characters awaiting input
in the input buffer.

```
IF SYSTEM(14) THEN ...
```

The NULL Statement

The NULL statement is used almost exclusively as a mate for the THEN clause in an IF-THEN-ELSE statement. The NULL statement does absolutely nothing (this is what technical types call a "no-op"). It can be used as follows:

IF *conditional.expression* **THEN NULL ELSE** *statement*

Nested IF-THEN-ELSE Constructs

There are cases where "nested" IF statements are needed (Fig. 18-1). Special caution must be applied in terminating all of the initiators. Inevitably, you will run into something that appears even worse than this example. This is why there is the CASE statement, which simplifies these situations.

This brings up an important point. With a syntactical structure that is so flexible, some problems may crop up elsewhere; these problems typically occur by having one too many, or one too few END statements. For example, consider this case :

IF *conditional.expression* THEN<cr>	(starts level 1)
statement . . .	
IF *conditional.expression* THEN<cr>	(starts level 2)
statement . . .	
IF *conditional.expression* THEN<cr>	(starts level 3)
statement . . .	
END ELSE	(ends level-3 THEN)
statement . . .	(level-3 ELSE)
END	
statement(s)	(more code may go here)
END ELSE	(ends level-2 THEN)
statement . . .	*(level-2 ELSE)*
statement(s)	*(more code may go here)*
END ELSE	*(ends level-1 THEN)*
statement	(level-1 ELSE)
END	(ends level-1 ELSE)

Fig. 18-1. Nesting IF-THEN-ELSE structures.

```
001   IF        conditional.expression THEN statement
002         IF        conditional.expression THEN statement
003            IF        conditional.expression ELSE statement
004                  statement
005                  statement
006         END
007   END
008   more code
009   more code
010   END
```

The programmer may have forgotten one of the critical END statements in the nested IF-THEN. The effect is that the compiler erroneously thinks that the first END statement (at line 6) belongs to the third level, that the second END statement (at line 7) belongs to the second level, and that the third END statement (in this case, at line 10) belongs to the first level. This sneaks through the compiler without any problem, other than the effect of not working properly.

The PRECISION Statement

The PRECISION statement declares the number of positions to be carried in mathematical calculations. It needs to be declared only once. The normal default setting on most systems is 4 (four), if left undeclared. The maximum varies from system to system. Ultimate now allows a maximum of 9, McDonnell Douglas allows 6, and the rest of the generic machines (unless they have been changed) allow 4.

COMMENT SECTIONS REVISITED

In Chapter 2, comment sections were introduced. Many other useful pieces of information could have been included in the comment section, but only the first four lines were used throughout the examples. Among the other kinds of information which could be included are:

☐ Any external subroutines called by the program

☐ A list of files affected by the program

☐ A list of input variables (variables passed to a local or external subroutine)

☐ A list of output variables (variables returned from a local or external subroutine)

☐ Any special processing considerations, such as the need for special forms, a tape, an external select, etc.

☐ Security restrictions: port number, account name, time, date, security clearance level, etc.

☐ Revision history. This is simply a list of the last batch of changes made to the program, along with the date and initials of the programmer who made the changes.

DICTIONARY ENTRIES FOR YOUR BP FILE

Now that you have diligently followed the convention of filling out the comments section in each of your programs, they may be put to some practical use. This involves using the Editor to build attribute definition items in the DICT (dictionary) level of the BP file, as shown in Fig. 18-2.

Since these three attributes are the only ones that are of interest for the moment, these attribute definition items will suffice. Naturally, if you decide to use any of the other suggested items in your templates, attribute definition items should be placed in the dictionary to correspond with them.

Now build the "implicit" attribute defining items, which show themselves automatically.

```
>COPY DICT BP DESCRIPTION DATE AUTHOR<cr>
TO:1 2 3<cr>
```

ACCESS sentences may now be used on the BP file. For example:

```
>SORT BP BY DATE DATE DESCRIPTION AUTHOR<cr>
```

Item-id : DESCRIPTION

001	A	Attribute pointer type.
002	2	Attribute number containing description.
003	DESCRIPTION	Column heading above output.
004		null
005		null
006		null
007		null
008	T3,80	Text extract to skip the "*" and extract text.
009	T	Text justification to break between words.
010	30	Width of output column.

Item-id : DATE

001	A	Attribute pointer type.
002	3	Attribute number containing date last modified.
003	DATE	Column heading above output.
004		null
005		null
006		null
007	D2/	Date output conversion, output formatted MM/DD/YY.
008	T3,8]DI	Text extract to skip the "*" and extract the date, which is stored in external format. The "]" character is a value mark (control] or control-shift]), which takes the external date and pushes it through the "date internal" conversion to convert it to its internal equivalent.
009	R	Right justification.
010	8	Width of output column.

Item-id : AUTHOR

001	A	Attribute pointer type.
002	4	Attribute number containing initials.
003	AUTHOR	Column heading above output.
004		null
005		null

Fig. 18-2. Attribute definitions in the DICT portion of the BP file.

006	null
007	null
008 T3,3	Text extract to skip the "*" and extract text.
009 L	Left justification.
010 3	Width of output column.

---

or, for the report in order by program name:

>**SORT BP**<cr>

or, to direct the output to the printer, simply add a (P) option:

>**SORT BP (P)**<cr>

Instruction Syntax and Compatibility

KEEPING UP WITH THE MANUFACTURERS' CHANGES TO THE PICK/BASIC LANGUAGE IS NEARLY IMPOSsible, given that there are now about 30 licensees. The three main branches of development still remain:

1) Ultimate, which includes the Honeywell- and DEC-based systems.

2) McDonnell Douglas, which includes the REALITY, SPIRIT, and SEQUEL product lines.

3) Pick, which is essentially everybody else.

A few of the licensees have implemented some of each other's features, so you may have to check in your system reference manuals.

Syntactical or operational differences are noted throughout this appendix by means of *compatibility icons*:

Pick	*Ultimate*	*McDonnell Douglas*
P	U	M

The absence of icons accompanying a particular statement or feature indicates that it is common to all three developmental branches of Pick. (All licensees are invited to submit their enhancements for inclusion in subsequent editions.)

For unfamiliar terms, please refer to the glossary, which contains definitions of the standard terms used in the Pick System, along with the special terms that were created during the writing of this guide.

Reprinted with permission from *The Pick Pocket Guide* (copyright 1982 by Jonathan E. Sisk.)

FORMAT OF PICK/BASIC PROCESSING COMMANDS

Described below are the standard forms of the PICK/BASIC processing commands.

>**ED** *filename itemlist* {(options)}*
>**EDIT** *filename itemlist* {(options)}*

Activates the editor process for entry of any file-resident item in the system (e.g., programs, PROCs, data items, etc.).

>**EED** *filename itemlist* {(options)}*
>**EEDIT** *filename itemlist* {(options)}*

Activates the editor process for entry of any file-resident item in the system (i.e., programs, PROCs, data items, etc.). EED and EEDIT compress all occurrences of three or more blanks or asterisks in a line into a more compact form for storage on disk. When these have been used on a PICK/BASIC program, it must then be compiled with the EBASIC command. (EED, EEDIT, and EBASIC are available only on Ultimate and McDonnell Douglas Systems).

Here are the options for ED, EDIT, EED, and EEDIT:

A   Activates the Assembly formatter. Equivalent to the AS editor command.   **P** **U**

P   Directs output to system printer, via spooler.   **P** **U**

M   Activates the Macro expansion function. Equivalent to the M editor command.   **P** **U**

S   Suppresses the display of line numbers in normal edit mode, or suppresses object code display when the assembly formatter is "on." Equivalent to the S editor command.   **P** **U**

Z   Suppresses the "Top" and "EOI" messages.

About PICK/BASIC Source Code Files. The file containing PICK/BASIC source code must be defined as a two-level file, that is, it must have both a DICTionary and DATA section. The (D-pointer) entry in the MD defining the location of the dictionary must have a "DC" in line one, as this defines the pointer file area for storing object code.

About Object Pointers. Once a program has been compiled, an entry is placed in the dictionary. This "pointer" item defines the virtual location where the object code is actually stored. The name of the pointer item is the same as that of the source program itself. It has the following format:

Attribute	*Description*
1. CC	Object pointer identifier.
2. fid	First frame-id of object.
3. "modulo"	Number of frames of object.
4. (null)	
5. (time/date)	Time/date of compile. **P** **U**

The Pick System prevents the use of the Editor on these object pointers. Use the LIST-ITEM or SORT-ITEM command on the DICT of the source file to examine them.

>**BASIC** *filename itemlist* {(options)}*
>**COMPILE** *filename itemlist* {(options)}*

`P` `U`

Note: The BASIC verb, and any verb for that matter, may be copied to a different name in the MD, provided that the choice of the new name does not already exist.

>**EBASIC** *filename itemlist* {(options)}*

`U` `M`

Activates PICK/BASIC compiler for translation of source code into object code. May only be used on programs that were entered with the EED or EEDIT verb.

Ultimate and McDonnell Douglas Only: The EBASIC command is used on programs entered with the EED or EEDIT commands.

Ultimate Only: See also the PICK/BASIC statements $INCLUDE, $CHAIN, $NODEBUG, and $ *. PICK/BASIC now allows for blank lines. These are occasionally useful for visual separation of code segments.

Here is a list of the available options:

A   Outputs assembled PICK/BASIC object code.   `P` `U`

B   Compiles with backward compatibility.   `M`

C   Compiles object code without end-of-line characters.   `P` `U`

E   Outputs error lines only.   `P` `U`

L   Lists program as it compiles

M   Generates program map.

N   Activates NOPAGE function on output to terminal.

P   Directs output to system printer, via spooler.

Q   Activates PAGE mode on errors.   `P` `U`

S   Suppresses symbol table generation.   `P` `U`

X   *Pick and Ultimate Only:* Cross-references all variables and places entries
     in the BSYM file.

     McDonnell Douglas Only: Cross-references all variables and places entries
     in the CSYM file.

ACTIVATING A PICK/BASIC PROGRAM

`U`

"Compile And Go" Programs. Available only on Ultimate systems, "Compile and Go" programs are vaguely similar to PROCs. They are placed into the MD, and must have either the word "PROGRAM" or "PROG" on the first line of the program. Once filed through the Editor, they are activated just as if they were cataloged, simply by entering the name of the program.

Compiled PICK/BASIC Programs. PICK/BASIC programs compiled via the COMPILE or BASIC command are activated as follows:

>**RUN** *filename itemname {arguments} { (options}*

This executes a compiled PICK/BASIC program. Note that arguments may be passed into the program directly from the TCL command.

Here is a list of the available options:

A   Prohibits entry into PICK/BASIC debugger; aborts on error conditions. **P U**

D   Enters PICK/BASIC debugger prior to execution. Important when parameters are passed in a CALL statement.

E   Enters debugger on any error condition.

F   Enters debugger on any error condition. **M**

I   Inhibits variable initialization.

N   Activates NOPAGE function, on output to terminal.

P   Directs output from PRINT statements to system printer, via spooler.

S   Suppresses run-time warning messages. (Very useful for demonstrations.)

T   Inhibits creation of tape label on tape writing operations. **M**

ABOUT CATALOGING PROGRAMS

Programs in PICK/BASIC may be placed in a "catalog" with the following command:

>CATALOG *filename itemlist** { (L})

Effectively, this command creates a "verb" from a compiled PICK/BASIC program, by placing an entry in the current account's Master Dictionary that allows execution of the program by entering the program name at TCL. It is required for any program defined as an external subroutine.

Ultimate Only: See also the "Compile and Go" programs explained above. Also note that the L option is used when the program being cataloged has the same name as the account in which it resides. This option prevents this program from being automatically executed as a logon procedure each time the account is entered.

McDonnell Douglas Only: Each program must be individually cataloged.

ACTIVATING A COMPILED AND CATALOGED PICK/BASIC PROGRAM

Once a program has been cataloged, it may be activated by typing the program name at the TCL prompt character:

>*programname {arguments} { (options) }*

Ultimate Only: Arguments may be passed directly from the TCL command into the program. Note also that the CATALOG command no longer checks to see whether or not there is source for the program, as long as the object code exists.

Ultimate and Pick: It is not necessary to CATALOG a program each time it is compiled. Here is a list of the options available with this form of the command:

A   Prohibits entry into PICK/BASIC debugger; aborts on error conditions. **P U**

D	Enters PICK/BASIC debugger prior to execution. Important when parameters are passed in a CALL statement.
E	Enters debugger on any error condition.
F	Enters debugger on any error condition.
I	Inhibits variable initialization.
N	Activates NOPAGE function, on output to terminal.
P	Directs output from PRINT statements to system printer, via spooler.
S	Suppresses run-time warning messages. (Very useful for demonstrations.)
T	Inhibits creation of tape label on tape writing operations.

>DECATALOG *filename itemlist**

Removes verb entry from current account's Master Dictionary and deletes object code created via a previous compile-and-catalog process. May be used to delete object code even if the program has not previously been cataloged.

:DELETE-CATALOG *itemlist**

Removes verb entry from current account's Master Dictionary and deletes object pointer from POINTER-FILE, which was put there during a previous CATALOG process. Each program must be decataloged separately. In other words, "*" may not be specified as an itemlist.

Note also the following special operations which are supported on McDonnell Douglas systems:

:BREF { (P) }

Activates procedure to produce a cross-reference listing of variables and labels in the CSYM file, put there by using the X option with the BASIC command.

:BVERIFY *itemlist** {*acctname*} { *(options)* }

Compares file-resident object code (*$program.name*) to its corresponding (catalog) entry. Options:

A	Lists all mismatches.
P	Directs output to printer, via spooler.

:PRINT-CATALOG *filename itemlist** {*acctname*}

Displays the time and date program(s) in catalog space were last compiled successfully. Also displays the precision specified in program, the source file, and item-ids (program names).

:PRINT-HEADER *filename itemlist** { (P) }

Displays the time and date that file-resident object code program(s) were last compiled successfully. Also displays the precision, source file, and item-ids (program names).

Catalogs a list or screen item that subsequently may be shared among multiple programs as constant data. Must be referenced in program with the SHARE statement.

OPERATORS AND OTHER RESERVED CHARACTERS

The following keyboard characters have special meanings in the PICK/BASIC language:

Character	*Meaning/Example*

:   1) Print line delimiter

```
PRINT "The current time is " : TIME()
```

2) Concatenation operator

```
WHOLE.NAME = FIRST.NAME : " " : LAST.NAME
```

;   Source line delimiter. Must be followed by a valid PICK/BASIC instruction.

```
ITEM.COUNTER=0 ; * Reset number-of-items counter
```

@   A string function which is used for cursor control when directing output to a CRT.

```
PRINT@(-1) :@(20,0) :"Main Menu" :@(58,0) :TIMEDATE()
```

McDonnell Douglas Only: The full range of "(-n)" options is not yet available.

,   Alternate print line delimiter. Puts 18 spaces between expressions being printed.

```
PRINT "Name" , "Address" , "Phone"
```

Also used to separate parameters in functions:

```
PRINT OCONV(DATE(),"D2")
```

and to separate arguments being passed to or from external subroutines:

```
CALL PROCESS.SAMPLE(AMOUNT,SUBTOTAL,GRAND.TOTAL)
```

!   Remark or comment indicator. (Same as * or REM statement)

```
100 ! Start Main Loop
```

Also used as a logical "or" statement. (Same as an "OR")

```
IF ANSWER = "QUIT" ! ANSWER = "END" THEN STOP
IF ANSWER = "QUIT" OR ANSWER = "END THEN STOP
```

&   Logical "and" statement. (Same as an "AND")

```
IF OPTION > 1 & OPTION < 10 THEN GOTO 10 ELSE STOP
IF OPTION > 1 AND OPTION < 10 THEN GOTO 10 ELSE STOP
```

=   Logical comparative operator for "equal to."

```
IF ANSWER = "YES" THEN PRINTER ON
```

Also used to assign a value to a variable or constant.

```
TODAY = DATE()
```

Logical comparative operator for "not equal to." (Same as using the > < or < > symbols).

```
IF ANSWER # "NO" THEN PRINTER ON
```

–   Mathematical operator for subtraction.

```
PROFIT = SALES - EXPENSES
```

+   Mathematical operator for addition.

```
TOTAL.EXPENSES = DIRECT.EXPENSES + INDIRECT.EXPENSES
```

/   Mathematical operator for division.

```
AVERAGE.SALARY = TOTAL.SALARY / NUMBER.OF.EMPLOYEES
```

*   Mathematical operator for multiplication.

```
GROSS.PAY = HOURLY.RATE * * HOURS.WORKED
```

Also used to indicate remark or comments when used as the first character on a source line.

```
* Now prepare to process employee deductions
```

^   Mathematical operator for exponentiation.

```
MAXIMUM.VALUE = BASE.FACTOR ^ POWER.FACTOR
```

<   Logical comparative operator for "less than."

```
IF RESPONSE>0 THEN PRINT "Response must be positive!"
```

Also used as a subscript indicator in dynamic arrays.

```
EQU CUSTOMER.NAME.ATTRIBUTE TO 1
PRINT CUSTOMER.ITEM<CUSTOMER.NAME.ATTRIBUTE>
```

>   Logical comparative operator for "greater than."

```
IF HOURS.WORKED > 40 THEN OVERTIME.FLAG = TRUE
```

Also used as a subscript indicator in dynamic arrays.

```
EQU CUSTOMER.ADDRESS.ATTRIBUTE TO 2
CUSTOMER.ITEM<CUSTOMER.ADDRESS.ATTRIBUTE>=NEW.ADDRESS
```

'   String delimiter. Used to indicate literal text.

```
PRINT 'Please enter the check amount ' :
```

"   String delimiter. Used to indicate literal text.

```
PRINT "Do you want the report printed ? " :
```

Note that for the most part, single quotes (') and double quotes (") are interchangeable. The HEADING and FOOTING statements in PICK/BASIC are particular about how quotes are used.

[*n,n*]   Text extraction (substring) indicator. These always travel in pairs. When the "open" (left) bracket is used, it must be "closed" with the right bracket.

```
IF ANSWER[1,1] = "Y" THEN STOP
```

216

The arguments within the brackets are expressions which derive numeric values. The first argument is the beginning position of the character within the string being affected. The second argument indicates the number of characters to retrieve. For example:

```
PHONE.NUMBER = "714-555-1212"
PRINT "AREA CODE = " : PHONE.NUMBER[1,3]
```

The above line prints "714".

```
PRINT "PHONE = " : PHONE.NUMBER[5,8]
```

The above line prints "555-1212".

( ) Function delimiter. These characters are required with virtually every intrinsic function in PICK/BASIC.

```
PRINT@(-1) :TIMEDATE() :@(25,0) :"Inventory maintenance"
```

Additionally, each reference to a dimensioned array element requires the parentheses. (See the coverage of the DIM statement for more information on dimensioned arrays.)

```
PRINT OCONV(INVOICE.ITEM(PAYMENT.DATE),"D2/")
```

Finally, parentheses are used to change the standard precedence of mathematical expressions. See "Precedence of Operators."

SPECIAL RESERVED WORDS

Any word that is part of the PICK/BASIC language should be avoided for use as a variable name. While it might work, the resulting code could be ambiguous to other programmers who support it, and that's no guarantee that it will work forever.

Compatibility note: Some of the words listed in Table A-1 may be unique to one particular version of the system, such as Ultimate. To be on the safe side, try to avoid using these words because of the possibility of future implementation on your system.

PRECEDENCE OF OPERATORS

Listed below are the precedences of all the arithmetic, relational, and other operators in the PICK/BASIC language:

Symbol	Precedence	Operation
^	1	Exponentiation

Table A-1. PICK/BASIC Reserved Words.

!	*	=	@
ABORT	ABS	ALPHA	AND
ASCII	BEGIN CASE	BREAK	CALL
CASE	CAT	CHAIN	CHAR
CLEAR	CLEARFILE	CLOSE	COL1
COL2	COM	COMMON	COS
COUNT	DATA	DATE	DCOUNT
DEL	DELETE	DIM	DISPLAY
DO	DTX	EBCDIC	ECHO
ELSE	END	END CASE	ENTER
EOF	EQ	EQU	EQUATE
ERROR	EXECUTE	EXIT	EXP
EXTRACT	FADD	FCMP	FDIV
FFIX	FFLT	FIELD	FMUL
FSUB	FOOTING	FOR	GE
GET	GOSUB	GOTO	GO TO
GT	HEADING	ICONV	IF
INDEX	INPUT	INPUTCLEAR	INS
INSERT	INT	LE	LEN
LET	LN	LOCATE	LOCK
LOOP	LT	MAT	MATCHES
MATCH	MATREAD	MATREADU	MATWRITE
MATWRITEU	MOD	NEXT	NE
NOT	NULL	NUM	OCONV
ON GOSUB	ON GOTO	OPEN	OR
PAGE	PRECISION	PRINT	PRINTER
PRINTERR	PROCREAD	PROCWRITE	PROGRAM
PROMPT	PUT	PWR	READ
READNEXT	READT	READU	READV
READVU	RELEASE	REM	REPEAT
REPLACE	RETURN	RETURN TO	REWIND
RND	RQM	SADD	SCMP
SDIV	SEEK	SELECT	SEQ
SIN	SMUL	SPACE	SQRT
SSUB	STEP	STOP	STORAGE
STR	SUBROUTINE	SYSTEM	TAN
THEN	TIME	TIMEDATE	TO
TRIM	UNLOCK	UNTIL	WEOF
WHILE	WRITE	WRITET	WRITEU
WRITEV	WRITEVU		

Symbol	Precedence	Operation
*	2	Multiplication
/	2	Division
+	3	Addition
−	3	Subtraction
	4	Masking
	5	Concatenation
	6	Relational operators
	7	And/or

For program clarity, it may be useful to use parentheses in complex mathematical operations, rather than relying on the precedence of the operator. Expressions are evaluated in order of precedence unless placed within parentheses. Expressions within the innermost parentheses are evaluated first.

LOGICAL EXPRESSIONS

Logical operators typically appear between conditional expressions in an IF-THEN or IF-THEN-ELSE construct. They have the property of determining when the THEN or ELSE clause is taken.

When conditional expressions are separated by a logical OR, or its "!" equivalent, the expressions are mutually exclusive. If either expression evaluates true, then the THEN statement (or statements) is executed. For example:

```
IF X = 1 OR X = "Y" THEN...
```

When conditional expressions are separated by a logical AND, or its "&" equivalent, the expressions are mutually dependent. If both expressions evaluate true, then the THEN statement (or statements) is executed. For example:

```
IF X > 1 AND X < 10 THEN...
```

SUBSTRING EXPRESSIONS

The expression shown below allows the extraction of a "fixed" string of characters from within another string of characters:

variable[*beginning.expression,length.expression*]

The *beginning.expression* evaluates to a number indicating the starting position within the string, and the *length.expression* evaluates to a number indicating the number of characters to be retrieved.

ARRAY REFERENCE EXPRESSIONS

Dimensioned Array Reference. References to dimensioned (static) arrays may take either of the following forms:

array.variable (*amc.expression*)
array.variable (*numeric.expression, numeric.expression*)

Dimensioned arrays have a maximum of two dimensions and must first be defined with a DIM or DIMENSION statement.

Dynamic Array Reference. References to dynamic arrays can take any of the following forms:

variable < *amc.expression* >
array.variable < *amc.expression,vmc.expression* >
array.variable < *amc.expression,vmc.expression,svmc.expression* >

Also see the DEL, DELETE, EXTRACT, INS, INSERT, LOCATE, and REPLACE statements.

PATTERN MATCHING RELATIONAL OPERATORS

The MATCH or MATCHES pattern-matching relational operators may be invoked in either of the following ways:

expression **MATCH** *match.expression*
expression **MATCHES** *match.expression*

See MATCH and MATCHES in the alphabetic listing of PICK/BASIC instructions.

LOGICAL OPERATORS

The logical operators available in PICK/BASIC are:

< or LT	Less than
> or GT	Greater than
< = or LE	Less than or equal to
> = or GE	Greater than or equal to
= or EQ	Equal to
# or NE	Not equal to
< > or > <	Not equal to

CONCATENATION OPERATORS

Strings may be concatenated (linked end-to-end) in either of the following two ways:

string.expression **CAT** *string.expression*
string.expression : *string.expression*

MASKING FUNCTION

The masking function performs formatting of output data values, using the following general format:

PRINT *variable mask.expression*

where *mask.expression* elements include:

Justification . . .
{number of digits after decimal} . . .
{scaling factor} . . .
{Z (suppresses leading zeros)} . . .
{, (inserts commas where appropriate)} . . .
{credit/debit indicator} . . .
{$ (appends dollar sign)} . . .
fill character . . .
{length}

The scaling factor defaults to the PRECISION statement of the program. If the length of the mask is omitted, the actual length of the field is used. Here are the other types of masks:

Justifications:

R   Right justified
L   Left justified

Credit/Debit Indicators:

C   Outputs CR after negative value
D   Outputs DB after positive values
E   Outputs "<" before and ">" after negative values
M   Outputs "−" after negative values
N   Suppresses leading minus sign on negative numbers

Special Fill Characters:

%n   Fills with *n* zeros.
#n   Fills with *n* blanks.
*n   Fills with *n* asterisks.

(Any other character may be substituted as a fill character.)

Here are two examples of masking:

```
PRINT X "R#12"

PRINT Y "L#15"
PRINT Z "R#12Z,E$*12"
```

PICK/BASIC STATEMENTS AND FUNCTIONS

The difference between PICK/BASIC statements and functions is relatively simple; If the syntax requires that the instruction be followed by a set of parentheses (optionally containing an argument or arguments), then it is a *function*. For example, the following are functions:

ABS (*numeric.expression*)
RND (*numeric.expression*)

ICONV (*string.expression,conversion.expression*)

Any instruction that does *not* have to be followed by a set of parentheses is a *statement*. For example:

PRINT X
INPUT Y
EXECUTE SENTENCE

The balance of this section is an examination (in alphabetical order) of the PICK/BASIC statements and functions.

! (Exclamation Point)

Logical "OR" statement. Also used to define user-specified remarks. See "Logical Expressions," or just use an OR.

* (Asterisk)

Mathematical operator (multiplication); also used to define user-specified remarks. Example of use in multiplication:

```
X = 10 * 20
```

Example of use as a remark (or comment) statement:

```
100 * Mainline ....
```

When used as a remark, the entire line is ignored by the compiler.

@ (The "At" Sign)

Cursor control (intrinsic) function. See the PRINT @ statement for arguments. Here is a typical usage:

```
PRINT @(-1) : @(20,0) : "Enter Customer"
```

Note: McDonnell Douglas does not yet support the full set of intrinsic functions for the @ sign.

$ * text   `U`

Places specified text into object code of PICK/BASIC program.

$CHAIN {filename} itemname   `U`

Instructs the compiler to link the current source code to the specified item in the optionally specified file. If *filename* is omitted, the current file is assumed.

$INCLUDE {filename} itemname   `U`

Instructs the compiler to retrieve the item specified and to include its source code in the program being compiled. If the filename is omitted, the current file is assumed.

$NODEBUG   `U`

Prevents end-of-lines (EOL) from being included in object code and suppresses generation of the symbol table. Note that the PICK/BASIC debugger is virtually useless once this has been performed on a program. The equivalent of this function is the use of the "C" and "S" options with the BASIC or COMPILE command.

ABORT *errmsg#*
ABORT *errmsg#,"parameter"{,"parameter" . .}*

Terminates program and PROC(s). The parameter(s) are passed to the error message handler and displayed with the message stored in the message number indicated by *errmsg#*. Any message in the ERRMSG file may be used. See also the STOP statement.

ABS(*numeric.expression*)

Returns the absolute value of the numeric expression in parentheses.

ALPHA(*expression*)

Returns a one (true) if *expression* contains only alphabetic characters, or zero (false) if it contains any non-alphabetic characters.

ASCII(*expression*)

Converts an EBCDIC expression to its ASCII equivalent. The inverse of EBCDIC.

BEGIN CASE

Initiates the CASE statement. For example:

BEGIN CASE
    CASE *conditional.expression*
     statement(s)
    CASE *conditional.expression*
     statement(s)
    .
    .
END CASE

See the CASE statement.

BREAK ON

Enables the break key on the CRT.

BREAK KEY ON

Disables the break key on the CRT.

BREAK OFF

Disables the break key on the CRT.

BREAK KEY OFF　　　　　　　　　　　　　　　　　　　　　　　　　　　**M**

Disables the break key on the CRT.

BREAK *expression*　　　　　　　　　　　　　　　　　　　　　　　　　　**P**

Disables the break key when *expression* evaluates false (zero). Enables the break key when *expression* evaluates true (non-zero).

CALL *cataloged-program-name*
CALL *cataloged-program-name(argument)*
CALL *cataloged-program-name(argument,argument, . . .)*

Transfers program control, either directly or indirectly, to an external subroutine, passing all arguments in list. Arguments must be separated by commas; there is a maximum of about 200 arguments. Example of a direct CALL:

```
CALL PROCESS.LINES(ID,ORDER.ITEM(1))
```

Example of an indirect CALL:

```
PROGRAM.VARIABLE = "PROCESS.LINES"
CALL @PROGRAM.VARIABLE(ID,ORDER.ITEM(1))
```

Avoid using this form due to high overhead.
　　Ultimate Only: When passing many arguments to an external subroutine, they may be placed on multiple source lines. When using this form, each line must *end* with a comma. The last argument must still be followed with a closing (right) parentheses.

CASE *conditional.expression*
CASE *conditional.expression* ; *statement* {; *statement* . . .}

Conditional execution function, based on whether the value being tested meets the criterion (or criteria) defined in the conditional expression. For example:

```
BEGIN CASE
   CASE conditional.expression
      statement(s)
         .
         .
         .
   CASE conditional.expression
      statement(s)
         .
         .
         .
   CASE 1
      statement(s)
         .
END CASE
```

CASE 1 is typically used at the end of a set of CASE statements as the condition to perform if none of the other CASE statements are executed.

CAT or :

Concatenation operator; used to join strings.

CHAIN *TCL-expression*

Transfers control to TCL, which interprets and executes the command defined in the expression. Note that control does not return to the program. See also the EXECUTE statement.

CHAR (*numeric.expression*)

Returns the ASCII character equivalent of a numeric value. The inverse of SEQ.

CLEAR

Initializes all variables to zero. Avoid using this, as it makes debugging programs nearly impossible.

CLEARFILE {**ON ERROR** *statement(s)*}
CLEARFILE *file.variable* {**ON ERROR** *statement(s)*}

Deletes all items in specified file variable, just like the TCL CLEAR-FILE command. The default file variable is cleared if no file variable is specified.
Ultimate Only: Only the Ultimate system allows the ON ERROR condition, which is taken if the file is remote (accessed through UltiNet) and the file can't be cleared due to a network error condition; in this instance, SYSTEM(0) contains the UltiNet error message number.

CLOSE {**ON ERROR** *statement(s)*}
CLOSE *file.variable* {**ON ERROR** *statement(s)*}

Closes a file variable previously opened with an OPEN statement. The default file variable is closed if no file variable is specified.
Ultimate Only: Only the Ultimate system allows the ON ERROR condition, which is taken if the file is remote (accessed through UltiNet) and the file can't be cleared due to a network error condition; in this instance, SYSTEM(0) contains the UltiNet error message number.

COL1( )

Returns the numeric column position of the character preceding the substring retrieved in the most recently executed FIELD statement.

COL2( )

Returns the numeric column position of the character following the substring retrieved in the most recently executed FIELD statement.

COM *variable{,variable. . .}*
COMMON *variable{,variable. . .}*

Indicates data elements to share among programs executed by a CHAIN, ENTER, or CALL statement; also defines the storage order for variables.

Note: When using a CHAIN or ENTER statement to initiate another run-time PICK/BASIC program, the ''I'' option must be used with the RUN command (at TCL) to prevent the reinitialization of variables in workspace and to keep the COMMON area intact. Suggestion: Don't use COMMON in conjunction with CHAIN OR ENTER.

COS(*numeric.expression***)**

Calculates the cosine of the angle specified in the numeric expression, and returns the results in degrees.

COUNT(*string.expression1,string.expression2***)**

Returns the number of occurrences of *string.expression2* within *string.expression1*.

CRT
CRT *expression*

Directs output unconditionally to the terminal. Functions like the PRINT statement, but is not affected by the (P) option used with the RUN command at TCL; the PRINTER ON statement; nor the HEADING, FOOTING, and PAGE statements.
Ultimate Only: See the DISPLAY statement.

DATA *expression{,expression, . . .}*

Holds value(s) for use by subsequent input requests initiated from CHAIN, ENTER, EXECUTE, or INPUT statements.

DATE( )

Returns current system date in internal format.

DCOUNT(*string.expression1,string.expression2***)**

Returns the number of occurrences of the delimiter specified by *string.expression2* within *string.expression1*. The *string.expression2* parameter must be any character being treated as a delimiter, including the system delimiters like attribute marks, value marks, and subvalue marks. The difference between this statement and the COUNT statement is that the value 1 is added to the result unless the string referenced in *string.expression1* is null.

DEBUG

Transfers control to PICK/BASIC symbolic debugger upon execution.

DEL *array.variable < amc.expression >*
DEL *array.variable < amc.expression,vmc.expression >*
DEL *array.variable < amc.expression,vmc.expression,svmc.expression >*

Deletes specified attribute, value, or subvalue from a dynamic array. See also the DELETE intrinsic function.

DELETE(*array.variable,amc.expression*)
DELETE(*array.variable,amc.expression,vmc.expression*)
DELETE(*array.variable,amc.expression,vmc.expression,svmc.expression*)

Deletes specified attribute, value, or subvalue from a dynamic array. In this form, the DELETE is always on the right side of an equals (=) sign.

DELETE *id.expression* {**ON ERROR** *statement(s)*}
DELETE *file.variable,id.expression* {**ON ERROR** *statement(s)*}

Deletes specified item-id expression from optionally specified file variable.
Ultimate Only: Only the Ultimate system allows the ON ERROR condition, which is taken if the file is remote (accessed through UltiNet) and the file can't be cleared due to a network error condition; in this instance, SYSTEM(0) contains the UltiNet error message number.

DIM *array.variable(dimension)*
DIM *array.variable(dimension1,dimension2)*

Defines a dimensioned array. In the first form, a single-dimensional vector is established. In the second form, a two-dimensional matrix is established. The two-dimensional vector has *nothing* to do with the handling of multivalues or subvalues in conjunction with the MATREAD or MATREADU statements. For example:

```
DIM CUSTOMER.ITEM(15)
```

This defines the array CUSTOMER.ITEM and reserves 15 storage locations for holding the corresponding attributes when retrieved with the MATREAD or MATREADU statement.

DISPLAY
DISPLAY *expression*

Directs output unconditionally to the terminal. Functions like the PRINT statement, but is not affected by the (P) option used with the RUN command at TCL; the PRINTER ON statement; nor the HEADING, FOOTING, and PAGE statements. Note that output may not be directed with the OUT. function in the EXECUTE statement.
Pick Only: See the CRT statement.

DO

Initiator for the REPEAT portion of the LOOP statement. See the LOOP-WHILE and the LOOP-UNTIL statements.

EBCDIC(*expression*)

Converts an ASCII expression to its EBCDIC equivalent. The inverse of ASCII.

ECHO OFF

Disables terminal character echo mode. Characters entered on the keyboard are not displayed on the terminal.

ECHO ON

Enables terminal character echo mode. All characters entered on the keyboard are displayed on the terminal.

ECHO *expression*

Enables terminal character echo mode when *expression* evaluates as true. Disables terminal character echo mode when *expression* evaluates as false.

ELSE

Precedes statements to execute when the IF clause evaluates as false, typically:

IF *conditional.expression* {**THEN** *statement(s)*} {**ELSE** *statement(s)*}

See the section on the THEN-ELSE construct.

END

Used as a terminator in two ways. As a *physical program end*, it is not required in PICK/BASIC source code (except on McDonnell Douglas systems), but is helpful for program readability:

```
. . . statements . . .
. . . body of program . . .
. . . statements . . .
END
```

As the *logical end* of a multiline IF-THEN or IF-THEN-ELSE construct, typically:

```
IF conditional.expression THEN
    statement(s)
    .
    .
    .
END
```

The presence of terminating END statements is mandatory. See the section on THEN-ELSE construct at the end of this appendix.

END CASE

Terminates the CASE statement, typically:

BEGIN CASE
  CASE *conditional.expression*
    statement(s)
      .
      .
      .
  CASE *conditional.expression*
    statement(s)
      .
      .
  CASE 1
    statement(s)
      .
  END CASE

ENTER *cataloged-program-name*
ENTER *@programname.variable*

Transfers control to specified cataloged program (but may *not* be used from a subroutine). See also the COMMON statement.

EOF(ARG.)

Tests the argument list (provided following the program name during execution) for an end-of-file condition and returns the current status. This returns a "true" (1) if the last GET statement tried to read beyond the end of the argument list; otherwise a "false" (0) is returned. See also the GET statement.

EOF(MSG.)

Tests the error message list (associated with programs initiated from an EXECUTE statement) for an end-of-file condition and returns the current staus. This returns a "true" (1) if the last GET statement tried to read beyond the end of the error message list; otherwise a "false" (0) is returned. See also the GET statement.

EQU{ATE} *symbol* **TO** *constant*{,*symbol* **TO** *constant* . . .}
EQU{ATE} *variable* **TO** *variable*

Performs constant or variable assignment at compile time. A *symbol* is similar to a variable name, with the exception that it may not be modified by placing it to the left of the equal sign in an assignment expression. Here are four examples:

```
EQUATE CLEAR.SCREEN TO CHAR(12)
EQUATE BELL TO CHAR(7)
EQUATE ATTRIBUTE.MARK TO CHAR(254)
EQUATE CUSTOMER.NAME.ATTRIBUTE TO 1
```

EXECUTE *TCL.expression* {**RETURNING** *return.variable*} . . .
   . . . {**CAPTURING** *capture.variable*}

                                                                              P

Issues any valid TCL expression, and continues execution of the program at the next line upon completion. The TCL expression may be any valid TCL command, including ACCESS sentences, verbs, PROCs, or other cataloged PICK/BASIC programs. Any input that may be needed by the EXECUTE statement may be provided with the DATA statement.

The optional RETURNING clause is used to contain any error message item-ids that may have been generated as a result of the EXECUTE statement. Each error message item-id is delimited by a space when more than one is present. See also the SYSTEM function, argument 17.

The optional CAPTURING clause is used to direct the output from a process into a variable. Carriage return/line feed combinations are converted to attribute marks, which allows the variable to be treated like a dynamic array. "Clear screens" (form feeds) are converted to nulls.

Note that control does not return from an EXECUTE statement that issues an OFF or LOGTO command. Also, each level of EXECUTE builds a new process workspace area; as the number of levels increase, so do disk space requirements.

EXECUTE *expression*   **U** **M**

EXECUTE *expression* ,/ / *redirection-indicator*

EXECUTE *expression* ,
    / / *redirection-indicator*

EXECUTE *expression* ,
    / / *redirection-indicator*
    / / *redirection-indicator*

Issues any valid TCL expression, and continues execution of the program at the next line upon completion. The TCL expression may be any valid TCL command, including ACCESS sentences, verbs, PROCs, or other cataloged PICK/BASIC programs.

The optional *redirection-indicator* tells the program how to handle the input or output required by the executed TCL expression. It may be contained in the same physical source line, or moved to the next line, as shown in the formats listed above.

The possible choices for composing the *redirection-indicator* are:

IN. < *expression*

This indicates that input is to be provided by the PICK/BASIC *expression*. If multiple pieces of information are to be passed, each piece has to be separated by an attribute mark. For example:

```
EXECUTE "COPY INVOICE-FILE " : INV.ID,
  // IN. < "(ARCHIVE-INVOICE-FILE"
```

Output may be redirected to the specified PICK/BASIC expression (typically a variable) via this indicator:

OUT. > *expression*

If multiple lines of output are to be passed, each is delimited by an attribute mark. For example:

```
EXECUTE "WHO",
   // OUT. > PORT.ACCOUNT
```

To pass a select list (typically a list of item-ids) to the specified PICK/BASIC expression (typically a variable), use this form:

SELECT. > *expression*

For example:

```
EXECUTE "SSELECT CUST-FILE BY ZIP",
   // SELECT. > CUST.LIST
```

To pass a select list (typically a list of item-ids) from the specified PICK/BASIC expression (typically a variable):

SELECT. < *expression*

For example:

```
EXECUTE "LIST CUST-FILE NAME ZIP",
   // SELECT. < CUST.LIST
```

Note that in both cases of the SELECT. that a select list may *not* be used in a subsequent EXECUTE statement.

EXIT

Transfers control out of a loop. Upon execution, control resumes with the next executable instruction after the REPEAT statement. See the LOOP-WHILE and LOOP-UNTIL statements.

EXP (*numeric.expression*)

Returns the exponential of the *numeric.expression*, that is, *e* (2.7717) raised to the power of the numeric expression notated (*e^numeric.expression*). The inverse of LN.

EXTRACT

The EXTRACT statement is used to retrieve an individual attribute, value, or subvalue from an item. There are two ways to do this; the "old" way involves the use of the EXTRACT function, while the "new" way involves the use of the "< >" characters acting as dynamic array reference characters.

"Original (Old) Form A"

EXTRACT (*array.variable,amc.expression*)

"New Improved Form A"

231

array.variable<amc.expression>

"Original (Old) Form B"

EXTRACT (*array.variable,amc.expression,vmc.expression*)

"New Improved Form B"

array.variable<amc.expression,vmc.expression>

"Original (Old) Form C"

EXTRACT (*array.variable,amc.expression,vmc.expression,svmc.expression*)

"New Improved Form C"

array.variable<amc.expression,vmc.expression,svmc.expression>

Here are several examples. Both of these statements do the same thing:

```
PRINT EXTRACT(CUSTOMER.ITEM,1,0,0)
PRINT CUSTOMER.ITEM<1>
```

Both statements display attribute one of the dynamic array variable CUSTOMER.ITEM. If there are multivalues or subvalues in this attribute, each will be displayed, along with the special "reserved" delimiter used to separate them. The two statements below also are the same:

```
PRINT EXTRACT(CUSTOMER.ITEM(1),1,2,0)
PRINT CUSTOMER.ITEM(1)<1,2>
```

Both of these statements display value two from attribute one in the dynamic array variable CUSTOMER.ITEM.

FADD (*expression1,expression2*)   **U**

Adds two floating point numbers and returns result as a floating point number. Both numbers *must* be floating point; otherwise an error message is displayed and the result returned is OEO. See also the FFLT and FCMP functions.

FCMP (*expression1,expression2*)   **U**

Compares the floating point number derived from *expression1* to the floating point number derived from *expression2,* returning −1 if the first is less than the second 0 if they are equal, and 1 if the second is greater than the first.

FDIV (*expression1,expression2*)   **U**

Divides the floating point number derived from *expression1* by the floating point number derived from *expression2,* returning the result as a floating point number. Both numbers *must* be floating point; otherwise an error message is displayed and the result returned is OEO. See also the FFLT and FCMP functions.

232

FFIX *(expression)*
FFIX *(expression,n)*

Fixes a floating point number, returning the value of the floating point number derived from *expression* as a string number. This is typically used on a floating point number generated with the FADD, FDIV, FMUL or FSUB functions. The expression *must* produce a floating point number.

In the second form, *n* may be any integer number which indicates the number of positions to permit after the decimal point. When omitted, the result will have as many positions as necessary. When specified, and the result produces more digits than allowed for by *n,* all digits after the *n*th position are truncated with *no* rounding taking place.

FFLT *(expression)*

Converts a number (or string number) into a floating point number. The maximum number of digits in the number derived by the expression is 13; any additional digits are truncated. This is typically used to prepare a number for use with the FADD, FDIV, FMUL, and FSUB functions. If the number derived from the expression is not valid, an error message is displayed and the result returned is OEO.

FIELD *(string.expression,search.delimiter,numeric.expression)*

Returns a substring from a string expression, by specifying a delimiter and the desired occurrence. The search delimiter may not be a reserved system delimiter (attribute mark, value mark, or subvalue mark). See also the COL1( ) and COL2( ) functions. Two examples follow:

```
GL.ACCOUNT = "02*4000*11"
COMPANY.CODE = FIELD(GL.ACCOUNT,"*",1)
```

This indicates that everything up to the first asterisk in GL.ACCOUNT should be assigned to the variable COMPANY.CODE. As a result, COMPANY.CODE afterward will contain the value "02".

```
ACCT.NUMBER = FIELD(GL.ACCOUNT,"*",2)
```

This indicates that everything from the first to the second asterisk should be stored in the variable ACCT.NUMBER. Thus, ACCT.NUMBER afterward would contain the value "4000".

FMUL *(expression1,expression2)*

Multiplies the floating point number derived from *expression1* by the floating point number derived from *expression2,* returning the result as a floating point number. Both numbers *must* be floating point; otherwise an error message is displayed and the result returned is OEO. See also the FFLT and FCMP functions.

FOOTING *expression*
FOOTING *"{{text} {'options'}...}"*

Designates text to output at the bottom of each page. Multiple options may be enclosed in the same set of single quotes, as in this expression:

```
FOOTING "'LC'Page 'PN' Printed at 'TL'"
```

Here is a list of the options:

' '	Outputs (one) single quote.
'C'	Centers output line.
'C n'	Centers output line in a line length of *n* positions.
'D'	Current date (Format *dd mmm yyyy*).
'L'	Issues carriage return/line feed
'P'	Current page number, right justified in a field of four blanks.
'P'	Current page number, left justified.
'PN'	Current page number, left justified.
'PP'	Current page number, right justified in a field of four blanks.
'T'	Current time and date (Format *hh:mm:ss dd mmm yyyy*).

FOR-NEXT

Incremental loop function. The syntax is:

FOR *variable* = *start.expression* **TO** *end.expression* {**STEP** *expression* }
    statement(s)
    .
    .
NEXT *variable*

The STEP function indicates the value to increment the counter variable on each pass. The default step is one.

FOR-NEXT-UNTIL

Conditional incremental loop function, which executes until the conditional expression following the UNTIL clause evaluates as true (non-zero). The UNTIL statement *must* appear in the first line of the FOR-NEXT LOOP.

FOR *variable* = *start.expression* **TO** *end.expression*...
...{**STEP** *expression*} **UNTIL** *conditional.expression*
    statement(s)
    .
    .
NEXT *variable*

FOR-NEXT-WHILE

Conditional incremental loop function. Executes while the conditional expression following the

WHILE evaluates to a non-zero (true). The WHILE statement *must* appear in the first line of the FOR-NEXT loop.

> FOR *variable* = *start.expression* TO *end.expression*...
> ...{STEP *expression*} WHILE *conditional.expression*
> *statement(s)*
> .
> .
> NEXT *variable*

FSUB(*expression1,expression2*)

Subtracts the floating point number derived from *expression2* from the floating point number derived from *expression1,* returning the result as a floating point number. Both numbers *must* be floating point; otherwise an error message is displayed and the result returned is OEO. See also the FFLT and FCMP functions.

GET(ARG.) *variable* {THEN *statement*} {ELSE *statement*}
GET(ARG. , *expression*) *variable* {THEN *statement*} {ELSE *statement*}

Used to retrieve arguments from the ARG. redirection variable and store the result in the indicated variable. Arguments are provided with the command used to execute the program initially. In the second form, the expression derives an integer number indicating the position of the argument to retrieve. If the expression is omitted, the next argument is retrieved. See also GET(MSG.) and the EOF function.

Note that the THEN and ELSE constructs are allowed. The THEN branch is taken when the GET successfully retrieves an argument, and the ELSE branch is taken if unsuccessful.

GET(MSG.) *variable* {THEN *statement*} {ELSE *statement*}
GET(MSG. , *expression*) *variable* {THEN *statement*} {ELSE *statement*}

Used to retrieve messages from the MSG. redirection variable and store the result in the indicated variable. Messages are generated from the most recently issued EXECUTE statement. The MSG. redirection variable is reset to null prior to issuing an EXECUTE statement. In the second form, the expression derives an integer number indicating the position of the argument to retrieve. If the expression is omitted, the next message is retrieved. See also GET(ARG.) and the EOF function.

Note that the THEN and ELSE construct is allowed. The THEN branch is taken when the GET successfully retrieves a message, and the ELSE branch is taken if unsuccessful.

GOSUB *statement.label*

Transfers control to specified local subroutine. See also the RETURN statement. All systems support numeric labels:

```
GOSUB 8000
```

Ultimate and McDonnell Douglas (Release 5.2 and higher) Only: Note that statement labels may contain (or consist of) alphabetic characters; however, alphanumeric statement labels *must* begin with a letter. For example:

```
GOSUB PROCESS.LINE.ITEMS
```

In all systems the label itself must be followed by a colon (:).

GOTO *statement.label*
GO TO *statement.label*

Transfers control to specified statement label. (Some systems allow the ''GO'' form.) All systems support numeric labels:

```
GOTO 8000
```

Ultimate and McDonnell Douglas (Release 5.2 and higher) Only: Note that statement labels may contain (or consist of) alphabetic characters; however, alphanumeric statement labels *must* begin with a letter. For example:

```
GOTO PROCESS.LINE.ITEMS
```

On all systems, the label itself must be followed by a colon (:).

HEADING *expression*
HEADING *"{{text} {'options'}...}"*

Designates text to output at the top of each page. Multiple options may be enclosed in the same set of single quotes. For example:

```
HEADING "'LC'Page 'PN' Printed at 'TL'"
```

Here is a list of the options:

' '	Outputs (one) single quote.	
'C'	Centers output line.	P U
'Cn'	Centers output line in a line length of *n* positions.	U M
'D'	Current date (format *dd mmm yyyy*).	
'L'	Issues carriage return/line feed	
'P'	Current page number, right justified in a field of four blanks.	P U
'P'	Current page number, left justified.	M
'P N'	Current page number, left justified.	P U
'P P'	Current page number, right justified in a field of four blanks.	M
'T'	Current time and date (format *hh:mm:ss dd mmm yyyy*).	

ICONV(*expression,conversion.expression*)

Converts expression to internal format, according to the conversion code specified in the

236

conversion expression. Here are several examples:

```
INPUT CHECK.AMOUNT
CHECK.AMOUNT = ICONV(CHECK.AMOUNT,"MR2")
```
P U

```
INPUT CHECK.AMOUNT
CHECK.AMOUNT = ICONV(CHECK.AMOUNT,"MD2")
```
U M

```
INPUT CHECK.DATE
CHECK.DATE = ICONV(CHECK.DATE,"D")
```

Any conversion (or correlative) available in ACCESS may be used with the ICONV and OCONV statements, with the exception of the "A" and "F" correlatives. Here are brief descriptions of the available conversions and correlatives:

Code	Function	
D	Date conversion	
G	Group Extract	
L	Length	
MCA	Mask Characters Alpha (returns all letters)	**P U**
MC/A	Mask Characters Non-Alphabetic	**P U**
MCN	Mask Characters Numeric (returns all numbers)	**P U**
MC/N	Mask Characters Non-Numeric	**P U**
MCT	Mask Characters to upper and lower case	**P U**
ML	Mask, left-justified	
MP	Mask, packed decimal	
MR*n*	Mask, right-justified. Normally used with *n,* which indicates the number of decimal positions after the decimal point	**P U**
MT	Mask Time	
MX	Mask Hexadecimal	
P	Pattern match	
R	Range	
T	Text Extraction	
T	File Translation (Don't even think about it. Use any form of the READ statement instead.)	
U*xxxx*	User Mode Exit (*caveat emptor!*)	

(Note that conversion codes differ considerably between Pick and McDonnell Douglas machines. Consult your system reference manuals.)

IF *conditional.expression* **THEN** *statement(s)* {**ELSE** *statement(s)*}

Performs conditional execution of one or more statements. See the section on the THEN/ELSE Construct.

INCLUDE {*filename*} *itemname*

Instucts the compiler to retrieve the item specified and to include its source code in the program being compiled. If the *filename* is omitted, the current file is assumed.

INDEX(*string.expression,substring,numeric.expression*)

Searches a string expression for the occurrence of the specified substring indicated in the numeric expression. Returns the starting column position of the matched substring. If the specified substring is not found, then 0 is returned. For example:

```
TEST = INDEX("ABCDEFG","D",1)
```

This returns the value 4 to the variable called TEST, since the first occurrence of "D" was found in the fourth position of the string.

INPUT *variable*{, *length.expression*} {:}

Prompts for the input of data from the terminal, using the default prompt character (?), or the character previously defined with the PROMPT statement.

The *length.expression* indicates the length of input to accept; a carriage return/line feed is automatically issued when the length of the argument in the length expression is satisfied. The optional colon (:) character inhibits the automatic cr/lf when completing the input, and the cursor remains positioned after the entered value.

INPUT @(*x,y*):*variable*{,*length.expression*}...
    ...{*mask.expression*}

Prompts for the input of data from the terminal, at the coordinates specified in the column (*x*) and row (*y*) parameters. Assigns input to specified variable after performing optional mask function. The length expression functions exactly like the standard INPUT statement.

If the data does not match the optionally specified mask expression, then the statement prompts again for input. Mask expressions may be any combination of conversions, pattern operators, or text justification. See the section on "Masking" near the beginning of this appendix.

INPUT {@(*x,y*)} {:}*variable*{,*length.expression*} {:}...   **U**
    ...{*mask.expression*} {__}{**THEN** *statement(s)*} {**ELSE** *statement(s)*}

Prompts for the input of data from the terminal, using the default prompt character (?), or the character previously defined by a PROMPT statement.

The "AT sign" (@) form of INPUT prompts for data input from the terminal, at the coordinates specified in the *x* (column) and *y* (row) parameters. Assigns input to specified variable after performing optional mask function. The optional colon (:) preceding the input variable indicates to display the "old" value of the variable being input.

The *length.expression* indicates the length of input to accept; a line feed is performed when the length of the argument is satisfied. The optional colon (:) character following *length.expression* inhibits the automatic carriage return and line feed when completing the input. The cursor remains positioned after the entered value.

If the input data value does not match the optionally specified mask expression, then the statement prompts again for input. Mask functions may be any combination of conversions, pattern-matching operators, or text justification. See the section on "Masking" near the beginning of this appendix.

The optional underscore (_) character, typically used in conjunction with the *length.expression*. It causes the terminal to sound its audible alarm when the number of characters entered exceeds the length expression.

Note that the THEN and ELSE constructs are permitted. The THEN branch is taken when at least one character of input is received; the ELSE branch is taken if no characters are received. In either case, the THEN and/or ELSE construct may be on single or multiple program lines. See the section on "Special Exceptions" at the end of the THEN/ELSE construct discussion.

INPUT *variable* **USING** *screen.variable...* **[M]**
...{,*source.expression* {**AT** *stepnum*} {**SETTING** *variable*}...
...**ELSE** *statement(s)*

Prompts for the input from a screen generated by the SCREENPRO processor into a dynamic array. The screen variable indicates which compiled screen (previously read from a file with a READ statement) is to be used.

The *source.expression* parameter supplies initial data to be passed to the processor; the *stepnum* indicates the associated screen step number at which processing is to begin (default is 1); and the SETTING parameter sets the specified variable to the current step number when a screen edit occurs. The ELSE statement(s) are executed when a screen exit occurs.

INPUTCLEAR **[U]**

Clears the type-ahead buffer. See also the PRINTERR statement.

INPUTERR *string.expression* **[P]**

Outputs message, defined in *string.expression,* on status (bottom) line of terminal. Used in conjunction with the PRINT @ statement.

INPUTNULL *character* **[P]**

Defines null character as specified character, which is recognized as a null on subsequent INPUT statements. Used in conjunction with INPUT @ statements. The default null character is an underscore (segment mark).

INPUTTRAP *string.expression* **GOSUB** *statement.label*{*,statement.label*}... **[P]**

Tests value of last executed INPUT @ statement. Upon execution, branches to statement label address of local subroutine that corresponds with location in statement label list.

INPUTTRAP *string.expression* **GOTO** *statement.label{,statementlabel}...*

Tests value of last executed INPUT @ statement. Upon execution, branches to statement label address that corresponds with location in statement label list.

INS *expression* **BEFORE** *variable < amc.expression >*   U M
INS *expression* **BEFORE** *variable < amc.expression,vmc.expression >*
INS *expression* **BEFORE** *variable < amc.expression,vmc.expression,svmc.expression >*

Inserts the expression into a specific location in a dynamic array. A "−1" may be specified as an *amc.expression*, *vmc.expression*, or *svmc.expression*, and *expression* will be inserted as the "last" element in the respective location.

The INSERT Function

Inserts the element referenced by *expression* into a specific location in a dynamic array, and has the following parametric forms:

INSERT(*array.variable,amc.expression;expression*)   P U

INSERT(*array.variable,amc.expression,vmc.expression;expression*)   P U

INSERT(*array.variable,amc.expression,vmc.expression,svmc.expression,...*

   ...expression)

Note: A "−1" may be specified as the *amc.expression, vmc.expression,* or *svmc.expression*. This causes *expression* to be inserted as the last element in the respective location.

INT(*numeric.expression*)

Returns the integer value of the numeric expression, that is, all the numbers to the left of the decimal point.

LEN(*string.expression*)

Returns the length of the string in the string expression.

LET(*variable = expression*

Assigns value of *expression* to specified variable. The LET statement is optional. The alternate, more commonly used form is:

variable = expression

which also works on all Pick-class systems.

LN(*numeric.expression*)

Returns the natural logarithm (base *e*) of the numeric expression. Inverse of EXP.

LOCATE(*expression,array.variable*{*,amc.expression,*{*vmc.expression*}};..
...*setvar*{*;sequence*}) {**THEN** *statement(s)*} **ELSE** *statement(s)*

Locates string expression (*expression*) in array referenced by *array.variable,* storing the positional value returned in *setvar.* If the string expression is not found, the value returned in *setvar* contains the position where the element should be inserted using the INS or INSERT function. See the section on the THEN/ELSE construct.

Listed below are the possible sequence parameters. (Note that the single quotes around parameters are required)

'AL'	Ascending, left-justified
'AR'	Ascending, right-justified
'DL'	Descending, left-justified
'DR'	Descending, right-justified

If no sequence parameter is specified, *setvar* position defaults to end of array element.

The use of the optional *amc.expression* and *vmc.expression* indicate whether the value returned into *setvar* is a value mark count or a subvalue mark count. If both are omitted, the value returned into *setvar* is an attribute mark count.

LOCATE *expression* **IN** *array.variable*{ {<*amc.expression*{*,vmc.expression*>}},...
...*startposition*} {**BY** *sequence*} **SETTING** *setvar* {**THEN** *statement(s)*}...
...**ELSE** *statement(s)*

Locates string expression (*expression*) in array referenced by *array.variable,* storing the positional value returned in *setvar.*

If the string expression is not found, the value returned in *setvar* contains the position where the element should be inserted using the INS or INSERT function. See the section on the THEN/ELSE construct.

In the latter form, the additional *startposition* parameter indicates the starting attribute, value, or subvalue position.

Listed below are the possible sequence parameters. (Note that the single quotes around parameters are required)

'AL'	Ascending, left-justified
'AR'	Ascending, right-justified
'DL'	Descending, left-justified
'DR'	Descending, right-justified

If no sequence parameter is specified, *setvar* position defaults to end of array element.

The use of the optional *amc.expression* and *vmc.expression* indicate whether the value returned into *setvar* is a value mark count or a sub-value mark count. If both are omitted, the value returned into setvar is an attribute mark count.

LOCK *locknumber.expression* {**ELSE** *statement(s)*}

Sets an execution (lock) flag in the range, (0-47 for Pick and Ultimate, 0-127 for McDonnell Douglas). This is used to prevent program re-entrancy, meaning that only one process may run this program at any given time. If the *locknumber.expression* evaluates to a number greater than 47 (or 127 for McDonnell Douglas), then the result is divided by 48 (or 128), and the *locknumber* is the remainder of the equation. The THEN clause is taken when the lock is already set. See the section on the THEN/ELSE construct.

LOOP {UNTIL}

Conditional loop function. Performs specified operations until the UNTIL clause evaluates as true (non-zero). Here are two examples of the parametric form:

LOOP {*statement(s)*} **UNTIL** *conditional.expression* **DO**
  statement(s)
  .
  .

REPEAT

LOOP
  statement(s)
UNTIL *conditional.expression* **DO**
  statement(s)
  .
  .

REPEAT

Ultimate Only: Note that the UNTIL portion of the LOOP construct is now optional. See also the EXIT statement.

LOOP {WHILE}

Conditional loop function. Performs specified operations while the WHILE conditional expression evaluates as true (non-zero). Here are two examples of the parametric form:

LOOP { *statement(s)*} **WHILE** *conditional.expression* **DO**
  statement(s)
  .
  .

REPEAT

LOOP
  statement(s)
WHILE *conditional.expression* **DO**
  statement(s)
  .
  .

REPEAT

Ultimate Only: Note that the WHILE portion of the LOOP construct is now optional. See also the EXIT statement.

MAT *array.variable* = *expression*
MAT *array.variable* = **MAT** *array.variable*

Initializes all the locations of a dimensioned array variable to the specified value(s). When assigning one matrix to another, both arrays must be dimensioned to the same size.

MATCH *matchstring*
MATCHES *matchstring*

Pattern matching operator. The *matchstring* may be a composite of literals and/or match operators, appended to length specifications. During processing, the value must be the exact length of the length specifications parameter. Listed below are the matchstring operators:

*n*A   Accept only *n* alphabetic characters.
*n*N   Accept only *n* numeric characters.
*n*X   Accept *n* wildcards (any character).
'literal'   Any literal string.

The *n* parameter specifies the length of the match operator string. A length specification of zero (0) allows any length of the following match operator. When combinations of matchstrings and literals are present, the entire matchstring must be enclosed in double quotes. Multiple matchstrings may be delimited with value marks. Shown below are examples of single and multiple pattern matches:

Single Pattern Match:

```
IF X MATCHES "3N'-'2N'-'4N" THEN
    PRINT "VALID SOCIAL SECURITY #"
END ELSE
    PRINT "INVALID SOCIAL SECURITY #"
END
```

Multiple Pattern Match:

```
IF X MATCHES "10N]1A9N" THEN...
```

The multiple-match example tests for ten numeric characters or one alphabetic character followed by nine numerics. Note that the character separating the two pattern matchstrings is a value mark.

MATINPUT *variable* **USING** *screen.variable*{*,source.array* { **AT** *stepnum*}...   **M**
    ...{**SETTING** *variable*} **ELSE** *statement(s)*

Prompts for the input from a screen generated by the SCREENPRO processor into a dynamic array. The screen variable indicates which compiled screen (previously read from a file with a MATREAD statement) is to be used.

The source array parameter supplies initial data to be passed to the processor; the *stepnum* indicates the associated screen step number at which processing is to begin (default is 1); and the SETTING parameter sets the specified variable to the current step number when a screen edit occurs. The ELSE statement(s) are executed when a screen exit occurs.

MATREAD *array.variable* **FROM** {*file.variable*}, *id.expression*...
    ...{**ON ERROR** *statement(s)*} {**THEN** *statement(s)* {**ELSE** *statement(s)*}

Reads the specified dimensioned array (item) from the optionally specified file variable, or the default file variable if none is specified, and stores one attribute per element into the array previously defined with a DIM statement. See also the MATREADU statement and the section on the THEN/ELSE Construct.

If more attributes are present in the item read than elements in the previously dimensioned array, then the extra attributes are inserted into the last array element, with each attribute delimited by an attribute mark. If the number of attributes read is less than the array size, then the remaining array elements are assigned null values.

Ultimate Only: Only the Ultimate system allows the ON ERROR condition, which is taken if the file is remote (accessed through UltiNet) and the file can't be cleared due to a network error condition; in this instance, SYSTEM(0) contains the UltiNet error message number.

MATREADU *array.variable* **FROM** {*file.variable*}, *id.expression...*
 ...{**ON ERROR** *statement(s)*} {**LOCKED** *statement(s)*}*...*
 ...{**THEN** *statement(s)* {**ELSE** *statement(s)*}

Reads the specified dimensioned array (item) from the optionally specified file variable, or the default file variable if none is specified, and stores one attribute per element into the array previously defined with a DIM statement.

If more attributes are present in the item read than elements in the previously dimensioned array, then the extra attributes are inserted into the last array element, with each attribute delimited by an attribute mark. If the number of attributes read is less than the array size, then the remaining array elements are assigned null values. See also the MATREAD statement and the section on the THEN/ELSE construct.

Ultimate Only: The MATREADU statement is identical to the MATREAD except that the item is "locked," preventing access to that item by any other process.

Pick and McDonnell Douglas Only: The MATREADU statement is identical to the MATREAD statement, except that the group in which the item resides is "locked," preventing access to any item in that group by any other process.

Ultimate Only: The LOCKED clause allows handling the case of contending with a group lock already being set when attempting the read; any statement(s) following the LOCKED clause will be executed if the read encounters a group lock. Only the Ultimate system allows the ON ERROR condition, which is taken if the file is remote (accessed through UltiNet) and the file can't be cleared due to a network error condition; in this instance, SYSTEM(0) contains the UltiNet error message number.

MATWRITE *array.variable* **ON** {*file.variable,*}*id.expression...*
 ...{**ON ERROR** *statement(s)*}

MATWRITEU *array.variable* **ON** {*file.variable,*}*id.expression...*
 ...{**ON ERROR** *statement(s)*}

Writes dimensioned array (item) into the specified file variable. If the file variable parameter is omitted, the default file variable is used. See also the RELEASE statement.

Pick and McDonnell Douglas Only: The MATWRITEU statement is identical to the MATWRITE statement, except that the group in which the item is written remains locked.

Ultimate Only: The MATWRITEU statement is identical to the MATWRITE statement, except that the item written remains locked. Only the Ultimate system allows the ON ERROR condition, which is taken if the file is remote (accessed through UltiNet) and the file can't be cleared due to a network error condition; in this instance, SYSTEM(0) contains the UltiNet error message number.

244

MOD(*dividend,divisor*)

Calculates the remainder (modulo) of the expression. Same as REM function.

NEXT *variable*

Terminates FOR-NEXT loop. See the FOR-NEXT statement.

FOR *variable* = *expression* **TO** *expression* {**STEP** *expression* }
   statement(s)
   .
   .

NEXT *variable*

NOT(*logical.expression*)

Returns "true" (1) if the expression evaluates to a zero; returns "false" (0) if the expression evaluates to a non-zero.

NULL

Performs no operation. Typically used in a single line IF-THEN-ELSE construct as in the following example:

IF *conditional.expression* **THEN NULL ELSE** *statement(s)* ...

NUM(*expression*)

Returns one (1) if the expression results in only numeric values; returns zero (0) if the expression contains any non-numeric characters.

OCONV(*expression,conversion.expression*)

Converts the expression to external format, according to conversion code specified in *conversion.expression*. Here are three examples:

```
PRINT OCONV(CHECK.AMOUNT,"MR2")
```
P U

```
PRINT OCONV(CHECK.AMOUNT,"MD2")
```
U M

```
PRINT OCONV(CHECK.DATE,"D")
```
P U

Any conversion (or correlative) available in ACCESS may be used with the ICONV and OCONV statements, with the exception of the "A" and "F" correlatives. Here are brief descriptions of the available conversions and correlatives:

Code	Function		
D	Date Conversion		
G	Group Extract		
L	Length		
MCA	Mask Characters Alpha (returns all letters)	P	U
MC/A	Mask Characters Non-Alphabetic	P	U
MCN	Mask Characters Numeric (returns all numbers)	P	U
MC/N	Mask Characters Non-Numeric	P	U
MCT	Mask Characters to upper and lower case	P	U
ML	Mask, left-justified		
MP	Mask, packed decimal		
MR*n*	Mask, right-justified. Normally used with *n*, which indicates the number of decimal positions after the decimal point	P	U
MT	Mask Time		
MX	Mask Hexadecimal		
P	Pattern match		
R	Range		
T	Text Extraction		
T	File Translation (Don't even think about it. Use any form of the READ statement instead.)		
U*xxxx*	User Mode Exit (*caveat emptor!*)		

(Note that conversion codes differ considerably between Pick and McDonnell Douglas machines. Consult your system reference manuals.)

ON *index.expression* **GOSUB** *statement.label*{*,statement.label...*}
ON *index.expression* **GOSUB** *statement.label,statement.label,...*   `U`

Transfers control to a local subroutine statement label according to the positional value of the index expression. The local subroutine must be terminated with a RETURN statement. If the index expression evaluates to a number less than one, or to a number greater than the number of statement labels, then nothing happens. Control passes to the next executable line in the program.

Ultimate Only: Note that statement labels in the Ultimate system may contain (or consist of) alphabetic characters. The first example below is legal on any Pick system, while the second applies only to Ultimate.


```
ON  RESPONSE  GOSUB  8000,9000,9500

ON  RESPONSE  GOSUB  SUB1,SUB2,SUB3
```

ON *index.expression* **GOTO** *statement.label*{,*statement.label,....*}

ON *index.expression* **GOTO** *statement.label,statement.label,...*

Transfers control to a statement label according to the positional value of the index expression. If the index expression evaluates to a number less than one, or to a number greater than the number of statement labels, then nothing happens. Control passes to the next executable line in the program.

Ultimate Only: Note that statement labels in the Ultimate system may contain (or consist of) alphabetic characters. The first example below is legal on any Pick system, while the second applies only to Ultimate.

```
ON RESPONSE GOTO 100,200,300,400,500

ON RESPONSE GOTO MAINLINE,WRAPUP
```

OPEN {**"DICT"**,} *file expression* {**TO** *file.variable*} **ON ERROR** *statement(s)*}...
    ...{**THEN** *statement(s)* **ELSE** *statement(s)*

Opens the specified filename expression and associates the file with the indicated file variable. If the "DICT" parameter is specified, then the dictionary level of the specified filename is opened and assigned to the file variable. If no file variable is specified, then the default file variable is opened and assigned. See the section on the THEN/ELSE construct.

Ultimate Only: Only the Ultimate system allows the ON ERROR condition, which is taken if the file is remote (accessed through UltiNet) and the file can't be cleared due to a network error condition; in this instance, SYSTEM(0) contains the UltiNet error message number.

PAGE
PAGE *expression*

Terminates the current page of output, prints the optional FOOTING, positions to top of form, and prints the optional HEADING. The optional *expression* may contain a number that indicates the new value for the page counter.

PRECISION *number-of-positions*

Defines number of decimal places to carry in results of mathematical expressions. The default precision is four (4).

Ultimate Only: The *number-of-positions* parameter must be in the range 0 to 9. Note that programs using string or floating point numbers ignore this statement.

McDonnell Douglas Only: The number-of-positions must be in the range 0 to 6.

PRINT ON *printfilenumber*

Directs printer output to one of 255 print reports in the range 0-254.

PRINT {@(*col*{,*row*}):} {*expression*{,*expression*}} {*mask.expression*}

Outputs literal or expression to the current output device. If the @ symbol is specified, the output is directed to the specified column and row coordinates. If nothing follows the PRINT statement, a blank line is output.

The comma between expressions specifies for the cursor to "tab right" 18 spaces before printing the next expression. The colon (:) between expressions and parameters specifies that expressions are concatenated; note that a colon must appear between the @(*col,row*) parameter and the following expression.

The mask expression may be any legal mask expression. See the section on the masking function. See also the PRINTER ON and EXECUTE statements.

Pick and Ultimate Only: Executing the PRINT @ statement in the form PRINT @(*n*), where *n* is a negative number, will activate one of the special terminal or printer control functions listed in Table A-2. (These features are relatively new to McDonnell Douglas systems; users please see your system manuals.)

Table A-2. PRINT @ Special Control Functions.

For Pick and Ultimate Only:

@(−1)	Clears screen and positions cursor in home position (0,0).
@(−2)	Positions cursor in home position (0,0).
@(−3)	Clears to end of screen from current cursor position.
@(−4)	Clears to end of line from current cursor position.
@(−5)	Enables blink function.
@(−6)	Disables blink function.
@(−7)	Enables protect function.
@(−8)	Disables protect function.
@(−9)	Moves cursor back one position.
@(−10)	Moves cursor up one line.

Ultimate Only:

@(−11)	Moves cursor down one line.
@(−12)	Moves cursor right one position.
@(−13)	Enables slave port.
@(−14)	Disables slave port.
@(−15)	Enables slave port in transparent mode.
@(−16)	Enables local print on slave port.
@(−17)	Enables underlining.
@(−18)	Disables underlining.
@(−19)	Enables inverse video.
@(−20)	Disables inverse video.
@(−21)	Deletes line.
@(−22)	Inserts line.
@(−23)	Scrolls entire screen up one line.
@(−24)	Enables boldface.
@(−25)	Disables boldface.
@(−26)	Deletes character.

@(−27)	Inserts blank character.
@(−28)	Enables character insert function.
@(−29)	Disables character insert function.

The following functions are for use with color terminals (listing format is Background/Foreground):

@(−30)	black/cyan	@(−49)	white/black
@(−31)	black/red	@(−50)	red/white
@(−32)	black/blue	@(−51)	red/green
@(−33)	black/green	@(−52)	prior/brown
@(−34)	black/magenta	@(−53)	prior/white
@(−35)	black/yellow	@(−54)	prior/red
@(−36)	black/white	@(−55)	prior/magenta
@(−37)	blue/red	@(−56)	prior/yellow
@(−38)	blue/green	@(−57)	prior/green
@(−39)	blue/white	@(−58)	prior/cyan
@(−40)	blue/yellow	@(−59)	prior/blue
@(−41)	blue/red	@(−60)	brown/prior
@(−42)	blue/cyan	@(−61)	white/prior
@(−43)	blue/magenta	@(−62)	black/prior
@(−44)	white/red	@(−63)	red/prior
@(−45)	white/green	@(−64)	blue/prior
@(−46)	white/blue	@(−65)	cyan/prior
@(−47)	white/cyan	@(−66)	magenta/prior
@(−48)	white/magenta		

The following additional functions are provided for use with letter-quality printers supported by Ultimate:

@(−101,n)	Sets Vertical Motion Index to n.
@(−102,n)	Sets Horizontal Motion Index to n.
@(−103)	Activates secondary (alternate) font.
@(−104)	Activates primary (standard) font.
@(−105)	Issues a half linefeed.
@(−106)	Issues a negative half linefeed.
@(−107)	Issues a negative linefeed.
@(−108)	Activates black ink.
@(−109)	Activates red ink. (Sometimes needed on P & L reports.)
@(−110)	Activates primary single (cut) sheet feeder.
@(−111)	Activates secondary single (cut) sheet feeder.
@(−112)	Activates tertiary single (cut) sheet feeder.
@(−113)	Activates standard print thimble.
@(−114)	Activates proportional space print thimble.

If problems are experienced when attempting the above functions, make sure that the *termtype* parameter is correctly set for the type of terminal being used. See the TERM and SET-TERM commands in the TCL section.

Note to McDonnell Douglas users: See the system manuals for the available options. (This is new.)

PRINTER CLOSE

Indicates that the current output is now complete, closes spooler entry, and releases control to the spooler.

PRINTER OFF

Directs output from subsequent PRINT statements to the terminal.

PRINTER ON

Directs output from subsequent PRINT statements to the system printer, via the spooler.

PRINTERR *expression*

Prints the message derived from the expression on the bottom line of the terminal screen. This message is automatically cleared before the next INPUT statement, and the type-ahead buffer is also cleared.

PROCREAD *variable* {THEN *statement(s)*} ELSE *statement(s)*

Reads the calling PROC's Primary Input Buffer and assigns its contents to the specified variable. *Ultimate and McDonnell Douglas Only:* When a successful read takes place, the variable is treated as a dynamic array. This means that every word from the Primary Input Buffer is delimited by an attribute mark.
Pick Only: When a successful read takes place, the variable is treated as one long string, with each word being delimited by a space.
The ELSE condition is taken when the program has not been executed from a PROC. Note that either a THEN or an ELSE construct must be present. See the section on the THEN/ELSE construct.

PROCWRITE *variable* {ELSE *statement(s)*}

Writes the variable to the calling PROC's Primary Input Buffer. See notes in PROCREAD about specific treatment by different versions of Pick. The ELSE statement(s) is (are) taken when the program was *not* run from a PROC.

PROGRAM {*program-name*}

Used as the first line in "compile-and-go" programs. These are placed in the MD and are immediately executable upon filing, just like a PROC. No compilation is needed. The optional *program-name* is ignored by the compiler.

PROMPT *expression*

Specifies the single character to display during subsequent INPUT statements that prompt for terminal input. The default prompt character is a question mark (?). A null prompt character may be defined with a PROMPT " " statement.

PUT(MSG.) *expression* {*,expression...*}

Allows the placement of messages in the MSG. redirection variable, and continues execution of the program. The first expression typically derives an error message id number, and the optional additional expressions derive parameters to pass into the error message handler. See also the GET and EOF functions.

PWR(*expression1,expression2*)

Raises value contained in *expression1* to the power of the value of *expression2*.
Ultimate Only: Note that this only works with standard numeric values, and *not* with string or floating point numbers.

READNEXT *id-variable*{*,posvar*} {**FROM** *selectvar*}...
...{**ON ERROR** *statement(s)*}$**THEN** *statement(s)*} **ELSE** *statement(s)*

Reads the next item-id from the active list and assigns it to the specified variable.
Pick and Ultimate Only: The list must have been retrieved by a SELECT, SSELECT, GET-LIST, or QSELECT command executed immediately before starting execution of the PICK/BASIC program that contains the READNEXT statement, or by a preceding SELECT or EXECUTE statement within the program.
McDonnell Douglas Only: The list must have been retrieved by a SELECT, SSELECT, GET-LIST, or FORM-LIST command executed immediately before starting execution of the PICK/BA-SIC program that contains the READNEXT statement, or by a preceding SELECT or EXECUTE statement within the program.
See also the (PICK/BASIC) SELECT statement and the section on the THEN/ELSE construct.
The position variable parameter indicates the position of the multivalue within an attribute, specified in an exploded sort, executed prior to the execution of the program. This allows multivalues to be retrieved in exploded sort sequence. The ELSE condition is executed if no selection was performed or when there are no more items in the list.
Ultimate Only: Only the Ultimate system allows the ON ERROR condition, which is taken if the file is remote (accessed through UltiNet) and the file can't be cleared due to a network error condition; in this instance, SYSTEM(0) contains the UltiNet error message number.

READ *array.variable* **FROM** {*file.variable,*} *id.expression*...
{**ON ERROR** *statement(s)*} {**THEN** *statement(s)*} **ELSE** *statement(s)*

Reads item from the optionally specified file variable and assigns each attribute to an array element in the dynamic array designated in *array.variable*. See also the READU statement and the section on the THEN/ELSE construct.
If the file variable parameter is not specified, the default file variable is used. The ELSE condition is taken when the item is not on file.
Ultimate Only: Only the Ultimate system allows the ON ERROR condition, which is taken if the file is remote (accessed through UltiNet) and the file can't be cleared due to a network error condition; in this instance, SYSTEM(0) contains the UltiNet error message number.

READU *array.variable* **FROM** {*file.variable,*}*id.expression*...
...{**ON ERROR** *statement(s)*} {**LOCKED** *statement(s)*}...
...{**THEN** *statement(s)*} **ELSE** *statement(s)*

Reads item from the optionally specified file variable and assigns each attribute to an array element in the dynamic array designated in *array.variable.* If the file variable parameter is not specified, the default file variable is used. The ELSE condition is taken when the item is not on file.

Ultimate Only: The READU statement is identical to the MATREAD statement, except that the item is "locked," preventing access to that item by any other process.

Pick and McDonnell Douglas Only: The READU statement is identical to the MATREAD statement, except that the group in which the item resides is "locked," preventing access to any item in that group by any other process.

Ultimate Only: The LOCKED clause allows handling the case of contending with a group lock already being set when attempting the read; any statement(s) following the LOCKED clause will be executed if the read encounters a group lock. Only the Ultimate system allows the ON ERROR condition, which is taken if the file is remote (accessed through UltiNet) and the file can't be cleared due to a network error condition; in this instance, SYSTEM(0) contains the UltiNet error message number.

READT *variable* {**THEN** *statement(s)*} **ELSE** *statement(s)*

Reads a tape record, and assigns the value returned to the specified variable. The length of the tape record is specified by the most recently executed T-ATT command. See the section on the THEN/ELSE construct. The ELSE condition is taken if the tape unit is not attached, or an end-of-file is encountered.

READV *variable* **FROM** {*file.variable,*} *id.expression,amc.expression*...
...{**ON ERROR** *statement(s)*} {**THEN** *statement(s)*} **ELSE** {*statement(s)*}

Reads item from the optionally specified file variable and assigns the value contained in the attribute number referenced in the attribute expression to the specified variable. The ELSE condition is taken if the item is not on file. See also the READVU statement and the section on the THEN/ELSE construct.

Ultimate Only: Only the Ultimate system allows the ON ERROR condition, which is taken if the file is remote (accessed through UltiNet) and the file can't be cleared due to a network error condition; in this instance, SYSTEM(0) contains the UltiNet error message number.

READVU *variable* **FROM** {*file.variable,*} *id.expression,amc.expression* . . .
 . . . {**ON ERROR** *statement(s)*} {**LOCKED** *statement(s)*} . . .
 . . . {**THEN** *statement(s)*} **ELSE** *statement(s)*

Reads item from the optionally specified file variable and assigns the value contained in the attribute number referenced in the attribute expression to the specified variable. The READVU statement is identical to the READV statement, except that a lock is set on the item. The ELSE condition is taken if the item is not on file. See also the READV statement and the section on the THEN/ELSE construct.

Ultimate Only: Only the Ultimate system allows the ON ERROR condition, which is taken if the file is remote (accessed through UltiNet) and the file can't be cleared due to a network error condition; in this instance, SYSTEM (0) contains the UltiNet error message number.

Ultimate and McDonnell Douglas Only: The LOCKED clause allows handling the case of contending with a group lock already being set when attempting the read. Any statement(s) following the LOCKED clause will be executed if the read encounters a group lock.

RELEASE {**ON ERROR** *statement(s)*}
RELEASE *id.expression* {**ON ERROR** *statement(s)*}
RELEASE *file.variable,id.expression* {**ON ERROR** *statement(s)*}

Releases the group locked with a previous MATREADU, READU, or READVU statement, in the optionally specified file variable. If the file variable and item-id expressions are both omitted, all groups currently locked by the current process are unlocked.

Ultimate Only: Only the Ultimate system allows the ON ERROR condition, which is taken if the file is remote (accessed through UltiNet) and the file can't be cleared due to a network error condition; in this instance, SYSTEM(0) contains the UltiNet error message number.

REM *text*

Defines user-specified remarks. Causes the entire source line to be ignored by the compiler. The characters, * or ! may be substituted for the REM statement.

REM*(dividend,divisor)*

Calculates the remainder (modulo) of two numeric expressions. Same as MOD function, except for McDonnell Douglas.

REPEAT

Terminates DO portion of LOOP-WHILE or LOOP-UNTIL statements. See the LOOP-WHILE or LOOP-UNTIL statements. For example:

LOOP {*statement(s)*}**UNTIL** *conditional.expression* **DO**
    statements(s)
    .
    .
    .
REPEAT

REPLACE*(array.variable,amc.expression;expression)*
REPLACE*(array.variable,amc.expression,vmc.expression;expression)*

REPLACE*(array.variable,amc.expression,vmc.expression,svmc.expression, . . .*
    . . . ,expression)
    string.expression < *array.variable*{*,vmc.expression*{*,svmc.expression*}} > = . . .
    . . . expression

Replaces the specified location within the dynamic array variable referenced by *array.variable* with the value referenced in *expression*. Note that " −1" may be specified as the *amc.expression, vmc.expression,* or *svmc.expression*. This causes the expression to be replaced as the last element in the respective location.

RETURN
RETURN TO *statement.label*

Terminates an internal or external subroutine. Control resumes with the statement following the CALL or GOSUB command. The TO clause may only be used with an internal subroutine, and transfers control to the specified statement label. This is *not* recommended, as it makes programs nearly impossible to figure out.

Ultimate Only: Note that statement labels in the Ultimate system may contain (or consist of) alphabetic characters.

REWIND {THEN *statements(s)*} ELSE *statement(s)*

Rewinds the magnetic tape on the attached unit. The ELSE condition is taken if the tape unit is not ready or attached with a T-ATT command. See the section on the THEN/ELSE construct.

RND*(numeric.expression)*

Generates a random number between 0 and the value specified in *numeric.expression*, minus one.

RQM
RQM *number.seconds*
RQM *military.time*

Puts the program to "sleep" for some period of time. While sleeping, program execution is suspended. Normally, so is the break key. This happens to be the same as the SLEEP statement. In the first form, when no argument is specified, the program sleeps for one second before continuing execution.

In the second form, when an integer number follows as the argument, the program sleeps for that number of seconds. For example, this statement:

```
RQM 300
```

puts the program to sleep for 5 minutes.

In the final form, the statement may be followed by a legal "military" (24-hour) time. This is like leaving a wake-up call. For example:

```
RQM 8:00
```

puts the program to sleep until 8:00 A.M. For times after noon, use the 24-hour form:

```
RQM 17:00
```

This suspends execution until 5:00 P.M.

SADD*(expression,expression)* U

Adds two string numbers and returns the result as a string number. If either number is not a string number, an error message is displayed and the result returned is zero (0).

SCMP*(expression1,expression2)* U

Compares the string number derived from *expression1* to the string number derived from *expression2*, returning " −1" if the first is less than the second, "0" if they are equal, and "1" if the second is greater than the first. If either number is not a string number, an error message is displayed and the result returned is zero (0).

SDIV*(expression1,expression2)* U

Divides the string number derived from *expression1* by the string number derived from

254

expression2, returning the result as a string number. Both numbers must be string numbers; otherwise an error message is displayed and the result returned to zero (0).

SEEK(ARG.) {**THEN** *statement*} {**ELSE** *statement*}
SEEK(ARG. , *expression*) {**THEN** *statement*} {**ELSE** *statement*}

Used to locate arguments from the ARG. redirection variable. Arguments are provided with the command used to initially execute the program. See also the GET(ARG.) and SEEK(MSG.) functions.

In the second form, the expression derives an integer number indicating the position of the argument to locate. If the expression is omitted, the next argument is located. See also the EOF function. Note that the THEN/ELSE construct is allowed. The THEN branch is taken when the SEEK successfully locates an argument, and the ELSE branch is taken if it is unsuccessful.

SEEK(MSG.) {**THEN** *statement*} {**ELSE** *statement*}
SEEK(MSG. , *expression*) {**THEN** *statement*} {**ELSE** *statement*}

Used to locate messages from the MSG. redirection variable. Messages are generated from the most recently issued EXECUTE statement. The MSG. redirection variable is reset to null prior to issuing an EXECUTE statement. See also the GET(MSG.) and SEEK(ARG.) functions.

In the latter form, the expression derives an integer number indicating the position of the message to retrieve. If the expression is omitted, the next message is located. See also the EOF function.

Note that the THEN/ELSE construct is allowed. The THEN branch is taken when the SEEK successfully locates a message, and the ELSE branch is taken if unsuccessful.

SELECT {*file.variable*} {**TO** *selectvar*} {**ON ERROR** *statement(s)*}

Creates a list of item-ids from the file specified in the file variable parameter, allowing sequential access to each item in the file. If the file variable parameter is not specified, the default file variable is used. See also the READNEXT statement. When used with the TO clause, the item list is assigned to the specified select variable.

Ultimate Only: Only the Ultimate system allows the ON ERROR condition, which is taken if the file is remote (accessed through UltiNet) and the file can't be cleared due to a network error condition; in this instance, SYSTEM(0) contains the UltiNet error message number.

SEQ(*expression*)

Converts an ASCII character to its numeric equivalent. The inverse of CHAR.

SIN(*numeric.expression*)

Calculates the sine of the angle specified in the numeric expression, and returns the result in degrees.

SLEEP
SLEEP *number.seconds*
SLEEP *military.time*

Puts the program to ''sleep'' for some period of time. While sleeping, program execution is suspended. Normally, so is the break key. This happens to be the same as the SLEEP statement. In the first form, when no argument is specified, the program sleeps for one second before continuing execution.

255

In the second form, when an integer number follows as the argument, the program sleeps for that number of seconds. For example, this statement

    SLEEP 300

puts the program to sleep for 5 minutes.

In the final form, the statement may be followed by a legal "military" (24-hour) time. This is like leaving a wake-up call. For example:

    SLEEP 8:00

puts the program to sleep until 8:00 A.M. For times after noon, use the 24-hour form:

    SLEEP 17:00

This suspends execution until 5:00 P.M.

SMUL*(expression1,expression2)*

Multiplies the string number derived from *expression1* by the string number derived from *expression2*, returning the result as a string number. Both numbers must be string numbers; otherwise an error message is displayed and the result returned is zero (0).

SPACE*(numeric.expression)*

Generates a string of spaces whose length is equal to the value of the numeric expression.

SQRT*(numeric.expression)*

Calculates the square root of the number defined in the numeric expression.

SSUB*(expression1,expression2)*

Subtracts the string number derived from *expression2* from the string number derived from *expression1*, returning the result as a string number. Both numbers must be string numbers; otherwise an error message is displayed and the result returned is zero (0).

STOP
STOP *errmsg#,"parameter"*{*,"parameter"* . . }

Terminates program. The parameter(s) passed to the error message handler and displayed with the message stored in the message number indicated by *errmsg#*. Any message in the ERRMSG file may be used. See also the ABORT statement.

STORAGE *small-buffer, medium-buffer, large-buffer*

Allows changing the standard size of the buffers for storage of string variables. Each "buffer" reference must derive an integer number which is divisible by 10. The default buffer sizes are 50, 150 and 250 bytes, respectively. For example:

    STORAGE 100,250,500

STR*(expression,numeric.expression)*

Generates a string of the variable *expression* repeated the number of times specified in numeric expression. For example, the statement:

```
PRINT STR("*",79)
```

prints 79 asterisks at the current cursor (or print head) position.

SUBROUTINE *{(argumentlist)}*
SUBROUTINE *subroutinename{(argumentlist)}*

Defines a program as an external subroutine. This statement must appear as the first line in an external subroutine, and all arguments defined in the optional argument list must be delimited by commas (,). See also the CALL statement.

All external subroutines should be cataloged prior to execution.

SYSTEM*(expression)*

Interrogates the current value of pertinent system functions. Because this intrinsic function was added to the various implementations at different points in time, the arguments and features vary among systems. See Tables A-3 and A-4 for a breakdown.

TAN*(numeric.expression)*

Calculates the tangent of the angle specified in degrees by numeric expression.

THEN/ELSE

In-line initiator. See the section at the end of this appendix on the THEN/ELSE construct.

TIME( )

Returns the current system time in internal format. Internal time is represented as an integer number indicating the number of seconds past midnight.

TIMEDATE( )

Returns current system time and date in external format:

hh:mm:ss   dd mmm yyyy

TRIM*(string.expression)*

Removes all leading and trailing blanks from string expression, and leaves one blank wherever more than one blank was embedded within the string. For example:

```
STRING = "   1600     PENNSYLVANIA     AVENUE        "
STRING = TRIM(STRING)
```

After the TRIM, STRING would contain "1600 PENNSYLVANIA AVENUE".

(0)	Relates to last tape-handling error :

        1 If not attached.
        2 EOF detected on tape.
        3 Attempted to write null string.
        4 Attempted to write tape record longer than tape block size.
        5 Off line.
        6 Cartridge improperly formatted.

(1)   Returns 1 if system printer is enabled (via the RUN command ''P'' option, or the PRINTER ON statement).

(2)   Returns page width, as defined by TERM command.

(3)   Returns page length, as defined by TERM command.

(4)   Returns number of lines remaining to print on current page, based on current terminal characteristics previously defined with TERM command.

(5)   Returns current page number.

(6)   Returns current line counter.

(7)   Returns terminal type code, as defined by TERM command.

(8)   Returns block size at which tape was last attached.

(9)   Returns system serial number.

(10)   Returns type of machine on which program is running:

        D0 DEC-based without typeahead.
        D1 DEC-based with typeahead and regular memory.
        D2 DEC-based with typeahead and dual-ported memory.
        H0 Honeywell-based with WCS.
        H1 Honeywell-based with HPP.

(11)   Returns number of characters residing in typeahead buffer.

(12)   Returns last character entered through last INPUT statement.

Note: Options 4, 5, and 6 may only be used in conjunction with the HEADING and/or FOOTING commands within PICK/BASIC.

UNLOCK
UNLOCK *locknumber-expression*

    Resets an execution lock, in the range 0 to 47. If no locknumber is specified, all locks set by the program are unlocked. See also the LOCK statement.

UNTIL

    In-line initiator in a FOR-NEXT statement. Multiline initiator in a LOOP statement. See FOR-NEXT and LOOP-WHILE statements.

(0)	Relates to last tape-handling error:

      1 If not attached.
      2 Null variable.
    11 Record truncated.

(1)   Returns "1" if system printer is on.

(2)   Retrieves current page width, as defined by TERM command.

(3)   Retrieves current page length, as defined by TERM command.

(4)   Returns number of lines remaining to print on current page, based on current terminal characteristics previously defined with TERM command.

(5)   Retrieves current page number.

(6)   Retrieves current line number.

(7)   Retrieves current terminal type code, as defined by TERM command.

(8)   Returns block size at which tape was last attached.

(9)   Retrieves current CPU charge units count.

(10)   Checks the current stack (STON) condition. Returns "1" (one) if stack is on, or "0" (zero) if not on.

(11)   Checks status of list function. Returns "1" (one) if list is active, or "0" (zero) if no list is active.

(12)   Returns system time in milliseconds.

(13)   System RQM. One 50 ms delay as timeslice is terminated.

(14)   Returns number of bytes awaiting input in input buffer.

(15)   Returns verb option(s) in effect.

(16)   Returns number of levels of nested EXECUTE statements.

(17)   Returns ERRMSG item-ids from previous EXECUTE statement.

(100)   Returns release level on Pick XT and AT only.

Note: Options 4, 5, and 6 may only be used in conjunction with the HEADING and/or FOOTING commands within PICK/BASIC.

WEOF *{THEN statement(s)}* **ELSE** *statement(s)*

    Writes an end-of-file mark to tape. The ELSE condition is taken if the tape is not ready or attached. See the section on the THEN/ELSE construct.

WHILE

    In-line initiator in a FOR-NEXT statement. Multiline initiator in a LOOP statement. See FOR-WHILE and LOOP-WHILE statements.

WRITE *array.variable* **ON** {*file.variable,*}*id.expression* . . .
   . . . {**ON ERROR** *statement(s)*}

Writes the item from the dynamic array specified in *array.variable* into the specified file, using the item-id specified in the item-id expression. If the file variable parameter is not specified, the default file variable is used. See also the WRITEU statement.

*Ultimate Only:*Only the Ultimate system allows the ON ERROR condition, which is taken if the file is remote (accessed through UltiNet) and the file can't be cleared due to a network error condition; in this instance, SYSTEM(0) contains the UltiNet error message number.

WRITET *expression* {**THEN** *statement(s)*} **ELSE** *statement(s)*

Writes the value of the expression to tape. The ELSE condition is taken if the tape is not ready or attached. See the section on the THEN/ELSE construct.

WRITEU *array.variable* **ON** {*file.variable,*}*id.expression* . . .
   . . . {**ON ERROR** *statement(s)*}

Writes the item from the dynamic array specified in *array.variable* into the specified file, using the item-id specified in the item-id expression. If the file variable parameter is not specified, the default file variable is used. See also the WRITE statement.

The WRITEU statement is identical to the WRITE statement, except that the group in which the item is written remains locked. See also the RELEASE statement.

Ultimate Only: Only the Ultimate system allows the ON ERROR condition, which is taken if the file is remote (accessed through UltiNet) and the file can't be cleared due to a network error condition; in this instance, SYSTEM(0) contains the UltiNet error message number.

WRITEV *expression* **ON** {*file.variable,*}*id.expression,amc.expression* . . .
   . . .{**ON ERROR** *statement(s)*}

Writes the value of the expression into the attribute designated in the attribute expression parameter, using the item-id specified in the item-id expression parameter. If the file variable parameter is omitted, the default file variable is used. Note that this statement causes a READ to occur prior to the WRITEV, which accounts for its inefficiency. See also the WRITEVU statement.

Ultimate Only: Only the Ultimate system allows the ON ERROR condition, which is taken if the file is remote (accessed through UltiNet) and the file can't be cleard due to a network error condition; in this instance, SYSTEM (0) contains the UltiNet error message number.

WRITEVU *expression* **ON** {*file.variable,*}*id.expression,amc.expression* . . .
   . . .{**ON ERROR** *statement(s)*}

Writes the value of the expression into the attribute designated in the attribute expression parameter, using the item-id specified in the item-id expression parameter. If the file variable parameter is omitted, the default file variable is used. Note that this statement causes a READ to occur prior to the WRITEV, which accounts for its inefficiency. See also the WRITEV statement.

The WRITEVU statement is identical to the WRITEV statement, except that the group in which the item is written remains locked. See also the RELEASE statement.

Ultimate Only: Only the Ultimate system allows the ON ERROR condition, which is taken if the file is remote (accessed through UltiNet) and the file can't be cleared due to a network error condition; in this instance, SYSTEM(0) contains the UltiNet error message number.

THE THEN/ELSE CONSTRUCT AND ITS
IMPLICATIONS ON MULTILINE STATEMENTS

The following statements make use of the THEN/ELSE construct in PICK/BASIC:

All Systems:	Ultimate Only:
IF	GET
LOCATE	INPUT
MATREAD	LOCK
MATREADU	PUT
OPEN	SEEK
READ	
READNEXT	
READT	
READU	
READV	
READVU	
REWIND	
WEOF	
WRITET	

Ultimate Only: See the section entitled "Optional ELSE Clause Special Exceptions" at the end of this section.

The IF-THEN-ELSE Construct

Each of these statements are referred to as *initiators* of the THEN or ELSE clause that succeeds them. The possible syntactic structures are:

1)   *initiator* **THEN** *statements* **ELSE** *statements*

2)   *initiator* **THEN** *statements*

3)   *initiator* **ELSE** *statements*

When THEN and ELSE clauses are both present, the THEN clause may be considered to be the initiator of the ELSE clause. All other characteristics are identical, except that an ELSE clause may succeed a THEN clause. For simplicity's sake, this will cover only the case of the THEN clause.

Within the THEN clause, the THEN token is the initiator, which requires a terminator. The clause may exist on one or more than one line. The nature of the terminator varies between these cases.

Single-Line Form. If the THEN clause is complete in one physical line, its terminator is a <cr> or an ELSE token.

initiator **THEN** *statement(s)* <cr>

or

initiator **THEN** *statement(s)* **ELSE** *statement(s)* <cr>

The form for the single-line clause is:

    THEN *statement*; *statement*; . . . ;<cr>

or

    THEN *statement*; *statement*; . . . ;**ELSE**<cr>

The syntax of the ELSE clause is the same as that of the THEN clause, except that it may not be followed by another ELSE clause.

Multiline Form. If the THEN clause spans more than one physical line, the THEN token must immediately be followed by an EOL (End-Of-Line) character. This may be either a <cr> or a semicolon. In this case, the clause is terminated by END preceded by an EOL character.

    initiator **THEN** <cr>
        statement(s)<cr>
        statement(s)<cr>
        statement(s)<cr>
    END

There must be one or more statements between the THEN and its terminator. If there are several statements, they must be separated by EOL characters. If the THEN clause is the one-physical-line clause, the EOL character must be a semicolon. If the THEN clause spans more than one physical line, the EOL characters may be either (or both) <cr>'s or semicolons.

    The form of the multiline clause is:

    THEN EOL *statement* **EOL** *statement* **EOL EOL END EOL**

or

    THEN EOL *statement* **EOL** *statement* **EOL EOL END ELSE EOL** *statement* . . .
    . . . **EOL** *statement* **END EOL**

In this case, each EOL character may be either a <cr> or a semicolon. This means that a multiline clause may be contained in either one or more than one physical line. This case will normally appear as:

    THEN<cr>
        statement<cr>
        statement<cr>
        statement<cr>
    END<cr>

For program clarity, the statements are indented from the beginning of the initiator, and the THEN or END ELSE are outdented to the beginning of the initiator.

Multiple END Statements

Multiline statements may have more than one END statement. The END statement then becomes the initiator for the ELSE condition, as follows:

```
   initiator THEN<cr>
      statement<cr>
      statement<cr>
      statement<cr>
   END ELSE<cr>
      statement<cr>
      statement<cr>
      statement<cr>
   END
```

Multiple END ELSE sequences may be used, provided that each ends with an END statement.

Optional ELSE Clause Special Exceptions

Ultimate Only: The following five statements *cannot* be followed by an ELSE clause in a single-line IF-THEN-ELSE construct because of potential ambiguity to the compiler:

```
GET     PUT
INPUT   SEEK
LOCK
```

When any of these statements are to be used in an IF-THEN-ELSE construct, then the multiline form *must* be used.

Table A-5. Common User Exits.

U3060	Returns 8 hexadecimal characters as a value from a supplied string. Used by the PASSWORD program to encrypt passwords.
U3079	Converts PCB-FID (Primary Control Block frame-id) either way, in an ICONV or OCONV statement.
U0079	Returns the same output as the "WHERE" verb from TCL.
U0159	Extended math processor for floating point operations.
U018D	Disables break key. Note that this must be used with ICONV, rather than OCONV.
U1072	Activates "SORT" from PICK/BASIC.
U118D	Enables break key. Note that this must be used with ICONV, rather than OCONV.
U307A	Sleeps until specified military time. See the SLEEP or RQM statements in this appendix.
U407A	Sleeps for specified number of seconds. See the SLEEP or RQM statements in this appendix.
U50BB	Functions exactly like the WHO command in TCL, returning the current port number and account name.
U6072	Enables function to strip control characters from input.
U7072	Terminates printing of (PICK/BASIC) HEADING and forces stop of paging.
U9072	Disables function to strip control characters from input.
U90ED	Resets tape reel number to one.

PICK/BASIC USER EXITS

User exits are special functions that make direct references to assembler routines known as *modes*. They were added to fulfill needs outside the standard boundaries of the Ultimate system, and did so until they were replaced by system extensions. User exits have always been dangerous and, as long as they remain, they will continue to be. EXTREME caution is advised in using them. *Caveat emptor.*

The general form of a user exit is:

. . . = **OCONV**(*argument*, *"user-exit"*)

In other words, the user exits may be on the right side of an equals sign or after a PRINT statement. Table A-5 summarizes the available user exits.

APPENDIX

B

Sample Data
and Dictionary
for STAFF File

THE FOLLOWING (DATA) ITEMS SHOULD BE ADDED TO THE STAFF FILE. THIS CAN BE DONE USING THE editor, just like you did with the tutorial programs. Alternately, if you have completed Program Example 10, which deals with file input and output, then that program can be used to add these items to the STAFF file.

```
Item-Id 100                        Item-Id 101

001   THOMPSON, HUNTER             001   HEMINGWAY, ERNIE
002   C/O STARDUST HOTEL           002   C/O HARRYS BAR
003   LAS VEGAS                    003   FLORENCE
004   NV                           004   IT
005   77777                        005   6065
006   7026601000                   006   0206167890
007   8888                         007   7777
008   -6500                        008   -10000
009   15000                        009   25000
```

Item-Id **102**		Item-Id **103**	
001	STEINBECK, JOHN	001	ALLEN, WOODY
002	C/O CANNERY ROW HOTEL	002	300 CENTRAL PARK WEST
003	CARMEL	003	NEW YORK
004	CA	004	NY
005	94500	005	10019
006	4158858880	006	212UNKNOWN
007	6666	007	7000
008	-9000	008	-6000
009	12500	009	30000

Item-Id **104**		Item-Id **105**	
001	TRUDEAU, GARRY	001	KUBRICK, STANLEY
002	C/O WALDEN POND	002	C/O STANLEY HOTEL
003	WALDEN	003	ESTES PARK
004	MA	004	CO
005	08080	005	80808
006	6175554444	006	3035558888
007	7100	007	7050
008	-5500	008	-8500
009	35000	009	22500

Item-Id **106**	
001	HUSTON, JOHN
002	C/O RICKS AMERICAN BAR
003	CASABLANCA
004	CA
005	92303
006	7149987777
007	6800
008	-7700
009	19500

THE STAFF FILE ATTRIBUTE-DEFINING-ITEMS

The following items should be added to the dictionary of the STAFF file.

Item-Id	NAME	ADDRESS	CITY	STATE	ZIP
001	A	A	A	A	A
002	1	2	3	4	5
003	NAME	ADDRESS	CITY	STATE	ZIP
004					
005					
006					
007					
008	L	T	L	L	R
009	15	20	15	5	5

Item-Id	PHONE	RENEW.DATE	BIRTHDAY	HOURLY.RATE
001	A	A	A	A
002	6	7	8	9
003	PHONE	RENEW.DATE	BIRTHDAY	HOURLY.RATE
004				
005				
006				
007	ML((###) ###-####)	D2/	D2/	MR2,$
008	L	R	R	R
009	14	8	8	14

Additional
PICK/BASIC Programs

PROGRAM EXAMPLE 5A

```
001 * EX.005A
002 * CALCULATE NUMBER OF SHOPPING DAYS UNTIL CHRISTMAS...
003 * mm/dd/yy : date last modified
004 * JES : author's initials
005 *
006    PROMPT ":"
007 *
008    PRINT
009 *
010 * FIRST, FIGURE OUT CURRENT YEAR
011 *
012    CURRENT.YEAR = OCONV(DATE(),"DY")
013 *
014 * NOW GET INTERNAL DATE FOR CHRISTMAS OF THIS YEAR
015 *
016    INTERNAL.CHRISTMAS = ICONV("12-25-":CURRENT YEAR, "D")
017 *
018 * NOW GET JULIAN DATE FOR CHRISTMAS
019 *
020    JULIAN.CHRISTMAS = OCONV(INTERNAL.CHRISTMAS,"DJ")
021 *
022 * NOW PRINT TODAY'S DATE
023 *
```

```
024     PRINT "TODAY IS " : OCONV(DATE(),"D2/")
025 *
026 * NOW GET TODAY'S JULIAN DATE
027 *
028     JULIAN.TODAY = OCONV(DATE(),"DJ")
029 *
030 * THAT'S ENOUGH WORK, LET'S FIGURE OUT THE REST
031 *
032     NUMBER.OF.DAYS = JULIAN.CHRISTMAS - JULIAN.TODAY
033     PRINT "IT'S DAY " : JULIAN.TODAY : " OF THE YEAR"
034     IF NUMBER.OF.DAYS > 0 THEN
035        PRINT "THERE ARE " : NUMBER.OF.DAYS :
036        PRINT " SHOPPING DAYS UNTIL CHRISTMAS."
037     END ELSE
038        PRINT "YOU MAY AS WELL FORGET ABOUT IT. YOU MISSED IT"
039     END
040 * ADIOS
041     END
```

SNAKE

```
001 * SNAKE
002 * THE NEW IMPROVED SNAKE
003 * mm/dd/yy : date last modified
004 * JES : author's initials
005 *
006    DIM  XX(200), YY(200)
007    MAT XX = 0 ; MAT YY = 0
008    HEAD = 1
008    BORED = 10 ; * HIGHER "BORED" = FEWER DIRECTION CHANGES
009    X = INT(RND(12)) + 6
010    Y = INT(RND(40)) + 20
011    DX = INT(RND(2))
012    IF DX = 0 THEN DX = -1
013    DY = INT(RND(2))
014    IF DY = 0 THEN DY = -1
015 *
016    LOOP
017       PRINT @(-1) : "LENGTH OF SNAKE (2-200) = " :
018       INPUT LENGTH
019    UNTIL LENGTH > 1 AND LENGTH < 201 DO REPEAT
020 *
021    LOOP
022       PRINT "NUMBER OF SECONDS TO EXECUTE (5-120) = " :
023       INPUT SECONDS
024    UNTIL SECONDS > 4 AND SECONDS < 121 DO REPEAT
025 *
026    MILLER.TIME = TIME() + SECONDS
027    LOOP UNTIL TIME() >= MILLER.TIME DO
028       PRINT @(Y,X) : "*" : @(YY(HEAD),XX(HEAD)) : " " :
```

```
029      XX(HEAD) = X
030      YY(HEAD) = Y
031      HEAD = HEAD + 1
032      IF HEAD > LENGTH THEN HEAD = 1
033      X = X + DX
034      IF X <= 0 OR X >= 22 OR RND(BORED) < 1 THEN DX = -DX
035      Y = Y + DY
036      IF Y <= 0 OR Y >= 79 OR RND(BORED * 3) < 1 THEN DY = -DY
037   REPEAT
038   END
```

PROGRAM EXAMPLE 16

```
001 * EX.016
002 * MORE ON LOOPS: LOOP WHILE AND LOOP UNTIL
003 * mm/dd/yy : date last modified
004 * JES : author's initials
005 *
006    PROMPT ":"
007 *
008    EQU TRUE TO 1
009    EQU FALSE TO 0
010    PERIOD.COUNTER = 0
011    PRINCIPAL = 0
012    INTEREST.INCOME.TOTAL = 0
013 *
014 * GET PRINCIPAL AMOUNT
015 *
016    LOOP
017       PRINT "ENTER PRINCIPAL AMOUNT " :
018       INPUT PRINCIPAL
019    UNTIL NUM(PRINCIPAL) OR PRINCIPAL = "QUIT" DO REPEAT
020    IF PRINCIPAL = "QUIT" THEN STOP
021 *
022    PRINCIPAL = ICONV(PRINCIPAL,"MR2") ;* INTERNALLY CONVERT
023 *
024 * GET INTEREST RATE
025 *
026    LOOP
027       PRINT "ENTER INTEREST RATE " :
028       INPUT RATE
029    UNTIL RATE # "" OR NUM(RATE) OR RATE = "QUIT" DO REPEAT
030    IF RATE = "QUIT" THEN STOP
031 *
032 * GET NUMBER OF PERIODS
033 *
034    LOOP
035       PRINT "ENTER NUMBER OF COMPOUNDING PERIODS " :
036       INPUT PERIODS
```

```
037     UNTIL PERIODS # "" OR NUM(PERIODS) OR PERIODS="QUIT" DO REPEAT
038     IF PERIODS = "QUIT" THEN STOP
039 *
040 * PRINT HEADER LINE
041 *
042     PRINT "PERIOD" "L#10" : "PRINCIPAL" "L#20" : "INTEREST" "L#20"
043 *
044 * START CALCULATIONS
045 *
046     LOOP
047        PRINT PERIOD.COUNTER + 1 "L#10" :
048        INTEREST.INCOME = PRINCIPAL * RATE
049        PRINT OCONV(PRINCIPAL,"MR2,$") "L#20" :
050        PRINT OCONV(INTEREST.INCOME,"MR2,$") "L#20"
051        PRINCIPAL=PRINCIPAL+INTEREST.INCOME
052        INTEREST.INCOME.TOTAL=INTEREST.INCOME.TOTAL+INTEREST.INCOME
053        PERIOD.COUNTER = PERIOD.COUNTER + 1
054     UNTIL PERIOD.COUNTER = PERIODS DO REPEAT
055 *
056 * ALL DONE
057 *
058     END
```

PICK/BASIC
Error Messages

B0   *programname* **cataloged**

Displayed when cataloging a PICK/BASIC program.

B1   **Run-time abort at line** *linenumber*

B3   **String length exceeds 32,266 characters**

B10   **Variable has not been assigned a value; zero used!**

Displayed when executing a PICK/BASIC program that references a variable that has not previously been referenced. Also occurs when writing dimensioned arrays that have not been ''set'' to null with a MAT assignment.

B11   **Tape record truncated to tape record length!**

This occurs in programs that write tape records when a tape record exceeds the number of bytes at which the tape was attached.

B12   **File has not been opened**

Indicates that a read or write operation was attempted on a file that has not previously been opened with an OPEN statement.

B13 Null conversion code is illegal; no conversion done!

This means that the conversion code expression in an ICONV or OCONV statement evaluated to a "null" and that it did not do exactly what was expected.

B14 Bad stack descriptor

Indicates that the number of arguments passed with a CALL statement differ from the number of arguments in the SUBROUTINE statement in the external subroutine. Also occurs when a file variable is used as an operand.

B15 Illegal opcode: *opcode*

Try recompiling the program.

B16 Non-numeric data when numeric required; zero used!

Typically occurs when a mathematical function is attempted on a string variable.

B17 Array subscript out-of-range

This fatal error occurs when referencing a subscript less than zero or greater than the number of subscripts (attributes) declared in the DIM or DIMENSION statement that established storage space for the dimensioned array.

B18 Attribute number less than −1 is illegal

Occurs when the attribute expression of the READV or WRITEV statement evaluates to a negative number.

B19 Illegal pattern

Indicates a meaningless pattern in a MATCH or MATCHES statement.

B20 COL1 or COL2 used prior to executing a FIELD stmt; zero used!

This means that a reference was made to either the COL1 ( ) or COL2 ( ) functions prior to issuing a FIELD statement.

B22 Illegal value for STORAGE statement

Indicates that an argument of the STORAGE statement is less than 10, or not divisible by 10.

B23 Program *programname* **must be recompiled**

Means that the object code being executed is not compatible with the current release of the operating system.

B24 Divide by zero illegal; zero used!

This indicates that a number was attempted to be divided by zero. Check the divisor to make sure that it has been assigned a value.

B25 Program *programname* has not been cataloged

This message displays when a CALL statement is issued, referring to an external PICK/BASIC program subroutine which has not been cataloged.

B26 UNLOCK attempted before LOCK

This indicates that an attempt was made to UNLOCK one of the 48 system execution locks prior to its having been locked.

B27 RETURN executed with no GOSUB

This typically occurs when an internal subroutine is executed without having been transferred to with a GOSUB statement, causing the RETURN statement to force this error.

B28 Not enough work space

This typically occurs when running a large PICK/BASIC program that may be dealing with one or more large data items. Program size is limited to 32,000 bytes. The solution is to break the program into smaller subroutines until this limitation is removed from the Pick System.

B30 Array size mismatch

This occurs when a mainline program and an external subroutine both refer to the same dimensioned array, but each declares a different number of attributes. Also occurs in a "MAT copy" (MAT A = MAT B) when the number of vectors are different.

B31 Stack overflow

This occurs when a program calls too many nested subroutines.

B32 Page heading exceeds maximum of 1400 characters

A HEADING statement in PICK/BASIC cannot exceed 1400 characters.

B33 Precision declared in subprogram *programname* is different from that declared in the mainline program

This indicates that there is a PRECISION statement in an external subroutine that specifies a different number of decimal places than that of the PRECISION statement in the mainline program.

B34 File variable used where string expression expected

This indicates that some reference was made to a variable that has been declared as a file variable in an OPEN statement.

B41 Lock number is greater than 47

This means that the expression evaluated in the LOCK statement contained a number greater than 47. PICK/BASIC divides the number by 48 and the remainder is used as the lock number.

B100 Compilation aborted; no object code produced

This is displayed when a compile fails for any reason. As a general rule of thumb, ignore all but the *first* message that displays when a compile fails. Find and fix the problem indicated with the first message and then recompile.

B101 Ambiguous ELSE clause

This indicates that a statement with an optional ELSE clause is used in a single-line IF statement.

B102 Bad statement

This compile-time error indicates that there is something syntactically wrong with the line displayed immediately above this message. Look for misspelled statements and/or unclosed quotes or parentheses.

B103 Label *label* is missing

Displayed when a GOTO statement refers to a statement label that cannot be located in the program. Make sure that the statement label is the *first* executable parameter on the line. If it follows an asterisk, for example, it will never be seen by the compiler. This also occurs when a reference to a dimensioned array is made without indicating a subscript (vector).

B104 Label *label* is doubly defined

Indicates that there are two occurrences of the same statement label.

B105 *variable* has not been dimensioned

This displays when a non-dimensioned variable is treated as a dimensioned variable.

B106 *variable* has been dimensioned and used without subscripts

This is displayed when a reference is made to a dimensioned array without being followed by a subscript (attribute) specification.

B107 LOOP statement nested too deep

Indicates that a LOOP statement is nested within too many outer LOOP statements.

B109 Variable missing in "NEXT" statement

This occurs when the NEXT statement is not followed by the variable declared in the FOR statement.

B110 END statement missing

This often occurs when the END statements do not "balance" in a program, meaning that there may be a missing END statement somewhere in a series of IF-THEN clauses.

B111 EXIT used outside of LOOP statement

Indicates that an EXIT statement occurred *outside* of a LOOP / REPEAT clause.

B112 REPEAT missing in LOOP statement

This means that the REPEAT statement cannot be located for the initiating LOOP statement.

B113 Terminator missing

This displays when a line containing quoted literals is missing one or more of the quote marks, or when "garbage" follows a legal statement.

B114 Maximum number of variables exceeded

PICK/BASIC allows for about 3200 variables in a program. This is normally enough for most people. If not, try moving some of the variables to an external subroutine.

B115 label *label* is used before the equate stmt

This occurs when a reference is made to a constant prior to its being declared with the EQU or EQUATE statement.

B116 label *label* is used before the COMMON stmt

All variables must be declared in the COM or COMMON statement prior to being used in a program. This can be avoided, as can other problems, by *not* using the COMMON statement.

B117 label *label* is missing a subscript list

This displays when a reference is made to a dimensioned array variable without indicating a subscript (attribute) specification.

B118 label *label* is the object of an EQUATE statement and is missing

Indicates that the variable after the TO portion of an EQU statement has not been declared, or is used elsewhere in the program.

B119 Warning - precision value out of range - ignored

Indicates that a precision less than zero (0) or greater than nine (9) was attempted.

B120 Warning - multiple precision statements - ignored!

This non-fatal error message indicates that more than one PRECISION statement is specified in the program. All but the first are ignored.

276

B121 Label *label* is a constant and cannot be written into.

This occurs when an attempt is made to change the value of a constant declared in an EQU or EQUATE statement.

B122 Label *label* is improper type

Indicates an invalid expression follows the TO in an EQU or EQUATE statement.

B124 Label *label* has literal subscripts out of range

Indicates a reference to a subscript (attribute) greater than the number of subscripts declared for the array in the DIM or DIMENSION statement; alternately, may indicate a subscript of less than one.

B125 No source statements found; no object code produced

Indicates a source item with no source lines.

B126 ELSE clause missing

Indicates that an ELSE clause is missing in a statement where it is required.

B127 NEXT missing

Indicates that the NEXT statement in a FOR-NEXT loop is missing.

B128 Item *itemname* not found

Indicates that the itemname specified in an $INCLUDE or $CHAIN directive has been omitted.

B129 Illegal: program name same as dictionary item name

There may *not* be a program in a file with the same name as the file.

B199 Source file must have separate DICT and DATA sections

Indicates that the PICK/BASIC source file has only a dictionary level. A data section must be created.

B209 File is update protected

Indicates that an update (write operation) was attempted on an update-restricted file.

B210 File is access protected

Indicates that a read operation was attempted on a read-restricted file.

B222 'CSYM' is not a file name or needs a data level

This displays when the pointer to the CSYM file is missing or improperly defined in the MD of the current account.

The PICK/BASIC
Interactive Debugger

THE PICK/BASIC DEBUGGER IS USED FOR TRACING EXECUTION LOCATIONS AND VARIABLES IN PICK/BASIC programs.

Symbol Definitions

Each variable referred to in a program produces a *symbol,* which is used to refer to that particular variable throughout the rest of the program and through functions within the debugger. The symbol definitions are automatically defined during the compile process and are with the executable object code in the dictionary level of the program file.

Activating the PICK/BASIC Debugger

The PICK/BASIC debugger is basically activated one of two ways, either voluntarily or involuntarily.

Voluntary Debugger Entry. In the voluntary form, the debugger is entered upon pressing the break key while running a PICK/BASIC program. It may also be entered prior to execution of a program with the ''D'' option:

```
>RUN BP HELLO (D)<cr>
*E1
*
```

If the program has been cataloged, then this form changes to:

```
>HELLO (D)<cr>
*El
*
```

Fatal Error Conditions. In the involuntary form, a PICK/BASIC program enters the debugger whenever a "fatal" error condition is encountered, like when an attempt is made to read from a file that has not previously been opened. When a fatal condition is encountered, the program "breaks" and displays something to this effect:

Innn

[nnn]text.of.fatal.error.message
```
*
```

The "I" in I*nnn* indicates that an "interrupt" has occurred in the program at line *nnn*, the corresponding source program line. The "B*nnn*" is the BASIC error message item-id, as retrieved from the ERRMSG file. The text next to the message attempts to explain the reason why the program crashed and burned.

Nonfatal Error Conditions. A "non-fatal" error condition is one in which a program error of some sort has been detected, but is not considered serious enough to warrant terminating the program. The classic case of such a condition is the infamous message:

```
[B***] VARIABLE HAS NOT BEEN ASSIGNED A VALUE!   ZERO USED.
```

Although the error does not stop the program, it still should be corrected. Sometimes it is difficult to "catch" the message being displayed, like when it flashes past just before a screen clearing operation.

Another option is provided to force all error conditions, whether normally considered fatal or not, to enter the debugger. This is the "E" option, and here is how it is used:

```
>RUN MY.PROGRAMS TEST.PROG (E)<cr>
```

(program starts running . . . .)
(Bang! It breaks!)

```
[B***] VARIABLE HAS NOT BEEN ASSIGNED A VALUE!   ZERO USED.
*
```

USING THE DEBUG STATEMENT

In the tedious debugging phase of writing programs, it might be necessary to insert one or more DEBUG statements within the program at potential trouble spots. When the DEBUG statement is executed, the program immediately enters the debugger, where variables may be interrogated and logic can be traced. Naturally, once the problems have been detected and corrected, then the DEBUG statements should be removed from the version that will go into production.

Prompt Character

The prompt character, an asterisk (*), appears in the leftmost column of the terminal display screen, indicating that the debugger is ready to accept any legal command.

Term Conventions

The following two abbreviations are used in command templates for the PICK/BASIC debugger:

op   Abbreviation for operator. Used in setting "breakpoints" with the "B" command. (See the following section on operators.)

var   Abbreviation for variable name. The actual name of the variable, as defined in the program source code.

Operators

The operators listed below perform logical comparison functions.

=   Equal to
>   Greater than
<   Less than

> =   Greater than or equal to

< =   Less than or equal to
Not equal to

Referencing, Displaying and Changing Variables

While in the debugger, any individual variable may be displayed. For example, let's suppose that there was a variable called AMOUNT.DUE, and you wanted to display its current value. You would enter:

```
*/AMOUNT.DUE<cr>
```

This would locate and display its current value, and allow you the option of changing it:

```
*/AMOUNT.DUE 12500=_
```

Note that when the cursor remains to the right of the "=" symbol, anything you enter will replace the current value of the variable. Issuing a carriage return while on the right side of the equal sign leaves the current value intact.

Referencing Dimensioned Arrays

If a dimensioned array variable is requested without also providing a subscript, then all elements in the array are individually displayed and the current value of any element may be changed. Pressing Return will "step" down to the next element until the last element is reached or the break key is pressed. For example, suppose there were a dimensioned array named CUSTOMER.ITEM:

```
*/CUSTOMER.ITEM<cr>
*CUSTOMER.ITEM(1) PROPELLER HEAD ENTERPRISES=<cr>
*CUSTOMER.ITEM(2) 1400 W. 147TH ST=<cr>
*CUSTOMER.ITEM(3) CHICAGO=<cr>
```

```
*CUSTOMER.ITEM(4) IL=<cr>
*CUSTOMER.ITEM(5) 60609=<break>
*
```

Individual subscripts in dimensioned arrays may also be examined and optionally changed. For example, the instruction:

```
*/CUSTOMER.ITEM(1)<cr>
```

might display:

```
*/CUSTOMER.ITEM(1) PROPELLER HEAD ENTERPRISES=<cr>
```

Once again, the current value may be replaced.

In the rare event of needing to reference a two-dimensional array, the syntax calls for both coordinates, as in the following example:

```
*/TAX.TABLE.ITEM(3,2)
```

Listing All Program Variables

A complete list of every variable defined in the program can be obtained with the command:

```
*/*<cr>
```

Note, however, that when all variables are being displayed, you are not given the chance to change any of them. Again, they must be requested individually to be changed.

Zone Output Specification

The following command sets left and right margins for output zone limits of debugger display:

*[{*leftmargin,rightmargin*}]

The [command followed immediately by a <cr> removes zone limits.

PICK/BASIC Debugger Command

*?

*$

Displays current program name, execution line number, and object code verification status.

Bvar operator variable

Bvar operator "literal"

The B command sets program breakpoints contingent either on a match between the contents

281

of specified variables, or on a specified variable matching a literal. For example:

```
*BREPORT.DATE=TODAY
*BCHECK.AMOUNT>0
*BEMPLOYEE.DEPARTMENT="ACCOUNTING"
```

In the first example, the program breaks and enters the debugger when the current value of RE-PORT.DATE matches the current value of TODAY; in the second, the program breaks when the value of CHECK.AMOUNT becomes greater than 0; and in the third, the break occurs when EMPLOYEE.DEPARTMENT contains the string "ACCOUNTING". Note that strings containing alphabetic or punctuation characters must be enclosed in quotes, but numeric "constants" do not.

*B$*operator linenumber*

The "$" symbol is a special means of referring to a source line number. This provides the ability to enter the debugger, for example, when a certain program line is executed. For example:

```
B$=45
```

This instructs the debugger to be entered before executing line 45 of the program.

```
B$>40
```

This causes the debugger to be activated before executing line 40 and then to reactivate itself before each subsequent program line is executed, until this breakpoint condition is removed.

As breakpoint conditions are entered into the breakpoint table, a plus (+) character is displayed for each breakpoint successfully entered, until the table is full. The maximum number of breakpoints is four.

Note that the spaces between the arguments in the above syntax illustrations are simply there for readability—they are not allowed when actually composing breakpoints, as shown in the following examples:

```
*B$=45                  (OK)
*BCHECK.SUM # CRC.TOTAL (wrong)
```

*D

Displays the contents of the Break and Trace tables.

*DE
*DEBUG

Transfers control to the system debugger; see your system manuals for available commands.

E{numberlines}*

Specifies the number of instructions to execute prior to returning to debugger command level. Followed immediately by a <cr>, The E command disables previous iteration counter setting.

*END

Terminates program execution and returns control to TCL.

*G {*linenumber*}

"Go to" function. Transfers control to a specific program (source) line number. Followed immediately by a carriage return, the G command resumes program execution from the current program line number. Note that if the program was compiled without EOL (End-Of-Line) characters, then the only number allowable for the "Go to" is one (1).

*K {*breakpoint-number*}

Kills a breakpoint previously set with the B command, and removes the entry from the breakpoint table. Followed immediately by a < cr >, the K command removes all breakpoint entries from the table.

*L {*startingline-numberlines*}
*L {*numberlines*}
L{}
*L

Displays source code program lines, beginning from specified starting line number, or from current position if no starting line number is specified. The L command followed by an asterisk displays the entire program. Followed immediately by a < cr >, the L command displays the current program source code line. (See also the Z command.)

*LP

Toggles the line printer bit, either directing debugger output to the terminal screen or the spooler.

*N {*numbertimes*}

Instructs the debugger to ignore breakpoints for the next number of times they are encountered. The N command followed immediately by a < cr > resets the bypass, and breakpoints are processed at each occurrence.

*OFF

Terminates program execution, logs process off system, and returns control to the logon message.

*P

Toggles the LISTFLG function, either enabling or disabling output display.

*PC

Closes the currently open spooler file entry, releasing control to spooler.

*R

Removes the top return stack address of local subroutine from stack, causing the program to return from current subroutine as though a RETURN statement had been encountered.

*S

Displays the contents of the subroutine stack.

*T{*var*}

Sets a trace table entry, instructing the debugger to display the specified data element, along with the contents of the break and trace tables, on each break. A plus (+) character is displayed for each trace table entry successfully entered into the table, up to a maximum of six entries. Entering the T command without parameters toggles the trace function on or off.

*U{*trace table entry*}

Removes trace table entries previously specified with the T command. A minus (−) character is displayed for each trace table entry successfully removed from the table. Followed immediately by a <cr>, the U command clears all trace table entries previously specified with the T command.

*V

Verifies PICK/BASIC object code. No longer serves any useful function.

*Z {**DICT**} *filename itemname*

*Z<cr>

FILE/PROG NAME?*filename itemname*

Specifies that the debugger should use the symbol table defined for the program referenced in itemname, in the specified filename. Only required when the source code for the program is in a different file than the object code. Entered without parameters, the Z command prompts for the *filename* and *itemname*.

Glossary

< cr >—The standard abbreviation for "carriage return." On some keyboards, this key is called "Enter" or "Newline" or "Line Feed." This is the key that you typically press to let the system know that your command or input is to be considered finished, and is ready for processing.

ABS frames—A frame which contains the executable object code of the Pick Operating System. The name is derived from "ABSolute location," since everything within the frame is addressable by an absolute location, derived by taking the frame number (fid) and displacement (offset) into the frame.

ACCESS—The data retrieval language used to produce reports with English-like sentences; also called RECALL, ENGLISH, INFO/ACCESS, etc. Not covered in this book.

accounts—Accounts are collections of logically related files, much like departments within a company. Each department has its own set of file cabinets. The name of the account is also the "logon," that is, it is entered at the "LOGON PLEASE" message to gain access to the system. In the account's MD also are verbs, miscellaneous connectives and modifiers, and PROCs.

amc.expression—Abbreviation for *Attribute Mark Count* expression. An expression or constant that derives a number which indicates the position of an attribute within an item.

array—An array is a fancy name for an item, as seen in PICK/BASIC. The Pick System allows its "three-dimensional" record structure: items are composed of attributes, which are in turn composed of values, and they in turn may be composed of subvalues. A *dynamic array*, accomplished in a program with a READ statement, is a means of dealing with an item that may have a variable number of array elements. A *dimensioned array* is characterized by having a predetermined number of elements, declared with the DIM statement.

array.variable—A variable used to contain an item, whether a dynamic or dimensioned array. Loaded through a READ or MATREAD statement.

attribute—An attribute is usually an object or a collection of logically related objects, like an address or list of addresses, within an item.

attribute mark—The reserved character from the ASCII character set used to indicate the end of an attribute and the beginning of another. Normally, these characters are "transparent," meaning that, for the most part, you will never see them. If you went looking for them, however, here's what you would find: In its conventional display form, it looks like an "up- arrow" (^); in hexadecimal, its representation is FE, but it is output as 5E; and in decimal, its representation is 254.

To produce an attribute mark from the keyboard requires "control up-arrow," i.e., <control>^. Sometimes the up-arrow key is located as an uppercase character (usually when the ^ symbol appears above the 6 key on the numeric keys above the alphabetic keys). In this case, it takes a "control-shift-^" to produce the attribute mark. Fortunately, you won't have to do this very often.

attribute mark count—The relative number of an attribute within an item.

base fid—This is the "first" frame of the block of contiguous frames set aside for a file.

bit—Actually a contraction for *binary digit*. The logical representation of either a 1 or 0. When eight of these gang together, they are called a *byte*.

byte—A collection of eight bits, which together represent one of the 256 possible characters in the ASCII character set.

conversion—A code native to the ACCESS and PICK/BASIC languages which perform a "reversible mapping," according to the new definition of SMA. More practically, these are the special codes which alter or change the data from one format to another. For example, a money amount may be "externally converted" so that it displays the dollar sign, commas, and decimal point.

conversion.expression—An expression which derives a valid conversion code. Used exclusively in the ICONV and OCONV intrinsic functions.

correlative—According to SMA, not a reversible mapping. The basic difference between conversions and correlatives has classicly been where they were placed in attribute defining items. The general consensus is that if it has to be placed on line 7, then it is a conversion. If it only works on line 8, then it must be a correlative. Some of these codes work on *both* attributes. We are left to decide what to call these. "Convelatives," perhaps? The bottom line is that, currently, *all* of the codes, with the exception of the "A" (algebraic) and "F" (function) correlatives, may be used in the PICK/BASIC ICONV and OCONV functions, although most of them are not needed since there are specific instructions in PICK/BASIC to emulate their features.

CRT—Abbreviation for *cathode ray tube*. Better known as a "tube."

delimiter, reserved—This is the set of four special characters used to accomodate the variable-length record structure of the Pick System. They are: attribute mark (^), value mark (]), subvalue mark (\ ), and the segment mark (_). Note that all four of these characters are control characters. Generally, when these characters need to be used in programs, they are obtained through the CHAR function, referring to each character by its decimal equivalent.

delimiter, non-reserved—A delimiter is simply a predefined character used to separate other characters in a string. For example, each word in this sentence is "delimited" by a space. Any character may be treated as a delimiter.

dictionary—The level of the file system used to contain the attribute defining items for use in ACCESS sentences, as well as to define the actual location of the data section for a file via its data definition item, commonly called its *D- pointer*. Dictionaries are hardly ever used by PICK/BASIC programs, although they are capable of being used through the EXECUTE statement.

Editor—The process through which programs are entered into the computer. It allows items to be created, changed and deleted from any file.

ERRMSG—This is the file which contains the text of the error messages of the operating system. The messages from this file may be used through the STOP and ABORT statements.

fid—Contraction for *frame-id*, the logical address of a frame. The number of frames on a Pick computer is a function of how much disk is present. Each frame is given a unique number between 0 (zero) and *maxfid*, the ''last'' addressable frame.

files—Files are collections of logically related items, much like a file cabinet contains file folders made up of similar types of information. For example, in one file cabinet you may find file folders containing information about your customers, while in another cabinet may be the folders for your suppliers. In the Pick System, the number of items that can be put into a file is limited by the capacity of the disk. We will put all of the PICK/BASIC programs, which are each considered ''items,'' into a file called BP.

file.variable—The name by which a file is referenced during the OPEN statement and subsequently through READ, MATREAD, READV, WRITE, MATWRITE, and WRITEV statements.

frame—The basic division of the hard disk. The entire disk is divided into individual *pages* or *frames* of a predetermined length. In the classic Pick System, frames were 512 bytes, with the first 12 bytes of each frame being *reserved* for the ''linkage'' fields. Frame size now varies on Pick implementations.

frame-id—See *fid*.

functions—Instructions which invoke machine-level microprograms. They usually perform relatively complicated ''functions,'', like removing all extraneous blanks from a string or converting dates to alternate formats, serving part of a larger statement. See Chapter 1.

GFE—Abbreviation for *Group Format Error*, the absolute nemesis of all Pick machines. The presence of one or more GFE's indicate that the data structure has become corrupted for one of about 20 different possible reasons and that data loss may be imminent. As any true-blue programmer will testify, GFE's are almost always caused by hardware and/or power problems. Generally, the appearance of GFE's indicates that it's time to head for your favorite bar while the local team of witch doctors exorcises your machine. Contrary to popular belief, however, you do not have to do a full restore when these appear. Most of them can be corrected by relatively painless surgical procedures.

group—Typically, this is where GFE's hang out.

hashing—The method by which items are placed into, and retrieved from, a file. Each item-id is put through a *hashing algorithm* that mathematically determines which group in the file to look for, or put, an item. An alternate to the industry-standard *ISAM* (Incredibly Slow Access Method).

id.expression—An expression which represents an item-id, found in instructions which read, write, or delete items from files.

item—A collection of logically related attributes.

item-id—The unique item-identifier or ''key'' of an item in a file. See Chapter 1.

megabyte—Contraction of ''mega,'' meaning million, and ''byte,'' from the Latin *bitus,* which means the feeling it places on your checkbook. Typically used by salespeople to indicate the amount of disk or main memory storage they intend to sell you.

modulo—The number that indicates the number of groups in a file. Typically, talking about choosing modulo is a good way to start a heated argument in a room full of technical types.

PIB—Abbreviation for *Primary Input Buffer*.

PROC—The procedural language.

Q-pointer—A "fake" file pointer placed into the Master Dictionary (MD), typically with the Editor. Q-pointers allow access to files that "physically" reside elsewhere, like in another account, but may also be used to refer to files within any account.

segment mark—The reserved character from the ASCII character set used to indicate the end of an item or group. Normally, these characters are "transparent," meaning that for the most part you will never see them. If you went looking for them, however, here's what you would find: In its conventional display format, it looks like an underline (__); in hexadecimal, its representation is FF; and in decimal, its representation is 255.

> To produce a segment mark from the keyboard requires a "control underline", i.e., <control>__. Sometimes the underline key is located as an uppercase character (like when the "__" symbol appears above the "-" key on the numeric keys above the alphabetic keys). In this case, it takes a "control-shift-__" to produce the segment mark.

separation—The number, which goes hand-in-hand with modulo, to indicate the number of frames in each group. On all Pick systems, this defaults to one. Some schools of thought contend that it should be greater than one in some circumstances, but this again is like discussing religion or politics. Pick Systems (the company) has been trying to remove separation altogether for quite a while; on many implementations, if you change the separation to something other than one, with the intent of resizing the file, the system thinks that you were just kidding and changes it back to one for you.

statements—A statement is a list of words which comprise the detailed instructions on which the computer makes its decisions and performs its duties. It will normally consist of constants, variables, expressions, and/or the special commands of the PICK/BASIC language. PICK/BASIC allows multiple statements to be put on one physical line (attribute) if each statement is separated by a semicolon (;). See Chapter 1.

string.expression—An expression which derives a string of characters and/or numbers.

subvalue—An individual element of a value. Most schools of thought prefer to pretend that these don't even exist, since that's how the ACCESS retrieval language reacts to them.

subvalue mark—The reserved character from the ASCII character set used to indicate the end of one subvalue and the beginning of another. Normally, these characters are "transparent," meaning that for the most part you will never see them. If, however, you went looking for them, here's what you would find: In its ASCII appearance, it looks like a backslash (\ ); in hexadecimal, its representation is FC; and in decimal, its representation is 252.

> To produce a subvalue mark from the keyboard requires a "control backslash", i.e., <control> \ . Sometimes the backslash key is located as an uppercase character. In this case, it takes a "control-shift- \ " to produce the subvalue mark.

SYSPROG—By far, the most powerful, and dangerous account on any Pick system. This is the account from which most maintenance takes place, like the creation and deletion of accounts, backups and occasionally restores, and dealing with the spooler. The SYSPROG account is the only account which contains the full complement of verbs; it thus should be restricted to use by only those with a full appreciation of the unlimited damage it can wreak upon the rest of the system.

SYSTEM—The "top" level of the Pick file hierarchy. This file contains "pointers" to all accounts and system-level files.

TCL—Abbreviation for Terminal Control Language, the point from which all operations begin. Indicated with the " > " prompt character.

value—An individual element of an attribute. An attribute which contains more than one value is typically referred to as a "multivalued" attribute.

value mark—The reserved character from the ASCII character set used to indicate the end of an attribute and the beginning of another. Normally, these characters are "transparent," meaning that for the most part you will never see them. If you went looking for them, however, here's what you would find: In its ASCII appearance, it looks like a right square bracket; in hexadecimal, its representation is FD; and in decimal, its representation is 253.

To produce a value mark from the keyboard requires a "control right bracket," i.e., "<control>]". Sometimes the right bracket key is located as an uppercase character. In this case, it takes a "control-shift-]" to produce the value mark.

variable—A variable is a symbol into which data can be stored. As its name implies, the value, or contents, of a variable can change during program execution. In the earliest form of BASIC, variable names were typically single alphabetic characters for variables containing numbers and alphabetic characters preceded by a "$" for "string" variables. A "string" variable is a variable containing alphabetic and/or punctuation characters. In PICK/BASIC, variable names may be of any length and therefore should be descriptively named. Variable names must begin with an alphabetic character and may include alphabetic characters, periods and dollar signs.

Review Quiz Answers

HERE ARE THE ANSWERS TO THE QUIZZES AT THE END OF EACH EXAMPLE. GIVE YOURSELF ONE POINT for each question you answer.

Review Quiz 1

1) A symbol that contains data whose value may be changed.

2) >ED *filename item-id*

   or

   >EDIT *filename item-id*

3) >BASIC *filename item-id* (to compile the program)
   >RUN *filename item-id*

   or

   >BASIC *filename item-id*
   >CATALOG *filename item-id*
   > *item-id*

4) Non-executable statements which allow text comments to be inserted into the source code. Why? to explain variable names and usage, tricky logic, etc.

5) "$" or "."

290

6) STOP, if executed before physical end of program.
   END, if no more code.

7) An expression which derives a true or false. True is represented as numeric non-zero and false is zero or null.

8) None. It's a *hardware* problem.

Review Quiz 2

1) The PROMPT statement.

2) PROMPT ">"

3) An optional number at the beginning of a source line to which execution may be transferred with the GOTO or GOSUB statement.

4) GOTO *statement.label* (also GO TO *statement.label*)

   or

   GOSUB *statement.label*

5) MATCHES or MATCH

6) (a) "2N'-'4N'-'2N"

   (b) "1A4N'/'3N"

   (c) "1A0A','1A0A"

   (d) "2N'/'1N'/'2N" or "1N0N'/'1N0N'/'2N0N"

   (e) "1N0N'.'2N"

7) As a terminator for a multiline THEN or ELSE clause, or to terminate program execution (when the END compiler directive appears as the last statement in a program).

8) When they occur between quotes, and between keywords and variables in a statement.

9) In remarks, to provide visual "spacing" for making the programs more readable.

10) NUMBER.OF.EYES = COUNT("Mississippi","i")

    or

    PRINT COUNT("Mississippi","i")

Review Quiz 3

1) Precedence determines the answer in expressions which do not contain parentheses!

2) The REM *statement* is a remark, or comment. The REM function divides one number by a

second number, and returns the remainder of the operation. The REM function is always followed by parentheses, like all other functions.

3) Generates a random number.

4) (a) The line should read:

IF ANSWER = "Y" THEN PRINT "YES" ELSE PRINT "NO"

The END statement is not allowed in this single-line IF statement.

(b) The fragment should read:

```
IF ANSWER > 0 THEN
    PRINT "ANSWER > 0"
END ELSE
    PRINT "ANSWER < 0"
END
```

The END statement is required on any multiple-line IF statement.

(c) The code should read:

```
IF ANSWER = "N" THEN
    PRINT "ENTER ALTERNATE VALUE " :
    INPUT ALTERNATE.VALUE
    IF ALTERNATE.VALUE = "" OR ALTERNATE.VALUE <= 0 THEN
        PRINT "MUST BE ANSWERED OR POSITIVE !"
    END
END
```

The "interior," or "nested" IF statement must be terminated with an END statement.

Review Quiz 4

1) The EQUATE evaluates at compile time and requires less overhead at run time. The assignment evaluates at run time and is less efficient.

2) Statement A

3) COUNT determines the number of occurrences of a string within another string. DCOUNT determines the number of data items delimited by a given string.

4) Puts a process to sleep for some period of time. Give yourself an extra point on this one.

5) SLEEP 600

6) SLEEP 17:30

7) Returns the DECIMAL value of any ASCII character.

8) Generates a string of characters.

9) PRINT STR($"-"$,10)

   or

   PRINT STR(CHAR(45),10)

Review Quiz 5

1) Internal format is the way the computer views and stores data. External format is the human-readable form.

2) The ICONV function and the "D" conversion code.

3) To determine the day of the week:

```
BILL.DATE = ICONV(BILL.DATE,"D")
PRINT OCONV(BILL.DATE,"DWA")
```

or, if you really want some punishment:

```
PRINT OCONV(ICONV(BILL.DATE,"D"),"DWA")
```

To determine when the bill should be paid:

```
BILL.DATE = ICONV(BILL.DATE,"D")
DUE.DATE = BILL.DATE + 30
PRINT OCONV(DUE.DATE,"D2/")
```

4) PRINT OCONV(TIME( ),"MTHS") or PRINT OCONV(TIME( ),"MTH")

5) Generates a string of spaces.

6) The process of formatting output through the "mask" expression which follows the expression that it is to affect.

7) (a)   NAME   ADDRESS

   (b)   123   456

   (c)   NAMEL#15ADDRESS

8) *variable* = TIMEDATE( ) or PRINT TIMEDATE( )

9) When you go to a restaurant and your waiter says, "If you need anything else, my name is Pat," and you wonder what his name is if you *don't* need anything else.

Review Quiz 6

1) (a) PRINT CHAR(12) :   or   PRINT @(-1) :

   (b) PRINT @(3,15) : "HELLO THERE" :

(c) PRINT @(-4) :

2) INPUT *variable*,6

3) *variable* = ICONV("123456.78","MR2")

4) PRINT OCONV(5667788,"MR2,$")

5) The process of "linking" strings together, meaning that the strings are joined end to end to form a new string.

Review Quiz 7

1) The [and] characters are used in the text extraction or substring function. For example:

   ```
   IF RESPONSE[1,1] = "Y" THEN PRINT "THANK YOU"
   ```

2) Initiates the CASE construct.

3) CASE *conditional.expression*
      statement(s)

4) BREAK OFF and BREAK ON disable and enable the break key, respectively.

5) Disables the output of PRINT statements to the printer. All subsequent PRINT statements direct output to the screen.

6) PRINTER ON causes all subsequent PRINT statements to be routed to the spooler, and possibly from there to the printer. There is no effect on CRT statements.

7) >RUN *filename program.name* (P

   or

   >*cataloged.program.name* (P

8) Completes the current spooler entry (print job), and releases it to the spooler.

9) ECHO OFF disables the terminal "echo" function. All characters from this point on are not displayed on the screen as they are entered. ECHO ON enables the "echo" function.

Review Quiz 8

1) Searches through a string of characters delimited by a known delimiter, and returns a group (or field) of characters. Usually, the delimiter is not one of the reserved system delimiters.

2) NUMBER.DESTINATIONS = DCOUNT(DESTINATIONS,",")

   LAST.STOP = FIELD(DESTINATIONS,",",5)

3) Searches for a string of characters within another string of characters, and returns the starting character position of the string, if it is found.

294

4) PRINT INDEX(ALPHABET, "S ",1)

Review Quiz 9

1) The STEP factor changes the normal value by which the variable in the "NEXT variable" statement is incremented. The incremental value is normally 1.

2) FOR I = 1 TO 100 STEP 2
   - •
   - •
   NEXT I

3) FOR I = 100 TO 1 STEP −3
   - •
   - •
   NEXT I

Review Quiz 10

1) The OPEN statement locates and establishes a "physical" address to a file. It is used before referring to the file for input or output.

2) These are the special "reserved" delimiters used to separate attributes, values, and sub-values. They indicate the "end" of one location, and the "beginning" of another.

3) ARRAY = "BARNEY RUBBLE"
   ARRAY<2,1> = "PO BOX 77"
   ARRAY<2,2> = "141 BEDROCK PLACE"
   ARRAY<3> = "BEDROCK"
   ARRAY<4> = "PA"
   ARRAY<5> = 19104

4) PRINT ARRAY<1>
   PRINT ARRAY<2,1>
   PRINT ARRAY<2,2>
   PRINT ARRAY<3> : ", " : ARRAY<4> : " " : ARRAY<5>

5) After the first ICONV statement (note that the value is preceded by five attribute marks):

   ^^^^^15767

   The second ICONV statement produces:

   ^^]]10000^^^15767

6 READ, READU, MATREAD, MATREADU

7) OPEN "INVOICE-FILE" TO INVOICE.FILE ELSE

```
        PRINT "INVOICE-FILE IS NOT A FILE NAME"
        INPUT RESPONSE
        STOP
    END
    READ INVOICE.ITEM FROM INVOICE.FILE,"S1000" ELSE
        PRINT "INVOICE S1000 NOT ON FILE"
        INPUT RESPONSE
        STOP
    END
```

8) The THEN clause may be followed by a statement, or statements, to execute when the item is found on file.

9) The ELSE clause may be followed by a statement, or statements, to execute when the item is not found on file.

Review Quiz 11
Review Quiz 12

OK, so there were no quizzes for these two chapters.

Review Quiz 13

If your program works, and does everything that was asked for, you passed the quiz.

Review Quiz 14

1) The EXECUTE statement allows a PICK/BASIC program to issue any TCL command, and optionally return the results to the program.

2) The CAPTURING clause indicates where the output from the TCL process will be directed.

3) The HEADING defines the text to appear at the top of each page of output on an ACCESS or PICK/BASIC report.

4) HEADING "'LC'Aged Trial Balance Report   Page 'PLC'
   as of 'DL'"

5) The READNEXT statement retrieves the next item-id from a selected list of item-ids.

6) The PAGE statement issues a form feed between pages of output on a PICK/BASIC report.

Index

About the Author

JONATHAN E. SISK is president of JES & Associates of Newport Beach, Calif., a firm specializing in the Pick Operating System. He is the author of *The Pick Pocket Guide, The Ultimate Pocket Guide, The REALITY Pocket Guide, Exploring the Pick Operating System,* and other books on Pick-based systems. Mr. Sisk also conducts a popular series of seminars nationwide on various aspects of the Pick System, and is a frequent speaker at user groups and industry trade shows.

PICK/BASIC: A Programmer's Guide

The programs from *PICK/BASIC: A Programmer's Guide* by Jonathan E. Sisk (TAB Book No. 2845), are available on magnetic media. Each example is provided as a separate item and will save you hours of tedious data entry. Extra programs, not provided in the original text are also included for your amusement and study.

Please order the PICK/BASIC program disks or tapes directly from:

JES & Associates, Inc.
P.O. Box 19274
Irvine, CA 92713

All orders must be prepaid and include shipping and handling charges, and for California residents, 6% sales tax. MasterCard or VISA orders may be placed by calling (714) 548-2388.

The programs are available in two formats:

☐ 5.25-inch floppy diskettes, low density, for PC's and compatibles. The price for the diskette version is $25.00.
☐ Half-inch tapes, 1600BPI for most other Pick machines. The price for the half-inch tape version is $35.00. Streaming cartridge tapes are available for an extra $30 (for a total of $55). Please specify the type of machine you are using and the kind of magnetic media it requires.

Shipping and handling charges are $2.50 per order in the contiguous United States and orders are shipped via UPS ground. Next-day UPS is $7.50, and second-day UPS is $5.00. All orders outside the continental United States are shipped via First Class Air Mail and the cost is $7.50 per order.

Your Name _____

Company Name _____

Street Address _____

(No P.O. Boxes Please, unless outside United States)

City, State, Zip _____

Telephone _____

Type of Machine _____

Type of Media _____